MW00488202

Prentice Hall

GRAMMAR HANDBOOK

Grade 11

Upper Saddle River, New Jersey
Boston, Massachusetts
Chandler, Arizona
Glenview, Illinois

Prentice Hall Grammar Handbook Consulting Author

We wish to thank Jeff Anderson who guided the pedagogical approach to grammar instruction utilized in this handbook.

Grateful acknowledgment is made to the following for copyrighted material:

Alfred A. Knopf, Inc.
"The Negro Speaks of Rivers" from *The Collected Poems of Langston Hughes* by Langston Hughes, copyright © 1994 by The Estate of Langston Hughes.

Longman Publishing Group, A Division of Pearson Education, Inc.
"Writing in a Second Language" from *Writing: A Guide for College and Beyond (2nd Edition)* by Lester Faigley. Copyright © 2010 by Pearson Education, Inc.

Note: Every effort has been made to locate the copyright owner of material reproduced in this component. Omissions brought to our attention will be corrected in subsequent editions.

Credits

Cover
Photos provided by istockphoto.com

Illustrations
Dan Hubig

Photographs
All interior photos provided by Shutterstock, Inc.

ISBN-13: 978-0-13-363844-8
ISBN-10: 0-13-363844-8
5 6 7 8 9 10 V054 15 14 13

GRAMMAR

USAGE

CHAPTER 8 **Using Modifiers** **195**

CHAPTER 9 **Miscellaneous Problems in Usage** **207**

MECHANICS

Numbered tags like this **EL1** are used on instruction pages of the
Grammar Handbook to indicate where to find a related tip in the
English Learner's Resource.

THE PARTS *of* SPEECH

Use each part of speech to help you build sentences that are meaningful and interesting.

WRITE GUY *Jeff Anderson, M.Ed.*

WHAT DO YOU NOTICE?

Uncover the parts of speech as you zoom in on these sentences from the myth "The Earth on Turtle's Back" retold by Michael Caduto and Joseph Bruchac.

MENTOR TEXT

> She was not as strong or as swift as the others, but she was determined. She went so deep that it was all dark, and still she swam deeper.

Now, ask yourself the following questions:

- How do the two coordinating conjunctions in the first sentence link parts of the sentence?
- What is the purpose of the coordinating conjunction *and* in the second sentence?

In the first sentence, the word *or* connects the adjectives *strong* and *swift*. The word *but* connects two main, or independent, clauses. The first main clause is *she was not as strong or as swift as the others,* and the second is *she was determined*. In the second sentence, the word *and* connects two main clauses. The first main clause is *she went so deep that it was all dark,* and the second is *still she swam deeper.*

Grammar for Writers Pay attention to how each part of speech can help you craft memorable sentences. Less noticeable words like conjunctions and prepositions play just as important a role as prominent words like adjectives and adverbs.

I'm going to watch a movie or go to a friend's house.

Why not use and so that you can do both?

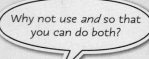

1.1 Nouns and Pronouns

Nouns and pronouns make it possible for people to label everything around them.

Nouns

The word *noun* comes from the Latin word *nomen*, which means "name."

RULE 1.1.1

> A **noun** is the part of speech that names a person, place, thing, or idea.

Nouns that name a *person* or *place* are easy to identify.

PERSON   Uncle Mike, neighbor, girls, Bob, swimmer, Ms. Yang, Captain Smith

PLACE   library, Dallas, garden, city, kitchen, James River, canyon, Oklahoma

The category *thing* includes visible things, ideas, actions, conditions, and qualities.

VISIBLE THINGS   chair, pencil, school, duck, daffodil, fort

IDEAS   independence, democracy, militarism, capitalism, recession, freedom

ACTIONS   work, research, exploration, competition, exercise, labor

CONDITIONS   sadness, illness, excitement, joy, health, happiness

QUALITIES   kindness, patience, ability, compassion, intelligence, drive

Concrete and Abstract Nouns

Nouns can also be grouped as *concrete* or *abstract*. A **concrete noun** names something you can see, touch, taste, hear, or smell. An **abstract noun** names something you cannot perceive through any of your five senses.

CONCRETE NOUNS	person, cannon, road, city, music
ABSTRACT NOUNS	hope, improvement, independence, desperation, cooperation

See Practice 1.1A

Collective Nouns

A **collective noun** names a *group* of people or things. A collective noun looks singular, but its meaning may be singular or plural, depending on how it is used in a sentence.

COLLECTIVE NOUNS			
army	choir	troop	faculty
cast	class	crew	legislature

Do not confuse collective nouns—nouns that name a collection of people or things acting as a unit—with plural nouns.

Compound Nouns

A **compound noun** is a noun made up of two or more words acting as a single unit. Compound nouns may be written as separate words, hyphenated words, or combined words.

COMPOUND NOUNS	
Separate	life preserver coffee table bird dog
Hyphenated	sergeant-at-arms self-rule daughter-in-law
Combined	battlefield dreamland porthole

Check a dictionary if you are not sure how to write a compound noun.

Common and Proper Nouns

Any noun may be categorized as either *common* or *proper*.
A **common noun** names any one of a class of people, places,
or things. A **proper noun** names a specific person, place, or thing.
Proper nouns are capitalized, but common nouns are not.
(See Chapter 10 for rules of capitalization.)

COMMON NOUNS	building, writer, nation, month, leader, place, book, war
PROPER NOUNS	Jones, Virginia, *Leaves of Grass,* Revolutionary War, White House, Mark Twain, France, June

A noun of direct address—the name of a person to whom you
are directly speaking—is always a proper noun, as is a family
title before a name. In the examples below, common nouns are
highlighted in yellow, and proper nouns are highlighted in orange.

COMMON NOUNS	My **mom** is a **doctor**.
	Our **teacher** is always early.
	My favorite person is my **grandma**.
DIRECT ADDRESS	Please, **Dad**, tell us a story before bed.
	Dad, can you take me there?
	Eva, please bring your vegetable dip when you come to the party.
FAMILY TITLE	**Aunt Deb** works in **Washington, D.C**.
	Grandpa bakes great fruit tarts, and his apple tart is my favorite.
	My favorite person is **Grandma Jones**.

See Practice 1.1B

PRACTICE 1.1A > **Identifying and Labeling Nouns as Concrete or Abstract**

Read each item. Then, label each item *concrete noun* or *abstract noun*, and write another similar concrete or abstract noun.

EXAMPLE   frustration

ANSWER   *abstract noun, exasperation*

1. coin
2. dreams
3. tennis racket
4. liberty
5. thought
6. information
7. beach
8. misery
9. toy
10. thrill

PRACTICE 1.1B > **Recognizing Kinds of Nouns (Collective, Compound, Proper)**

Read each sentence. Then, write whether the underlined nouns are *collective*, *compound*, or *proper*. Answer in the order the words appear.

EXAMPLE   <u>Sam</u> is one of four kids in his <u>family</u>.

ANSWER   *proper, collective*

11. Kristen's <u>brother-in-law</u> was raised in <u>Kentucky</u>.
12. The <u>station wagon</u> is so large, the entire <u>squad</u> could almost fit in it.
13. <u>Burt</u> hiked all the way to the top of the inactive volcano.
14. In <u>Montreal</u>, it seems that you are in the <u>minority</u> if you don't like hockey.
15. The field looked far away to some of the <u>crowd</u>.
16. I had to take my <u>great-grandfather</u> to see a doctor.
17. There was a <u>swarm</u> of bees behind our house.
18. The restaurant was named *<u>Timmy's</u>* after the owner.
19. <u>Tony</u> reads the <u>newspaper</u> as soon as he gets home.
20. The <u>audience</u> cheered loudly for the singer.

SPEAKING APPLICATION

Take turns with a partner. Name an object in the room, and say abstract nouns that could be used to describe it. Move on to another object and do the same.

WRITING APPLICATION

Using one common, one collective, one compound, and one proper noun from Practice 1.1B, write an original paragraph on any subject.

Pronouns

Pronouns help writers and speakers avoid awkward repetition of nouns.

RULE 1.1.2

> **Pronouns** are words that stand for nouns or for words that take the place of nouns.

Antecedents of Pronouns Pronouns get their meaning from the words they stand for. These words are called **antecedents.**

RULE 1.1.3

> **Antecedents** are nouns or words that take the place of nouns to which pronouns refer.

The arrows point from pronouns to their antecedents.

EXAMPLES   **Kristy** said **she** lost **her** list after the meeting.

When the **Woods** moved, **they** gave **their** furniture to me.

Attending the town concert was tiring, but **it** was fun!

Antecedents do not always appear before their pronouns, however. Sometimes an antecedent follows its pronoun.

EXAMPLE   Because of **its** history, **Jerusalem**, Israel, is my favorite city.

There are several kinds of pronouns. Most of them have specific antecedents, but a few do not.

See Practice 1.1C

Personal Pronouns The most common pronouns are the **personal pronouns.**

PERSONAL PRONOUNS		
	SINGULAR	PLURAL
First Person	I, me my, mine	we, us our, ours
Second Person	you your, yours	you your, yours
Third Person	he, him, his she, her, hers it, its	they, them their, theirs

In the first example below, the antecedent of the personal pronoun is the person speaking. In the second, the antecedent of the personal pronoun is the person being spoken to. In the last example, the antecedent of the personal pronoun is the thing spoken about.

FIRST PERSON **My** name is not Greg.

SECOND PERSON When **you** left, **you** forgot **your** wallet.

THIRD PERSON The car is new, but **its** windows are dirty.

Reflexive and Intensive Pronouns These two types of pronouns look the same, but they function differently in sentences.

REFLEXIVE AND INTENSIVE PRONOUNS		
	SINGULAR	PLURAL
First Person	myself	ourselves
Second Person	yourself	yourselves
Third Person	himself, herself, itself	themselves

REFLEXIVE   The children prepared **themselves** for the upcoming presentation.

INTENSIVE   Ricky Stanley **himself** wrote an account of the transformation.

See Practice 1.1D

Reciprocal Pronouns **Reciprocal pronouns** show a mutual action or relationship.

> **RULE 1.1.6**
>
> The **reciprocal pronouns** *each other* and *one another* refer to a plural antecedent. They express a mutual action or relationship.

EXAMPLES   The two students quizzed **each other**.

The class shared their answers with **one another**.

See Practice 1.1E

Demonstrative Pronouns **Demonstrative pronouns** are used to point out one or more nouns.

> **RULE 1.1.7**
>
> A **demonstrative pronoun** directs attention to a specific person, place, or thing.

There are four demonstrative pronouns.

DEMONSTRATIVE PRONOUNS	
SINGULAR	PLURAL
this, that	these, those

Demonstrative pronouns may come before or after their antecedents.

BEFORE **That** is the **country** I would like to visit.

AFTER I hope to visit **Texas** and **New Mexico**. **Those** are my first choices.

One of the demonstrative pronouns, *that*, can also be used as a relative pronoun.

Relative Pronouns

Relative pronouns are used to relate one idea in a sentence to another. There are five relative pronouns.

> A **relative pronoun** introduces an adjective clause and connects it to the word that the clause modifies.

1.1.8 RULE

RELATIVE PRONOUNS				
that	which	who	whom	whose

EXAMPLES She watched a **movie that** portrayed a character's childhood memories.

The **writer who** had lived it explained her childhood.

The **vacation**, **which** they knew would be exciting, was quickly approaching.

See Practice 1.1F

Read each sentence. Then, write the antecedent of each underlined pronoun.

EXAMPLE   My mother told me to give my sister <u>her</u> books.

ANSWER   *sister*

1. As the boy made his way up the hill, <u>he</u> whistled.

2. Tony must get <u>himself</u> ready soon if <u>he</u> wants to make it to the game.

3. Martin <u>himself</u> admitted to hiding the ball.

4. The three sisters packed <u>themselves</u> plenty of supplies for <u>their</u> weekend at camp.

5. <u>Those</u> are the dishes Mom likes, but <u>she</u> isn't sure the colors are right.

6. We rode in a cab <u>whose</u> driver told us about the city.

7. Conor told <u>himself</u> that there was nothing <u>he</u> could do about the bad weather.

8. I saw the outraged bull tossing <u>its</u> head and kicking wildly.

9. Terik and Colleen, allow <u>yourselves</u> one hour to get there.

10. <u>These</u> are the watches Miguel likes best.

Read each sentence. Then, write each pronoun, and label it *personal*, *reflexive*, or *intensive*.

EXAMPLE   Lucas spoke to the professor and persuaded him to delay the quiz.

ANSWER   *him — personal*

11. Jim was surprised when he learned the truth.

12. Just imagine yourself in a foreign land.

13. She didn't know the coat was mine.

14. With their love for rolling around in mud, pigs themselves aren't very clean.

15. You owe yourself a night out on the town.

16. Scientists are surprised themselves when they discover new species.

17. Robin made his decision.

18. The children themselves were responsible for making breakfast.

19. Everyone has different talents, and running track is one of hers.

20. The vast majority of worker bees sacrifice themselves for their queen.

SPEAKING APPLICATION

Take turns with a partner. Tell about someone you would like to meet and why. Use three or more pronouns that refer to that person. Your partner should identify the pronouns and their antecedents.

WRITING APPLICATION

Write a paragraph about a trip you have taken, using personal, reflexive, and intensive pronouns in your paragraph.

Read each sentence. Then, write the reciprocal pronoun in each sentence.

EXAMPLE   Linda and Fabio are going to help each other study for the midterms.

ANSWER   *each other*

1. The couple laughed at each other as they finished their meal.

2. My brothers and sisters are very fond of one another.

3. Talia and I have known each other for years.

4. Robert and Eileen wrote to each other for a long time.

5. I think we have learned a lot about one another this year.

6. Brian and Vallon supported each other through tough times.

7. They have each other, don't they?

8. We gave presents to one another.

9. Celia and Jennifer always say goodbye to each other.

10. They write to each other once a month.

Read each sentence. Then, write each underline pronoun and label it *demonstrative* or *relative*.

EXAMPLE   <u>These</u> are my two favorite records.

ANSWER   *These* — demonstrative

11. The quarterback <u>who</u> played last night was a close friend.

12. Jackson's father gave him an old watch <u>that</u> he had worn.

13. Marla, <u>whose</u> car was in the shop, rode with us to the dance.

14. The play <u>that</u> the cast performed was written by Alexis.

15. <u>This</u> belongs to my best friend.

16. <u>That</u> is the upper section of the stadium.

17. <u>Those</u> are the new shoes I want to buy.

18. The community meeting, <u>which</u> started at 7:00, ended hours later.

19. <u>These</u> are the library books I still have to return.

20. Sandy, <u>whom</u> I met this summer, is joining me for dinner.

SPEAKING APPLICATION

Take turns with a partner. Describe the relationship between two friends in a book that you have read. Show that you understand reciprocal pronouns by using some in your description. Your partner should listen for and identify the reciprocal pronouns that you use.

WRITING APPLICATION

Write a paragraph describing an upcoming school event, using at least two demonstrative and two relative pronouns.

Interrogative Pronouns

Interrogative pronouns are used to ask questions.

See Practice 1.1G

RULE 1.1.9

> An **interrogative pronoun** is used to begin a question.

The five interrogative pronouns are *what*, *which*, *who*, *whom*, and *whose*. Sometimes the antecedent of an interrogative pronoun is not known.

EXAMPLE   **Who** picked up the cups for the party?

Indefinite Pronouns

Indefinite pronouns sometimes lack specific antecedents.

RULE 1.1.10

> An **indefinite pronoun** refers to a person, place, or thing that may or may not be specifically named.

INDEFINITE PRONOUNS				
SINGULAR			**PLURAL**	**BOTH**
another	everyone	nothing	both	all
anybody	everything	one	few	any
anyone	little	other	many	more
anything	much	somebody	others	most
each	neither	someone	several	none
either	nobody	something		some
everybody	no one			

Indefinite pronouns sometimes have specific antecedents.

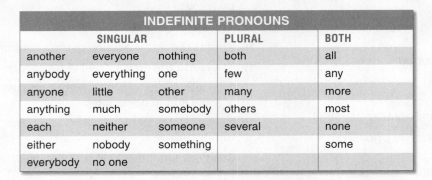

NO SPECIFIC ANTECEDENT   **Each** brought one friend.

SPECIFIC ANTECEDENTS   **One** of the **students** didn't pass.

Indefinite pronouns can also function as adjectives.

ADJECTIVE   **Few** authors are as famous as this one.

See Practice 1.1H

PRACTICE 1.1G > Recognizing Interrogative Pronouns

Read each sentence. Then, write the interrogative pronoun needed to complete the sentence.

EXAMPLE _____ needs a pen?

ANSWER *Who*

1. _____ of the Nelson boys plays soccer?
2. _____ led the symphony during the performance?
3. _____ led Tiffany to miss her brother's recital?
4. _____ was the total cost of your vacation?
5. _____ of the students came in late?
6. _____ 's going on?
7. _____ can we ask about adopting the kitten?
8. To _____ are you speaking?
9. _____ are those stickers?
10. _____ of the performances was canceled?

PRACTICE 1.1H > Identifying Indefinite Pronouns

Read each sentence. Then, write the indefinite pronoun(s) used in each sentence.

EXAMPLE All of the teachers met in the faculty staff room.

ANSWER *All*

11. Everyone had some of the fruit salad.
12. After the meeting, few of the attendees stayed to interview the speaker.
13. Most of the travelers were weary at the end of the day.
14. No one failed to make a contribution.
15. I believe that much could be accomplished at this point.
16. Do either of your backup plans sound reasonable?
17. Neither of the disks we had was formatted.
18. Everyone worked so hard during the campaign that no one left early.
19. Both of us agreed it should end in a tie.
20. There isn't much to do since everybody has finished.

SPEAKING APPLICATION

With a partner, take turns trying to find out what the other did over the weekend. Use interrogative pronouns in your questions.

WRITING APPLICATION

Rewrite sentences 11, 18, and 19, replacing the indefinite pronouns with different indefinite pronouns. Make sure that the new sentences still make sense.

1.2 Verbs

Every complete sentence must have at least one **verb**, which may consist of as many as four words.

A verb is a word or group of words that expresses time while showing an action, a condition, or the fact that something exists.

Action Verbs and Linking Verbs

Action verbs express action. They are used to tell what someone or something does, did, or will do. **Linking verbs** express a condition or show that something exists.

An action verb tells what action someone or something is performing.

ACTION
VERBS

Deanna **read** about European cities.

The stereo **blared** the lyrics of the new CD.

We **chose** to visit Austin and Houston.

They **remember** the book about Israel.

The action expressed by a verb does not have to be visible. Words expressing mental activities—such as *learn*, *think*, or *decide*—are also considered action verbs.

The person or thing that performs the action is called the *subject* of the verb. In the examples above, *Deanna*, *stereo*, *we*, and *they* are the subjects of *read*, *blared*, *chose*, and *remember*.

1.2.3 RULE

> A **linking verb** is a verb that connects its subject with a noun, pronoun, or adjective that identifies or describes the subject.

LINKING VERBS

The woman **is** a famous singer.

The chair **seems** to be clean.

EL6

The verb *be* is the most common linking verb.

THE FORMS OF *BE*			
am	am being	can be	have been
are	are being	could be	has been
is	is being	may be	had been
was	was being	might be	could have been
were	were being	must be	may have been
		shall be	might have been
		should be	shall have been
		will be	should have been
		would be	will have been
			would have been

Most often, the forms of *be* that function as linking verbs express the condition of the subject. Occasionally, however, they may merely express existence, usually by showing, with other words, where the subject is located.

EXAMPLE   Dinner **is** on the table.

Other Linking Verbs A few other verbs can also serve as linking verbs.

OTHER LINKING VERBS		
appear	look	sound
become	remain	stay
feel	seem	taste
grow	smell	turn

EXAMPLES

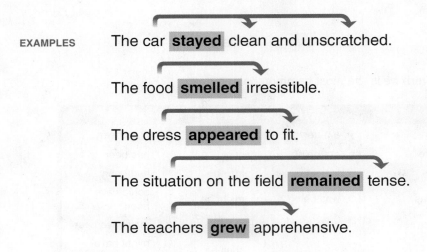

The car **stayed** clean and unscratched.

The food **smelled** irresistible.

The dress **appeared** to fit.

The situation on the field **remained** tense.

The teachers **grew** apprehensive.

Some of these verbs may also act as action—not linking—verbs. To determine whether the word is functioning as an action verb or as a linking verb, insert *am*, *are*, or *is* in place of the verb. If the substitute makes sense while connecting two words, then the original verb is a linking verb.

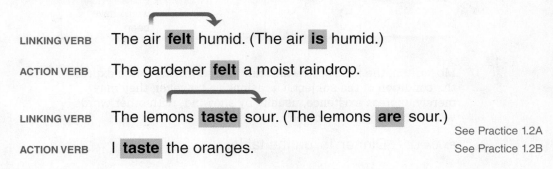

LINKING VERB   The air **felt** humid. (The air **is** humid.)

ACTION VERB   The gardener **felt** a moist raindrop.

LINKING VERB   The lemons **taste** sour. (The lemons **are** sour.)

ACTION VERB   I **taste** the oranges.

See Practice 1.2A
See Practice 1.2B

16   The Parts of Speech

> **PRACTICE 1.2A** **Identifying Action and Linking Verbs**

Read each sentence. Write the action verb in each sentence.

EXAMPLE   The telephone rings in both offices.

ANSWER   *rings*

1. Mary grew cucumbers during the summer.
2. The injured man stumbled into the hospital.
3. Brian memorized the opening line of his speech.
4. The kitten raced around the living room.
5. I pushed open the squeaky, old door.

Read each sentence. Write the linking verb in each sentence.

EXAMPLE   Milk spoils quickly unless it is refrigerated.

ANSWER   *is*

6. The express bus may be late this evening.
7. Our dinner tasted delicious.
8. The accident victim remained alert.
9. Your behavior should have been less rude.
10. The huge dog was ferocious.

> **PRACTICE 1.2B** **Distinguishing Between Action and Linking Verbs**

Read each sentence. Write *action* or *linking* for each underlined verb.

EXAMPLE   He <u>submitted</u> his latest poems for the contest.

ANSWER   *action*

11. The flowers <u>smelled</u> delightful.
12. Federick <u>leaned</u> back in his chair.
13. Camilla repeatedly <u>waved</u> at Aaron.
14. The room <u>seemed</u> dark and oppressive.
15. The famished swimmers <u>smelled</u> the bacon and eggs.
16. Jose will <u>buy</u> lunch for the four of us.
17. The cat <u>is</u> the neighborhood stray.
18. You should be <u>thinking</u> about college.
19. Arabella <u>seemed</u> to be a talkative person.
20. Jake <u>suffered</u> through the grueling match.

SPEAKING APPLICATION

Take turns with a partner. Tell about a television show you saw recently. Your partner should listen for and name three action verbs that you use.

WRITING APPLICATION

Write four sentences, two sentences with action verbs and two sentences with linking verbs. Then, exchange papers with a partner and underline the verbs in your partner's sentences. Label each verb *action* or *linking*.

Transitive and Intransitive Verbs

All verbs are either **transitive** or **intransitive,** depending on whether or not they transfer action to another word in a sentence.

> A **transitive verb** directs action toward someone or something named in the same sentence. An **intransitive verb** does not direct action toward anyone or anything named in the same sentence.

The word toward which a transitive verb directs its action is called the *object* of the verb. Intransitive verbs never have objects. You can determine whether a verb has an object by asking *whom* or *what* after the verb.

TRANSITIVE   Felix **hit** the ball.
(Hit what? ball)

We **ate** the hummus.
(Ate what? hummus)

INTRANSITIVE   The cast **practiced** on the stage.
(Practiced what? [no answer])

The mother **shouted** quickly.
(Shouted what? [no answer])

> Because linking verbs do not express action, they are always intransitive. Most action verbs can be either transitive or intransitive, depending on the sentence. However, some action verbs can only be transitive, and others can only be intransitive.

TRANSITIVE   I **wrote** a postcard from Florida.

INTRANSITIVE   The editor **wrote** quickly.

ALWAYS TRANSITIVE		European oranges **rival** those of America.

See Practice 1.2C

ALWAYS INTRANSITIVE	They **winced** at the sound of the thunder.

Verb Phrases

A verb that has more than one word is a **verb phrase.**

> A **verb phrase** consists of a main verb and one or more helping verbs.

RULE 1.2.6

Helping verbs are often called auxiliary verbs. One or more helping verbs may precede the main verb in a verb phrase.

VERB PHRASES I **will be taking** an extended vacation in Italy.

I **should have been watching** when I ran down the stairs.

All the forms of *be* listed in this chapter can be used as helping verbs. The following verbs can also be helping verbs.

OTHER HELPING VERBS			
do	have	shall	can
does	has	should	could
did	had	will	may
		would	might
			must

A verb phrase is often interrupted by other words in an sentence.

INTERRUPTED VERB PHRASES I **will** definitely **be taking** an extended vacation in Italy.

Should I **take** an extended vacation in Italy?

See Practice 1.2D

PRACTICE 1.2C ▷ Distinguishing Between Transitive and Intransitive Verbs

Read each sentence. Then, write *transitive* or *intransitive* for each underlined verb.

EXAMPLE   Keith <u>placed</u> the heavy metal box on his desk.

ANSWER   *transitive*

1. Clouds <u>swirled</u> near the top of the volcano.
2. After much delay, the judge <u>rendered</u> an unpopular decision.
3. For a good analysis, <u>read</u> *Understanding Fiction*.
4. Dimitri <u>rehearsed</u> his speech many times.
5. The runaway skateboard <u>careened</u> into a stone wall.
6. The orchestra <u>began</u> with a loud overture.
7. The townspeople <u>took</u> a siesta each afternoon.
8. The mother <u>smiled</u> at the infant in her arms.
9. The eel <u>slid</u> along the floor of the fishing boat.
10. The crew <u>ate</u> lunch under an old oak tree.

PRACTICE 1.2D ▷ Recognizing Verb Phrases

Read each sentence. Then, write the verb phrase in each sentence.

EXAMPLE   By now, we should have been in Houston.

ANSWER   *should have been*

11. The police department has already been notified.
12. We can expect a letter from them in a month.
13. The flood has not blocked the main highway.
14. Their roles have not been clearly defined.
15. Will you remind them of our change in plans?
16. The hunting dogs were howling with excitement.
17. The horses could not jump the high hedges.
18. She might have won with a better partner.
19. The ship will be sailing soon.
20. Ying should have known better than that.

SPEAKING APPLICATION

Take turns with a partner. Say two sentences with a transitive verb and two sentences with an intransitive verb. Your partner should identify each type of verb.

WRITING APPLICATION

Rewrite sentences 12 and 13, keeping the subject but changing the verb phrases. Make sure the sentences still make sense.

1.3 Adjectives and Adverbs

Adjectives and **adverbs** are the two parts of speech known as *modifiers*—that is, they slightly change the meaning of other words by adding description or making them more precise.

Adjectives

An **adjective** clarifies the meaning of a noun or pronoun by providing information about its appearance, location, and so on.

> An **adjective** is a word used to describe a noun or pronoun or to give it a more specific meaning.

1.3.1   RULE

An adjective answers one of four questions about a noun or pronoun: *What kind? Which one? How many? How much?*

EXAMPLES   **high-heeled** shoes (What kind of shoes?)

that car (Which car?)

five shirts (How many shirts?)

four inches of rain (How much rain?)

When an adjective modifies a noun, it usually precedes the noun. Occasionally, the adjective may follow the noun.

EXAMPLES   The professor was **impressed** with my prior knowledge.

I considered the professor **impressed**.

An adjective that modifies a pronoun usually follows it. Sometimes, however, the adjective precedes the pronoun as it does in the example on the next page.

AFTER   We were **sad** the restaurant was closed.

BEFORE   **Sad** that they had to say goodbye, they began to leave.

More than one adjective may modify a single noun or pronoun.

EXAMPLE   We hired an **efficient, knowledgeable** manager.

Articles Three common adjectives—*a, an*, and *the*—are known as **articles.** *A* and *an* are called **indefinite articles** because they refer to any one of a class of nouns. *The* refers to a specific noun and, therefore, is called the **definite article.**

INDEFINITE EXAMPLES	DEFINITE EXAMPLES
a daisy	the stem
an orchid	the mask

Remember that *an* is used before a vowel sound; *a* is used before a consonant sound.

EXAMPLES   **a** one-stoplight town (*w* sound)

                a universal feeling (*y* sound)

                an honest pastor (no *h* sound)

See Practice 1.3A

Nouns Used as Adjectives Words that are usually nouns sometimes act as adjectives. In this case, the noun answers the questions *What kind?* or *Which one?* about another noun.

NOUNS USED AS ADJECTIVES	
flower	flower garden
lawn	lawn mower

See Practice 1.3B

Proper Adjectives Adjectives can also be proper. **Proper adjectives** are proper nouns used as adjectives or adjectives formed from proper nouns. They usually begin with capital letters.

PROPER NOUNS	PROPER ADJECTIVES
Monday	Monday morning
San Francisco	San Francisco streets
Europe	European roses
Rome	Roman hyacinth

Compound Adjectives Adjectives can be compound. Most are hyphenated; others are combined or are separate words.

HYPHENATED **rain-forest** plants

water-soluble pigments

COMBINED **airborne** pollen

evergreen shrubs

See Practice 1.3C   SEPARATE **North American** rhododendrons

Pronouns Used as Adjectives Certain pronouns can also function as adjectives. The seven personal pronouns, known as either **possessive adjectives** or **possessive pronouns**, do double duty in a sentence. They act as pronouns because they have antecedents. They also act as adjectives because they modify nouns by answering *Which one?* The other pronouns become adjectives instead of pronouns when they stand before nouns and answer the question *Which one?*

> A pronoun is used as an adjective if it modifies a noun.

1.3.2 RULE

Possessive pronouns, demonstrative pronouns, interrogative pronouns, and indefinite pronouns can all function as adjectives when they modify nouns.

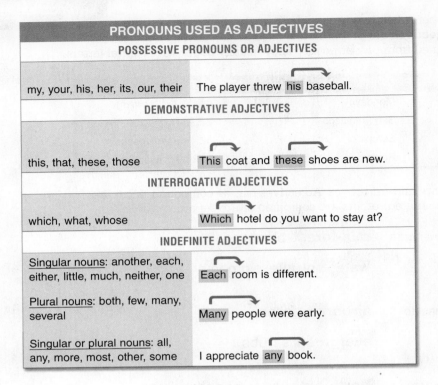

PRONOUNS USED AS ADJECTIVES

POSSESSIVE PRONOUNS OR ADJECTIVES	
my, your, his, her, its, our, their	The player threw his baseball.

DEMONSTRATIVE ADJECTIVES	
this, that, these, those	This coat and these shoes are new.

INTERROGATIVE ADJECTIVES	
which, what, whose	Which hotel do you want to stay at?

INDEFINITE ADJECTIVES	
<u>Singular nouns</u>: another, each, either, little, much, neither, one	Each room is different.
<u>Plural nouns</u>: both, few, many, several	Many people were early.
<u>Singular or plural nouns</u>: all, any, more, most, other, some	I appreciate any book.

Verb Forms Used as Adjectives Verb forms used as adjectives usually end in *-ing* or *-ed* and are called **participles.**

EXAMPLE   I petted the **barking** puppy.

Nouns, pronouns, and verb forms function as adjectives only when they modify other nouns or pronouns. The following examples show how their function in a sentence can change.

	REGULAR FUNCTION	AS AN ADJECTIVE
Noun	The new floor was wet.	I sat on the floor mat.
Pronoun	This was a peaceful house.	This house was peaceful.
Verb	The rain melted the ice	The melted ice flooded the gutter.

See Practice 1.3D

PRACTICE 1.3A **Recognizing Adjectives and Articles**

Read each sentence. Then, write the adjective(s) and the article(s) in each sentence.

EXAMPLE   I remember the man with the raspy voice.

ANSWER   *raspy; the, the*

1. The box with the yellow bow is a present.
2. An oral report is due next week.
3. A lizard has weak jaws.
4. The woman in the blue sneakers ran the fastest.
5. An error of judgement can result in bad consequences.
6. An author can also be a great illustrator.
7. A well-known theory is the theory of plate tectonics.
8. The colorful sign above the desk inspires me.
9. The small children ran down a field in the rain.
10. The nurse spoke in a soft voice.

PRACTICE 1.3B **Identifying Nouns Used as Adjectives**

Read each sentence. Then, write each noun that is used as an adjective and the noun that it modifies.

EXAMPLE   The school bus arrived.

ANSWER   *school, bus*

11. Next Monday is a vacation day.
12. The weather report called for snow today.
13. He received a laptop computer for his birthday.
14. This juice comes from Florida oranges.
15. My mother uses lots of household products.
16. My little sister enjoys story hour at the town library.
17. Dad picked up a magazine at the newspaper stand.
18. Magda put a spider crab in her metal bucket.
19. Our summer vacation is here at last.
20. Karell's new car has leather seats.

SPEAKING APPLICATION

Take turns with a partner. Tell about your favorite character from a book. Use different kinds of adjectives. Your partner should listen for and name the adjectives that you use.

WRITING APPLICATION

Write three sentences that have the following nouns: *weather, newspaper,* and *summer.* Then, write three additional sentences, using each noun as an adjective.

PRACTICE 1.3C ▶ Recognizing Proper and Compound Adjectives

Read each sentence. Then, identify each underlined adjective as *proper* or *compound*.

EXAMPLE   The <u>Navajo</u> weaver made a blanket.

ANSWER   *proper*

1. The quartet sang several <u>Irish</u> songs.
2. France is a part of the <u>European</u> continent.
3. We need to develop a <u>well-planned</u> activity.
4. The class watched a <u>Victorian</u> drama today.
5. The vanilla yogurt had a <u>long-lasting</u> flavor.
6. You must reference an <u>up-to-date</u> encyclopedia.
7. My family visited a <u>Hawaiian</u> island last summer.
8. Woven <u>Peruvian</u> blankets are warm.
9. My mother enjoys reading <u>self-help</u> books.
10. We bought <u>Indian</u> rugs at the import store.

PRACTICE 1.3D ▶ Recognizing Pronouns and Verbs Used as Adjectives

Read each sentence. Then, write each pronoun or verb used as an adjective and the noun that it modifies.

EXAMPLE   The carpenter fixed the dilapidated roof.

ANSWER   *dilapidated, roof*

11. The wailing baby could be heard by all of the shoppers.
12. Some potters use a shaping tool.
13. The remaining contestants were nervous.
14. The smiling bridesmaid happily displayed her fragrant bouquet.
15. The tugboat saved the sinking ship.
16. This computer is very fast.
17. The attending physician examined twenty patients last night.
18. The race cars waited at the starting line.
19. These ingredients are for the birthday cake.
20. Several plants bloomed after the rain.

SPEAKING APPLICATION

Take turns with a partner. Say sentences using the following words as adjectives: *French, American, self-starting,* and *ever-lasting.* Your partner should identify the nouns as proper or compound.

WRITING APPLICATION

Write four sentences, include pronouns used as adjectives and verbs used as adjectives.

Adverbs

Adverbs, like adjectives, describe other words or make other words more specific.

> An **adverb** is a word that modifies a verb, an adjective, or another adverb.

When an adverb modifies a verb, it will answer any of the following questions: *Where? When? In what way? To what extent?*

An adverb answers only one question when modifying an adjective or another adverb: *To what extent?* Because it specifies the degree or intensity of the modified adjective or adverb, such an adverb is often called an **intensifier.**

The position of an adverb in relation to the word it modifies can vary in a sentence. If the adverb modifies a verb, it may precede or follow it or even interrupt a verb phrase. Normally, adverbs modifying adjectives and adverbs will immediately precede the words they modify.

ADVERBS MODIFYING VERBS	
Where?	**When?**
The puppy played outside.	Sophie never ate her treats.
The puppy played there.	Later, we toured the farm.
The cat ran everywhere.	The puppy chews the bone daily.
In what way?	**To what extent?**
She quickly sold the puppy.	The landscapers were still working loudly.
She graciously let us hold her.	She always read with expression.
Joe left immediately after the show.	Be sure you wash completely after playing.

ADVERBS MODIFYING ADJECTIVES	ADVERBS MODIFYING ADVERBS
To what extent?	**To what extent?**
The price was quite reasonable.	They played very quietly today.
It wasn't an extremely hard choice.	I am not entirely sure about that.
The team was overly excited about the win.	Jodi was not completely finished with her paper.

Adverbs as Parts of Verbs Some verbs require an adverb to complete their meaning. Adverbs used this way are considered part of the verb. An adverb functioning as part of a verb does not answer the usual questions for adverbs.

EXAMPLES   The child **backed up** because she was scared.

Be sure to **point out** which painting is yours.

Jonathan had to **run out** to get some different color

paints.

See Practice 1.3E

Nouns Functioning as Adverbs
Several nouns can function as adverbs that answer the questions *Where?* or *When?* Some of these words are *home, yesterday, today, tomorrow, mornings, afternoons, evenings, nights, week, month,* and *year.*

NOUNS USED AS ADVERBS	
NOUNS	AS ADVERBS
Afternoons are always slower.	I nap afternoons.
My week off was relaxing.	Let's go shopping this week.
Tomorrow will be a busy day.	I will see them tomorrow at the show.

Adverb or Adjective?

Adverbs usually have different forms from adjectives and thus are easily identified. Many adverbs are formed by the addition of *-ly* to an adjective.

ADJECTIVES   The father looked **happy** .

The dog ran through the **open** door.

ADVERBS   The father looked at his daughters **happily** .

Paul and I discussed our concerns **openly** .

Some adjectives, however, also end in *-ly*. Therefore, you cannot assume that every word ending in *-ly* is an adverb.

ADJECTIVES   an **elderly** person

a **lively** debate

a **leisurely** stroll

oily fish

Some adjectives and adverbs share the same form. You can determine the part of speech of such words by checking their function in the sentence. An adverb will modify a verb, adjective, or adverb; an adjective will modify a noun or pronoun.

ADVERB   The ceremony ran **late** .

ADJECTIVE   We enjoyed the **late** -night dancing.

ADVERB   The bears walked **straight** through the camp.

See Practice 1.3F   ADJECTIVE   The line of students was **straight** .

PRACTICE 1.3E > Recognizing Adverbs

Read each sentence. Then, write the adverb in each sentence, and tell whether it modifies a *verb*, *adjective*, *or adverb*.

EXAMPLE   The man spoke sharply.

ANSWER   *sharply — verb*

1. The play was extremely funny.
2. Rafe was really trying to win.
3. We decided that we will go tomorrow.
4. That pitcher throws really hard and fast.
5. James will probably call us when he arrives.
6. Shawn runs quickly down the court.
7. My grandparents are exceedingly generous.
8. I could hardly believe how the book ended.
9. The dog is unusually alert this evening.
10. News of the wedding traveled rapidly.

PRACTICE 1.3F > Identifying Adverbs and the Words They Modify

Read each sentence. Then, write the adverb in each sentence and the word it modifies.

EXAMPLE   Sammy's bike is very fast.

ANSWER   *very, fast*

11. She was nearly starving after the camping trip.
12. Mom is an extremely early riser.
13. I predict that our team will be hugely victorious.
14. My new computer arrived yesterday from the seller.
15. The dog ferociously ate his meal.
16. She laughed loudly.
17. We couldn't help arriving so late.
18. Tatum hardly ever chats over the Internet.
19. I can barely see without my contact lenses.
20. The ecology club toiled hard to make Earth Day a success.

SPEAKING APPLICATION

Take turns with a partner. Tell about something that you enjoy doing. Your partner should name adverbs that you use.

WRITING APPLICATION

Use sentence 15 as a model to write three sentences of your own. Replace the adverb in sentence 15 with other adverbs.

1.4 Prepositions, Conjunctions, and Interjections

Prepositions and conjunctions function in sentences as connectors. **Prepositions** express relationships between words or ideas, whereas **conjunctions** join words, groups of words, or even entire sentences. **Interjections** function by themselves and are independent of other words in a sentence.

Prepositions and Prepositional Phrases

Prepositions make it possible to show relationships between words. The relationships may involve, for example, location, direction, time, cause, or possession. A preposition may consist of one word or multiple words. (See the chart on the next page.)

> **A preposition** relates the noun or pronoun that appears with it to another word in the sentence.

RULE 1.4.1

Notice how the prepositions below, highlighted in pink, relate to the words highlighted in yellow.

LOCATION   Paintings **are displayed around** the **house**.

TIME   Some artists aren't **famous for centuries**.

CAUSE   Karen is **late because of** the long **test**.

> **A prepositional phrase** is a group of words that includes a preposition and a noun or pronoun.

RULE 1.4.2

The noun or pronoun with a preposition is called the **object of the preposition.** Objects may have one or more modifiers. A prepositional phrase may also have more than one object. In the example below, the objects of the prepositions are highlighted in blue, and the prepositions are in pink.

EXAMPLE   Michael and Heather applied **for a marriage certificate on Monday**.

PREPOSITIONS

aboard	before	in front of	over
about	behind	in place of	owing to
above	below	in regard to	past
according to	beneath	inside	prior to
across	beside	in spite of	regarding
across from	besides	instead of	round
after	between	into	since
against	beyond	in view of	through
ahead of	but	like	throughout
along	by	near	till
alongside	by means of	nearby	to
along with	concerning	next to	together with
amid	considering	of	toward
among	despite	off	under
apart from	down	on	underneath
around	during	on account of	until
aside from	except	onto	unto
as of	for	on top of	up
as	from	opposite	upon
atop	in	out	with
barring	in addition to	out of	within
because of	in back of	outside	without

See Practice 1.4A

Preposition or Adverb?
Many words may be used either as prepositions or adverbs.
Words that can function in either role include *around*, *before*,
behind, *down*, *in*, *off*, *on*, *out*, *over*, and *up*. If an object
accompanies the word, the word is used as a preposition.

PREPOSITION   My friends gathered **around** the dog.

ADVERB   The dog ran **around** and **around**.

See Practice 1.4B

PRACTICE 1.4A > Identifying Prepositions and Prepositional Phrases

Read each sentence. Then, write each prepositional phrase, and underline each preposition.

EXAMPLE   I saw a rabbit in the thicket.

ANSWER   *in the thicket*

1. In the evening, my friends and I finished unpacking.
2. Tina arrived early for the concert.
3. The trunk beside the bed is full of old treasures.
4. Long ago, my grandfather fished in this lake.
5. The reference books are on the first floor of the library.
6. With a beep of the car's horn, Mom got my attention.
7. You're the one with the incredible golf swing!
8. We were all tired after the long trip.
9. The students waited patiently at the door.
10. The ball rolled toward the fence.

PRACTICE 1.4B > Distinguishing Between Prepositions and Adverbs

Read each sentence. Then, label the underlined word in each sentence as *preposition* or *adverb*.

EXAMPLE   I showed the new student <u>around</u>.

ANSWER   *adverb*

11. She asked me to wait <u>outside</u>.
12. Cars lined up <u>outside</u> the train station.
13. We got confused and drove <u>past</u> the entrance.
14. As we waited at the red light, we were shocked to see an elephant run <u>past</u>!
15. Subway trains roared beneath our feet, and skyscrapers towered <u>above</u>.
16. We could hear the geese honking <u>above</u> the clouds.
17. We put our rain gear <u>on</u> quickly.
18. Ducks paddled peacefully <u>on</u> the pond.
19. The doghouse is <u>behind</u> the garden.
20. When you went home, you left your homework <u>behind</u>.

SPEAKING APPLICATION

With a partner, take turns describing the locations of objects in the room. Your partner should listen for and identify the prepositional phrases that you use and the preposition in each phrase.

WRITING APPLICATION

Write a sentence using the word *inside* as a preposition. Then, write another sentence using *inside* as an adverb.

Conjunctions

There are three main kinds of conjunctions: **coordinating, correlative,** and **subordinating.** Sometimes a type of adverb, the **conjunctive adverb,** is also considered a conjunction.

A **conjunction** is a word used to connect other words or groups of words.

Coordinating Conjunctions The seven coordinating conjunctions are used to connect similar parts of speech or groups of words of equal grammatical weight.

COORDINATING CONJUNCTIONS						
and	but	for	nor	or	so	yet

EXAMPLES   My sister **and** mother ran the shop.

Bonnie left late, **so** I waited for her.

Correlative Conjunctions The five paired correlative conjunctions join elements of equal grammatical weight.

CORRELATIVE CONJUNCTIONS		
both . . . and	either . . . or	neither . . . nor
not only . . . but also	whether . . . or	

EXAMPLES   She was buying **both** a Yorkie **and** a poodle.

Neither Marco **nor** Liz came to the party.

I don't know **whether** to meet them for lunch **or** for dinner.

Subordinating Conjunctions Subordinating conjunctions join two complete ideas by making one of the ideas subordinate to, or dependent upon, the other.

SUBORDINATING CONJUNCTIONS			
after	because	lest	till
although	before	now that	unless
as	even if	provided	until
as if	even though	since	when
as long as	how	so that	whenever
as much as	if	than	where
as soon as	inasmuch as	that	wherever
as though	in order that	though	while

The subordinate idea in a sentence always begins with a subordinating conjunction and makes up what is known as a subordinate clause. A subordinate clause may either follow or precede the main idea in a sentence.

EXAMPLES We will be waiting for you at the airport **whenever** your plane arrives.

As soon as the speaker arrived, we started the lecture.

Conjunctive Adverbs Conjunctive adverbs act as transitions between complete ideas by indicating comparisons, contrasts, results, and other relationships. The chart below lists the most common conjunctive adverbs.

CONJUNCTIVE ADVERBS		
accordingly	finally	nevertheless
again	furthermore	otherwise
also	however	then
besides	indeed	therefore
consequently	moreover	thus

Punctuation With Conjunctive Adverbs Punctuation is usually required both before and after conjunctive adverbs.

EXAMPLES   The exam was unusually hard. **Furthermore** , there were topics that we didn't cover in class.

Bonnie was an excellent sculptor; **however** , painting was her favorite medium.

I left early; **nevertheless** , I still got there late.   See Practice 1.4C

Interjections

Interjections express emotion. Unlike most words, they have no grammatical connection to other words in a sentence.

An **interjection** is a word that expresses feeling or emotion and functions independently of a sentence.

Interjections can express a variety of sentiments, such as happiness, fear, anger, pain, surprise, sorrow, exhaustion, or hesitation.

SOME COMMON INTERJECTIONS				
ah	dear	hey	ouch	well
aha	goodness	hurray	psst	whew
alas	gracious	oh	tsk	wow

EXAMPLES   **Ouch** ! Those peppers burned my mouth.

Wow ! That was close!

Oh ! I didn't see it.

Whew ! What a relief to finish the long race.   See Practice 1.4D

PRACTICE 1.4C	Identifying Different Conjunctions

Read each sentence. Then, write the conjunction in each sentence, and label it *coordinating*, *correlative*, *subordinating*, or *conjunctive*.

EXAMPLE   As soon as the rain stopped, we went out.

ANSWER   *As soon as* — subordinating

1. I wanted to go to the concert, but I could not.

2. Both my brother and my sister play soccer.

3. My cousin has been traveling since he graduated.

4. It began to snow; therefore, the game was canceled.

5. When the winner was announced, Gaby cheered.

6. My dog Comet follows me wherever I go.

7. He had to leave; otherwise, he'd miss his train.

8. Julio swam well; indeed, he won every race.

9. Either you tell me, or I'll find out from someone else.

10. I like living here because the ocean is nearby.

PRACTICE 1.4D	Supplying Interjections

Read each sentence. Then, write an interjection that shows the feeling expressed in the sentence.

EXAMPLE   _____, the cat got out!

ANSWER   *Oh, no*

11. _____, where did I leave my keys?

12. _____, is that someone famous?

13. _____! We won again!

14. _____, that salesperson is calling again!

15. _____, the queen has produced an heir!

16. _____! I don't approve of that behavior.

17. _____! I thought we'd never get out of there.

18. _____! I tripped and sprained my ankle.

19. _____, come in out of the rain.

20. _____, wait for me!

SPEAKING APPLICATION

Take turns with a partner. Tell about something that you did with a friend. Your partner should name conjunctions that you use and tell what kind of conjunction each one is.

WRITING APPLICATION

Write three sentences using interjections.

1.5 Words as Different Parts of Speech

Words are flexible, often serving as one part of speech in one sentence and as another part of speech in another.

Identifying Parts of Speech

To *function* means "to serve in a particular capacity." The function of a word may change from one sentence to another.

RULE 1.5.1

The way a word is used in a sentence determines its part of speech.

The word *well* has different meanings in the following sentences.

As a Noun	The well was overflowing.
As a Verb	After winning the tournament, tears welled in Meena's eyes.
As an Adjective	Tia didn't feel well yesterday.

Nouns, Pronouns, and Verbs A **noun** names a person, place, or thing. A **pronoun** stands for a noun. A **verb** shows action, condition, or existence.

The chart below reviews the definition of each part of speech.

PARTS OF SPEECH	QUESTIONS TO ASK YOURSELF	EXAMPLES
Noun	Does the word name a person, place, or thing?	Their trip to Yellowstone Park delighted Tina.
Pronoun	Does the word stand for a noun?	They lent the car to him.

PARTS OF SPEECH	QUESTIONS TO ASK YOURSELF	EXAMPLES
Verb	Does the word tell what someone or something did? Does the word link one word with another word that identifies or describes it? Does the word show that something exists?	We played tennis. That game was fun. Our host appeared relaxed. Our guest is here.

See Practice 1.5A

The Other Parts of Speech An **adjective** modifies a noun or pronoun. An **adverb** modifies a verb, an adjective, or another adverb. A **preposition** relates a noun or pronoun that appears with it to another word. A **conjunction** connects words or groups of words. An **interjection** expresses emotion.

PARTS OF SPEECH	QUESTIONS TO ASK YOURSELF	EXAMPLES
Adjective	Does the word tell *what kind, which one, how many,* or *how much?*	Those two fruit bars have an unusual taste.
Adverb	Does the word tell *where, when, in what way,* or *to what extent?*	Go home. Apply now. Walk very slowly. I am extremely excited.
Preposition	Is the word part of a phrase that includes a noun or pronoun?	Behind the fence, the children were on the swings.
Conjunction	Does the word connect other words in the sentence or connect clauses?	Both Sara and I will cook because they need food; besides, it will be fun!
Interjection	Does the word express feeling or emotion and function independently of the sentence?	Hey, where's that from? Wow! That was a bargain!

See Practice 1.5B

Read each sentence. Then, label the underlined word *noun*, *pronoun*, or *verb*.

EXAMPLE   Ted lives in the biggest house in <u>our</u> neighborhood.

ANSWER   *pronoun*

1. The senior musical was a big <u>hit</u> with the community.

2. The pitcher threw the ball, and Eduardo <u>hit</u> it out of the park.

3. Bart said <u>he</u> doesn't like jazz music.

4. <u>We</u> have a question for the teacher.

5. I hope no one <u>spots</u> me here when I should be sleeping.

6. Mom says a leopard never changes its <u>spots</u>.

7. I am so glad <u>our</u> project is finished.

8. Stephen offered to take his little cousin to the <u>park</u>.

9. I'll wait here while you <u>park</u> the car.

10. Ask your friends if <u>they</u> want to come in.

Read each sentence. Then, write which part of speech the underlined words are in each sentence.

EXAMPLE   Rosa didn't win the award, but an article was written <u>about</u> her in the <u>newspaper</u>.

ANSWER   *preposition, noun*

11. Mom is home, <u>but</u> Dad is not.

12. Let's stop and <u>visit</u> our friends <u>while</u> we're here.

13. <u>Hey</u>, where were <u>you</u> earlier?

14. She got <u>home</u> at three, and she's been studying ever <u>since</u>.

15. We stayed up to watch the <u>late</u> movie.

16. I was on time, but you arrived <u>late</u>.

17. <u>After</u> the storm, the air was <u>very</u> still.

18. Dad will talk to <u>him</u> <u>after</u> we get home.

19. Ted had an <u>early</u> breakfast and headed to school.

20. Have you <u>finished</u> your assignments <u>yet</u>?

SPEAKING APPLICATION

Take turns with a partner. Tell about something that you did earlier today. Your partner should identify the nouns, pronouns, and verbs that you use.

WRITING APPLICATION

Write the part of speech of each word in sentence 18.

CHAPTER 2

BASIC SENTENCE PARTS

Pair strong subjects and verbs to form creative sentences, and use descriptive complements to add interest.

WRITE GUY *Jeff Anderson, M.Ed.*

WHAT DO YOU NOTICE?

Focus on sentence parts as you zoom in on these lines from Act 4 of the play *The Crucible* by Arthur Miller.

MENTOR TEXT

> **Danforth,** *suspiciously:* What is he about here?
> **Herrick:** He goes among them that will hang, sir. And he prays with them. He sits with Goody Nurse now. And Mr. Parris with him.

Now, ask yourself the following questions:

- What is the sentence fragment in these lines, and what is missing that makes it a fragment?
- What reason do you think the playwright had for using a sentence fragment here?

The sentence fragment in these lines is *And Mr. Parris with him.* Although the line has a subject, *Mr. Parris*, it lacks a verb to make it a complete sentence. Miller probably decided to use a sentence fragment here because he wanted the dialogue to sound natural. People often use sentence fragments in conversation.

Grammar for Writers When you are writing formally, it is best to use complete sentences. However, if you are writing dialogue, it is acceptable to use an occasional sentence fragment to echo real speech.

All in a muddle. Completely fragmented.

Know what you mean. Me too.

2.1 Subjects and Predicates

A **sentence** is a group of words that expresses a complete unit of thought. *The cereal in the bowl* is not a complete unit of thought because you probably wonder what the writer wanted to say about the cereal. *The cereal in the bowl is soggy*, however, does express a complete unit of thought.

RULE 2.1.1 A **sentence** is a group of words that has two main parts: a complete subject and a complete predicate. Together, these parts express a complete thought or paint a complete picture.

EL9

The **complete subject** contains a noun, pronoun, or group of words acting as a noun, plus its modifiers. These words tell *who* or *what* the sentence is about. The **complete predicate** consists of the verb or verb phrase, plus its modifiers. These words tell what the complete subject is or does.

COMPLETE SUBJECTS	COMPLETE PREDICATES
Snakes	slither.
A bell-clanging streetcar	moved through the turn.
Wood or cellulose	makes a delicious meal for a termite.
The candidate's approach to fiscal problems	impressed the voters attending the rally.

Sometimes, part of the predicate precedes the complete subject.

EXAMPLES

At midnight , the cluster of stars
complete   complete subject
was visible .
predicate

Tonight my book club
complete complete subject
visited a coffee shop .
predicate

See Practice 2.1A

Simple Subjects and Predicates

The most essential parts of a sentence are the **simple subject** and the **simple predicate.** These words tell you the basics of what you need to know about the topic of the sentence. All of the other words in the sentence give you information about the simple subject and simple predicate.

2.1.2 · RULE

> The **simple subject** is the essential noun, pronoun, or group of words that acts as a noun in a complete subject. The **simple predicate** is the essential verb or verb phrase in a complete predicate.

Note: When sentences are discussed in this chapter, the term *subject* will refer to a simple subject, and the term *verb* will refer to a simple predicate.

SUBJECTS	VERBS
Small shoes	fit nicely into the closets.
Many Broadway shows	have used colored lights to show effect.
Jars of honey	were hanging from the tree branch.
A colorful sign	covered the door.
The author's editor	published all of her books.
Studies of other cultures	have certainly revealed much about their lifestyles.

In the last example, the simple subject is *studies,* not *cultures; cultures* is the object of the preposition *of.* Objects of prepositions never function as simple subjects. In this same example, the simple predicate is a verb phrase. In addition, the word *certainly* is not part of the simple predicate because it does not provide essential information.

See Practice 2.1B

PRACTICE 2.1A ▷ **Recognizing Complete Subjects and Predicates**

Read each sentence. Then, rewrite the sentence, and draw a vertical line between the complete subject and the complete predicate.

EXAMPLE   The player with the ball tagged the runner.

ANSWER   *The player with the ball | tagged the runner.*

1. My friends are starting a business.

2. We will need a tent and some sleeping bags.

3. Arriving at the mall, we saw a crowd near the main entrance.

4. Everyone has an opportunity to get involved.

5. The beginning of the book was not very interesting.

6. The path across the desert was hot and dusty.

7. The pilot flew the hot-air balloon above the hilltops.

8. They learned to water ski on the lake this summer.

9. An old dog slept on the front porch.

10. My father has written many stories of his childhood.

PRACTICE 2.1B ▷ **Identifying Simple Subjects and Predicates**

Read each sentence. The complete subject is underlined. The rest of the sentence is the complete predicate. Write the simple subject and simple predicate.

EXAMPLE   <u>That girl on the diving board</u> is in my Spanish class.

ANSWER   *girl, is*

11. <u>Three of us from the hiking club</u> traveled across the country.

12. <u>Mrs. Irwin</u> finished painting her house today.

13. <u>The price of that car</u> is more than I can pay.

14. <u>The tiny bird</u> was rescued by one of our neighbors.

15. <u>The temperature</u> rarely falls below freezing in southern Florida.

16. <u>Three homes on our block</u> were recently sold.

17. <u>Tanya</u> wanted to e-mail her parents.

18. <u>A child holding a paper bag</u> stared up at me.

19. <u>Too many errors</u> have been left in this report.

20. <u>A terrible blizzard</u> took people by surprise that winter.

SPEAKING APPLICATION

Take turns with a partner. Tell about something interesting that happened to you. Your partner should tell the complete subject and complete predicate in each of your sentences.

WRITING APPLICATION

Write a paragraph about your favorite place to visit. In each sentence, underline the simple subject, and double underline the simple predicate.

Fragments

A **fragment** is a group of words that does not contain either a complete subject or a complete predicate, or both. Fragments are usually not used in formal writing. You can correct a fragment by adding the parts needed to complete the thought.

> A **fragment** is a group of words that lacks a subject or a predicate, or both. It does not express a complete unit of thought.

2.1.3 RULE

FRAGMENTS	COMPLETE SENTENCES
bowl of cherries (complete predicate missing)	The bowl of cherries was eaten quickly. (complete predicate added)
splash in water (complete subject missing)	Children splash in water. (complete subject added)
from the playground (complete subject and predicate missing)	Kids from the playground swarmed into the house. (subject and complete predicate added)

In conversations, fragments usually do not present a problem because tone of voice, gestures, and facial expressions can add the missing information. A reader, however, cannot ask a writer for clarification.

Fragments are sometimes acceptable in writing that represents speech, such as the dialogue in a play or short story. Fragments are also sometimes acceptable in elliptical sentences.

> An **elliptical sentence** is one in which the missing word or words can be easily understood.

2.1.4 RULE

EXAMPLES   Until June.

Why such an anxious face?

Don't be sad!

Locating Subjects and Verbs

To avoid writing a fragment, look for the subject and verb in a sentence. To find the subject, ask, "Which word tells *what* or *who* this sentence is about?" Once you have the answer (the subject), then ask, "What does the subject do?" or "What is being done to the subject?" This will help you locate the verb.

In some sentences, it's easier to find the verb first. In this case, ask, "Which word states the action or condition in this sentence?" This question should help you locate the verb. Then ask, "*Who* or *what* is involved in the action of the verb?" The resulting word or words will be the subject.

EXAMPLE   Dogs often eat dry and wet food.

To find the subject first, ask, "Which word or words tell what or whom this sentence is about?"

ANSWER   Dogs (*Dogs* is the subject.)

Then ask, "What do dogs do?"

ANSWER   eat (*Eat* is the verb.)

To find the verb first, ask, "Which word or words state the action or condition in the sentence?"

ANSWER   eat (*Eat* states the action, so it is the verb.)

Then ask, "Who or what eats?"

ANSWER   Dogs (*Dogs* is the subject.)

To easily locate the subject and verb, mentally cross out any adjectives, adverbs, and prepositional phrases you see. These words add information, but they are usually less important than the simple subject and verb.

EXAMPLE   O̶u̶r̶ **flowers** **should grow** r̶a̶p̶i̶d̶l̶y̶
             simple subject   verb phrase
             i̶n̶ ̶t̶h̶e̶ ̶n̶e̶x̶t̶ ̶t̶e̶n̶ ̶w̶e̶e̶k̶s̶.

Sentences With More Than One Subject or Verb

Some sentences contain a **compound subject** or a **compound verb,** or a subject or verb with more than one part.

> **A compound subject** consists of two or more subjects. These subjects may be joined by a conjunction such as *and* or *or*.

EXAMPLES   The **campers** and **hikers** carried water bottles.

Cars, motorcycles, and **trucks** are all employing new fuel technology.

Neither the **teacher** nor the **student** looked happy.

> **A compound verb** consists of two or more verbs. These verbs may be joined by a conjunction such as *and, but, or,* or *nor*.

EXAMPLES   I neither **wrote** them nor **called** them.

Kelly **left** work and **ran** to dance class.

The baby **screamed** and **cried** through the entire play.

Some sentences contain both a compound subject and a compound verb.

See Practice 2.1C
See Practice 2.1D

EXAMPLES   **Jill** and **Peter** **planned** the party but **disagreed** on what food to serve.

The **chef** and his **student** **eyed** their staff, **turned** warily, and **walked** into the kitchen.

| PRACTICE 2.1C | Locating Subjects and Verbs |

Read each sentence. Then, write subjects(s) and verb(s) in each sentence. Underline the subject.

EXAMPLE   All of my relatives live and work in the Southwest.

ANSWER   *All; live, work*

1. Either Max or Ellen will get the best grade.
2. In this theater, the best seats are on the right.
3. The salad and drinks are in the refrigerator.
4. Pete mixed water into the paint and spread it on the canvas.
5. The thunder and lightning signaled a violent storm.
6. Haley gave it her best and won the contest.
7. Plumbers and electricians can make a very good living.
8. We left early and sped home to make sure everything was all right.
9. They held a meeting on the first night of camp.
10. Bud made corn bread and took it to the party.

| PRACTICE 2.1D | Fixing Sentence Errors |

Read each fragment. Then, use each fragment in a sentence.

EXAMPLE   in the morning

ANSWER   *I eat breakfast in the morning.*

11. sang a song
12. the statue in front of the school
13. at lunch
14. another clean shirt
15. with my help
16. wrote a poem
17. at the beach
18. the truck
19. swam in the lake
20. our second try

SPEAKING APPLICATION

Take turns with a partner. Tell about your favorite possessions. Your partner should name the subject and the verb in each of your sentences.

WRITING APPLICATION

Write a fragment of your own. Use the fragment in three different sentences.

2.2 Hard-to-Find Subjects

While most sentences have subjects that are easy to find, some present a challenge.

Subjects in Declarative Sentences Beginning With *Here* or *There*

When the word *here* or *there* begins a declarative sentence, it is often mistaken for the subject.

> **Here** and **there** are never the subject of a sentence.

RULE 2.2.1

Here and *there* are usually adverbs that modify the verb by pointing out *where* something is located. However, *there* may occasionally begin a sentence simply as an introductory word.

In some sentences beginning with *here* or *there*, the subject appears before the verb. However, many sentences beginning with *here* or *there* are **inverted.** In an inverted sentence, the subject follows the verb. If you rearrange such a sentence in subject–verb order, you can identify the subject more easily.

INVERTED   There **are** the **groceries**. (verb–subject order)

REARRANGED   The **groceries are** there. (subject–verb order)

SENTENCES BEGINNING WITH *HERE* OR *THERE*	SENTENCES REARRANGED IN SUBJECT–VERB ORDER
There are the new condo buildings.	The new condo buildings are there.
Here is the ticket for the show.	The ticket for your show is here.
There is money in the jar.	Money is in the jar there.

> In some declarative sentences, the subject is placed after the verb in order to give the subject greater emphasis.

RULE 2.2.2

Because most sentences are written in subject–verb order, changing that order makes readers stop and think. Inverted sentences often begin with prepositional phrases.

SENTENCES INVERTED FOR EMPHASIS	SENTENCES REARRANGED IN SUBJECT–VERB ORDER
Toward the open doors rushed the hungry crowd.	The hungry crowd rushed toward the open doors.
Around the corner careened the racing bicyclist.	The racing bicyclist careened around the corner.

Subjects in Interrogative Sentences

Some interrogative sentences use subject–verb order. Often, however, the word order of an interrogative sentence is verb–subject.

EXAMPLES
Which **television** **gets** the best picture?
(subject–verb order)

When **are** **we** going there?
(verb–subject order)

> In interrogative sentences, the subject often follows the verb.

An inverted interrogative sentence can begin with an action verb, a helping verb, or one of the following words: *how, what, when, where, which, who, whose,* or *why*. Some interrogative sentences divide the helping verb from the main verb. To help locate the subject, mentally rearrange the sentence into subject–verb order.

INTERROGATIVE SENTENCES	REARRANGED IN SUBJECT–VERB ORDER
Is the Museum of Art open this afternoon?	The Museum of Art is open this afternoon.
Do they own that boat?	They do own that boat.
Where will the party be held?	The party will be held where?

Subjects in Imperative Sentences

EL9

The subject of an imperative sentence is usually implied rather than specifically stated.

> In imperative sentences, the subject is understood to be *you*.

IMPERATIVE SENTENCES	SENTENCES WITH *YOU* ADDED
First, tour the movie studios.	First, [you] tour the movie studios.
After the tour, come back for the rides.	After the tour, [you] come back for the rides.
Peri, show me the park map.	Peri, [you] show me the park map.

In the last example, the name of the person being addressed, *Peri*, is not the subject of the imperative sentence. Instead, the subject is still understood to be *you*.

Subjects in Exclamatory Sentences

In some **exclamatory sentences,** the subject appears before the verb. In others, the verb appears first. To find the subject, rearrange the sentence in subject–verb order.

> In exclamatory sentences, the subject often appears after the verb, or it may be understood.

EXAMPLES   What **do they know**!
(**They do know** what.)

Come now!
(Subject understood: [**You**] come now!)

In other exclamatory sentences, both the subject and verb may be unstated.

EXAMPLES   Lightning! ([**You watch** out for the] lightning!)

See Practice 2.2A
See Practice 2.2B

Bear! ([**I see**] a bear!)

PRACTICE 2.2A Identifying Hard-to-Find Subjects

Read each sentence. Then, write the subject of each sentence.

EXAMPLE   Here is your new car!

ANSWER   *car*

1. There is a strange odor in here.
2. Has the last bus left yet?
3. Near the center of town is the old courthouse.
4. Where can my umbrella be?
5. Here is the tool you were looking for.
6. In the forest sleep wild animals.
7. There are no bananas in the kitchen.
8. Will someone be available to answer questions?
9. Beyond the house is a small pond.
10. There goes the last of the geese.

PRACTICE 2.2B Locating Hard-to-Find Verbs

Read each sentence. Then, write the verb in each sentence.

EXAMPLE   Look for Gary's house.

ANSWER   *Look*

11. Can you verify the facts from the case?
12. Why would anyone tell such bad jokes?
13. In the morning, wake up happy.
14. Before the game, show me your special pitch.
15. With great stealth, the animal stalked its prey.
16. During a hurricane, can lightning strike?
17. Hey, take the bread out of the oven!
18. Where are your parents?
19. Against the wall stood the tall ladder.
20. At dusk, turn on the lights.

SPEAKING APPLICATION

Take turns with a partner. Say sentences that describe someone doing something. Your partner should name the subject in each of your sentences.

WRITING APPLICATION

Write three imperative sentences. Underline the subject and double underline the verb in each sentence.

2.3 Complements

Some sentences are complete with just a subject and a verb or with a subject, verb, and modifiers: *The crowd cheered.* Other sentences need more information to be complete.

The meaning of many sentences, however, depends on additional words that add information to the subject and verb. For example, although *The satellite continually sends* has a subject and verb, it is an incomplete sentence. To complete the meaning of the predicate—in this case, to tell *what* a satellite sends—a writer must add a **complement.**

> A **complement** is a word or group of words that completes the meaning of the predicate of a sentence.

2.3.1 RULE

There are five kinds of complements in English: **direct objects, indirect objects, object complements, predicate nominatives,** and **predicate adjectives.** The first three occur in sentences that have transitive verbs. The last two are often called **subject complements.** Subject complements are found only with linking verbs. (See Chapter 1 for more information about action and linking verbs.)

Direct Objects

Direct objects are the most common of the five types of complements. They complete the meaning of action verbs by telling *who* or *what* receives the action.

> A **direct object** is a noun, pronoun, or group of words acting as a noun that receives the action of a transitive verb.

2.3.2 RULE

EXAMPLES   I **visited** the **Kennedy Space Center**.
direct object

Ice and **hail broke** the **gutters** this winter.
direct object

Direct Objects and Action Verbs The direct object answers the question *Whom?* or *What?* about the action verb. If you cannot answer the question *Whom?* or *What?* the verb may be intransitive, and there is no direct object in the sentence.

EXAMPLES   The sprinters **can run** around the track.
(Ask, "Sprinters can run *what*?" No answer; the verb is intransitive.)

The top **spun** around the table.
(Ask, "The top spun *what*?" No answer; the verb is intransitive.)

In some inverted questions, the direct object may appear before the verb. To find the direct object easily, rearrange inverted questions in subject–verb order.

INVERTED
QUESTION   Which **shows** **did** **they** **see**?
            direct object

REARRANGED
IN SUBJECT–
VERB ORDER   **They** **did see** which **shows**?
                             direct object

Some sentences have more than one direct object, known as a **compound direct object.** If a sentence contains a compound direct object, asking *Whom?* or *What?* after the action verb will yield two or more answers.

EXAMPLES   The climbers **wore** **helmets** and
                            direct object

gloves.
direct object

The theater company **has performed** **plays**
                                      direct object

and **musicals** around the country.
    direct object

In the last example, *country* is the object of the preposition *around*. The object of a preposition is never a direct object.

Indirect Objects

Indirect objects appear only in sentences that contain transitive verbs and direct objects. Indirect objects are common with such verbs as *ask, bring, buy, give, lend, make, show, teach, tell,* and *write*. Some sentences may contain a compound indirect object.

> An **indirect object** is a noun or pronoun that appears with a direct object. It often names the person or thing that something is given to or done for.

2.3.4 RULE

EXAMPLES   The **professor gave** the **student** the corrected
                                                indirect object
paper .
direct object

I showed my **cousin** and **friend** the new
                    compound indirect object
DVD .
direct object

To locate an indirect object, make sure the sentence contains a direct object. Then, ask one of these questions after the verb and direct object: *To* or *for whom?* or *To* or *for what?*

EXAMPLES   The **instructor taught** our **class yoga** .
(The instructor taught yoga *to whom*? ANSWER: our class)

We bought our **puppy** a **bed** .
(Bought a bed *for what*? ANSWER: our puppy)

An indirect object almost always appears between the verb and the direct object. In a sentence with subject–verb order, the indirect object never follows the direct object, nor will it ever be the object of the preposition *to* or *for*.

EXAMPLES   **Erin sent** the **book** to **me** .
                            direct object object of preposition

Theo sent me the **DVD** .
            indirect object   direct object

Theo gave Dan a **review** of the song.
            indirect object direct object

See Practice 2.3A

Object Complements

While an indirect object almost always comes *before* a direct object, an **object complement** almost always *follows* a direct object. The object complement completes the meaning of the direct object.

> An **object complement** is an adjective or noun that appears with a direct object and describes or renames it.

A sentence that contains an object complement may seem to have two direct objects. However, object complements occur only with such verbs as *appoint, call, consider, declare, elect, judge, label, make, name, select,* and *think.* The words *to be* are often understood before an object complement.

EXAMPLES The **organizers** of the conference **declared it**
                                                              direct object
successful in the end.
object complement

The **coach appointed him captain**
                        direct object   object
                                        complement
of the team.

I consider Bonnie a loyal **friend** and
            direct object   object
                                     complement
sensitive **mother**.
object complement

Subject Complements

Linking verbs require **subject complements** to complete their meaning.

> A **subject complement** is a noun, pronoun, or adjective that appears with a linking verb and gives more information about the subject.

There are two kinds of subject complements: **predicate nominatives** and **predicate adjectives**.

Predicate Nominatives

The **predicate nominative** refers to the same person, place, or thing as the subject of the sentence.

> A **predicate nominative** is a noun or pronoun that appears with a linking verb and renames, identifies, or explains the subject. Some sentences may contain a compound predicate nominative.

RULE 2.3.7

EXAMPLES
Tara Penn **is** a **doctor** at the hospital.
predicate nominative

The **winner** of the show **will be** the **poodle**.
predicate nominative

Michael Stoll **was** a **coach** and former **hockey player**.
compound predicate nominative

Predicate Adjectives

A **predicate adjective** is an adjective that appears with a linking verb. It describes the subject in much the same way that an adjective modifies a noun or pronoun. Some sentences may contain a compound predicate adjective.

> A **predicate adjective** is an adjective that appears with a linking verb and describes the subject of the sentence.

RULE 2.3.8

EXAMPLES
Your **reasoning** **seems** **fair**.
predicate adjective

The **soccer player** **was** **fast**.
predicate adjective

The **ocean** **sounded** **loud** and **fierce**.
compound predicate adjective

The navy **uniforms** **are** **blue** and **white**.
compound predicate adjective

See Practice 2.3B

PRACTICE 2.3A ▷ Identifying Direct and Indirect Objects

Read each sentence. Then, write and label each direct object and indirect object.

EXAMPLE   The students brought posters.

ANSWER   *posters* — direct object

1. I promised James and Lara a trip to the park.
2. Tell the doctor your symptoms.
3. The teacher asked me a question.
4. Sasha bought a sweater and a pair of shoes.
5. Why did you tell him the secret?
6. Which program are you watching?
7. My family runs an Italian restaurant in the city.
8. Teach the children the poem.
9. What destination do you recommend?
10. After class, the teacher gave us the news.

PRACTICE 2.3B ▷ Locating Object and Subject Complements

Read each sentence. Then, write the complement, and label it *object complement* or *subject complement*.

EXAMPLE   The coach named Albert team leader.

ANSWER   *leader* — object complement

11. Mr. Johnson labeled the mail "First Class."
12. Suddenly, the old man seemed friendlier.
13. Sean became our neighbor last year.
14. Of all countries, India is the most beautiful.
15. Shelly painted her room blue.
16. Did you think the house was unusual?
17. She remained my friend for many years.
18. He is extremely sensitive to heat.
19. The principal appointed Ravi spokesperson.
20. Our teacher often calls us brilliant.

SPEAKING APPLICATION

Take turns with a partner. Tell about a family event. Your partner should name the direct object and indirect object, if any, in each of your sentences.

WRITING APPLICATION

Use sentences 11 and 12 as models to write similar sentences. Underline and label the complement in each of your sentences.

PHRASES *and* CLAUSES

Combine related clauses into sentences to add variety to your writing, and include phrases that add vivid description.

WRITE GUY *Jeff Anderson, M.Ed.*

WHAT DO YOU NOTICE?

Hunt for phrases as you zoom in on this sentence from the book *Moby-Dick* by Herman Melville.

MENTOR TEXT

> Silently obeying the order, the three harpooners now stood with the detached iron part of their harpoons, some three feet long, held, barbs up, before him.

Now, ask yourself the following questions:

- What participle modifies the noun *part* in the sentence?
- Which noun does the participial phrase *silently obeying the order* modify?

A participle is a form of a verb that can act as an adjective. In this sentence, *detached* is a participle that acts as an adjective modifying the noun *part*. The participial phrase *silently obeying the order* contains the present participle *obeying*; the entire phrase modifies the noun *harpooners*.

Grammar for Writers Writers can add or take away phrases and clauses to adjust their sentence lengths and to add information. Think of phrases and clauses as movable parts that help you form your sentences.

This adjective isn't enough on its own.

Well then, make it part of a phrase!

3.1 Phrases

When one adjective or adverb cannot convey enough information, a phrase can contribute more detail to a sentence. A **phrase** is a group of words that does not include a subject and verb and cannot stand alone as a sentence.

There are several kinds of phrases, including **prepositional phrases, appositive phrases, participial phrases, gerund phrases,** and **infinitive phrases.**

Prepositional Phrases

A **prepositional phrase** consists of a preposition and a noun or pronoun, called the object of the preposition. *Over their heads, until dark,* and *after the baseball game* are all prepositional phrases. Prepositional phrases often modify other words by functioning as adjectives or adverbs.

Sometimes, a single prepositional phrase may include two or more objects joined by a conjunction.

EXAMPLES   between the **shower** and the **sink**
preposition   object   object

with the **sand** and the **ocean**
preposition   object   object

beside the **grass** and **trees**
preposition   object   object

See Practice 3.1A

Adjectival Phrases
A prepositional phrase that acts as an adjective is called an **adjectival phrase.**

> An **adjectival phrase** is a prepositional phrase that modifies a noun or pronoun by telling *what kind* or *which one.*

ADJECTIVES	ADJECTIVAL PHRASES
An important book was displayed in the library.	A book of great importance was displayed in the library. *(What kind of book?)*
Mike had a hot sandwich.	Mike had a sandwich that was hot. *(What kind of sandwich?)*

Like one-word adjectives, adjectival phrases can modify subjects, direct objects, indirect objects, or predicate nominatives.

MODIFYING A SUBJECT The house **across the road** is for sale.

MODIFYING A DIRECT OBJECT Let's take a picture **of the Empire State Building**.

MODIFYING AN INDIRECT OBJECT I gave the people **on the trolley** a tour.

MODIFYING A PREDICATE NOMINATIVE Italy is a country **with many traditions**.

A sentence may contain two or more **adjectival phrases.** In some cases, one phrase may modify the preceding phrase. In others, two phrases may modify the same word.

EXAMPLES We bought tickets **for the rides** **in the park**.

The photograph **of the tree** **in the library** was beautiful.

Adverbial Phrases

RULE
3.1.2

> An **adverbial phrase** is a prepositional phrase that modifies a verb, an adjective, or an adverb by pointing out *where, why, when, in what way,* or *to what extent.*

ADVERBS	ADVERBIAL PHRASES
She drove swiftly. (Drove *in what way?*)	She drove with speed .
I was scared then. (Scared *why?*)	I was scared by the loud noise .
The hawk flew overhead. (Flew *where?*)	The hawk flew over our house .

Adverbial phrases can modify verbs, adjectives, or adverbs.

MODIFYING
A VERB   The coins rolled **across the table**.

MODIFYING
AN ADJECTIVE   Joan was worried **beyond belief**.

MODIFYING
AN ADVERB   He kept his comments deep **in his mind**.

An adverbial phrase may either follow the word it modifies or be located elsewhere in the sentence. Often, two adverbs in different parts of a sentence can modify the same word.

MODIFIES

EXAMPLES   A tiny village vanished **during the mudslide**.

MODIFIES

During the mudslide, a tiny village vanished.

MODIFIES   MODIFIES

After the game, we all gathered **in the hall**.   See Practice 3.1B

PRACTICE 3.1A > **Identifying Prepositional Phrases**

Read each sentence. Write the prepositional phrase in each sentence and underline the preposition.

EXAMPLE   The book cover on that novel is interesting.

ANSWER   *on that novel*

1. She wore a jacket of soft cashmere.
2. In the car, she began to sing softly.
3. I moved the trash cans across the driveway.
4. My parents arrived late for the gathering.
5. She worked on Tuesday.
6. The room in the attic has been empty for years.
7. I remember the man with the big smile.
8. The children were hungry after the play date.
9. The jacket with the silver buttons is hers.
10. The hotels in Las Vegas are very large and ornate.

PRACTICE 3.1B > **Identifying Adjectival and Adverbial Phrases**

Read each sentence. Write the adjectival or adverbial phrase. Then, label the phrase *adjectival* or *adverbial*.

EXAMPLE   You can make time for the things you want.

ANSWER   *for the things you want —* adjectival

11. A glass of water will satisfy your thirst.
12. Even ten years later, the memory still remains in my mind.
13. Gillian sat by the pool and read her magazine.
14. Conduct rules for all employees must be followed.
15. Vanessa will take the test on Monday.
16. The man in the black shorts ran the fastest.
17. The study of dinosaurs is fascinating.
18. Ryan left for Mexico.
19. Bruno was very excited about the good news.
20. The team with the red caps is ours.

SPEAKING APPLICATION

With a partner, take turns describing the location of the furniture in the classroom. Your partner should listen for and name three prepositions that you use.

WRITING APPLICATION

Show that you understand the function of adjectival and adverbial phrases. Write sentences using the adjectival and adverbial phrases in any four sentences from Practice 3.1B. Read your sentences to a partner, who should identify the phrases as you speak.

Appositives and Appositive Phrases

The term *appositive* comes from a Latin verb that means "to put near or next to."

Appositives Using **appositives** in your writing is an easy way to give additional meaning to a noun or pronoun.

RULE 3.1.3

> An **appositive** is a group of words that identifies, renames, or explains a noun or pronoun.

As the examples below show, appositives usually follow immediately after the words they explain.

EXAMPLES   Some members, **the old-timers**, don't like change.

The home team, **the Panthers**, won the tournament title.

Notice that commas are used in the examples above because these appositives are **nonessential.** In other words, the appositives could be omitted from the sentences without altering the basic meaning of the sentences.

Some appositives, however, are not set off by any punctuation because they are **essential** to the meaning of the sentence.

EXAMPLES   The poet **Lord Byron** was a British citizen.
(The appositive is essential because it identifies which specific poet.)

My neighbor **Beth** is a talented painter.
(The appositive is essential because you might have several neighbors.)

Note About Terms: Sometimes, the terms *nonrestrictive* and *restrictive* are used in place of *nonessential* and *essential*.

Appositive Phrases When an appositive is accompanied by its own modifiers, it is called an **appositive phrase.**

> An **appositive phrase** is a noun or pronoun with modifiers that adds information by identifying, renaming, or explaining a noun or pronoun.

RULE 3.1.4

Appositives and appositive phrases may follow nouns or pronouns used in almost any role within a sentence. The modifiers within an appositive phrase can be adjectives, adjective phrases, or other groups of words functioning as adjectives.

EXAMPLES   Mrs. Vanas, **my guidance counselor**, picked three colleges for me to visit.

Tara explained genetics, **the study of heredity and genes**.

ROLES OF APPOSITIVE PHRASES IN SENTENCES	
Identifying a Subject	Leonardo da Vinci, a famous artist, painted many murals.
Identifying a Direct Object	The chef prepared snails, a French delicacy.
Identifying an Indirect Object	I brought my cousin Isabella, a girl of seven, a DVD.
Identifying an Object Complement	I chose neon blue, an unusual color for a car.
Identifying a Predicate Nominative	My favorite snack is an orange, a citrus fruit.
Identifying the Object of a Preposition	Store the books in the basement, a cool, dry place.

Compound Appositives Appositives and appositive phrases can also be compound.

EXAMPLES The entire team—**writers**, **editors**, and **designers**—worked on the book.

All books, **fiction** and **non-fiction**, are on sale at the store.

Casey visited her favorite cities, **Paris**, **London**, and **Oslo**, on her summer vacation.

See Practice 3.1C

Grammar and Style Tip When **appositives** or **appositive phrases** are used to combine sentences, they help to eliminate unnecessary words. One way to streamline your writing is to combine sentences by using an appositive phrase.

TWO SENTENCES	COMBINED SENTENCE
New Jersey is located in North America. The state is an exporter of cranberries.	New Jersey, an exporter of cranberries, is located in North America.
The ballet was performed in the sixteenth and seventeenth centuries. It was first seen in the French king's courts.	The ballet, performed in the sixteenth and seventeenth centuries, was first seen in the French king's courts.
New York City is one of the busiest cities in the United States. It is located on the East Coast.	New York City, one of our busiest cities, is on the East Coast of the United States.

Read aloud the pairs of sentences in the chart. Notice how the combined sentences, which began as two choppy sentences, include the same information. However, they flow much more smoothly once the information in both sentences is clearly linked.

See Practice 3.1D

PRACTICE 3.1C > **Identifying Appositives and Appositive Phrases**

Read each sentence. Then, write the appositive or appositive phrase in each sentence.

EXAMPLE Jackie's favorite team, the Bulldogs, won the championship game.

ANSWER *the Bulldogs*

1. Miss Smith, a music teacher, decided to play on Broadway.
2. My favorite cousin, a circus performer, lives far away.
3. I sold my old car, the Road Warrior.
4. My sister Tonya just graduated from college.
5. I stared at her face, beaming with pride.
6. Her plants, all roses, are exquisite.
7. Gazpacho, a spicy soup, is my favorite.
8. Her favorite meal, roast chicken, will be served today.
9. Most people will never play polo, a challenging game.
10. My friends Tiffany and Jing are going with me.

PRACTICE 3.1D > **Using Appositives and Appositive Phrases**

Read each pair of sentences. Then, combine the sentences using an appositive or an appositive phrase.

EXAMPLE Austin is a rapidly changing city. It is the capital of Texas.

ANSWER *Austin, a rapidly changing city, is the capital of Texas.*

11. Dr. Kim is retiring. She is our family doctor.
12. A box was in the basement. It was small but large enough for the gift.
13. The birds sat within a foot of the window. They were cardinals.
14. She suffers from claustrophobia. Claustrophobia is a fear of enclosed spaces.
15. We finally reached the campsite. It was a meadow surrounded by trees.
16. Her hobby is gardening. It keeps her busy.
17. Ecuador is a country in South America. It straddles the equator.
18. The prize was a plastic magnet. It disappointed me.
19. The dress is on the bed. It is my favorite.
20. My brothers are Dean and Michael. They are very different people.

SPEAKING APPLICATION

Take turns with a partner. Read aloud an article from a newspaper. Your partner should listen and identify the appositives and appositive phrases in the article.

WRITING APPLICATION

Write two sentences about the same subject. Then, combine the sentences with an appositive or an appositive phrase.

Verbal Phrases

When a verb is used as a noun, an adjective, or an adverb, it is called a **verbal.** Although a verbal does not function as a verb, it retains two characteristics of verbs: It can be modified in different ways, and it can have one or more complements. A verbal with modifiers or complements is called a **verbal phrase.**

Participles

Many of the adjectives you use are actually verbals known as **participles.**

> **A participle** is a form of a verb that can act as an adjective.

The most common kinds of participles are **present participles** and **past participles.** These two participles can be distinguished from one another by their endings. Present participles usually end in *-ing (frightening, entertaining).* Past participles usually end in *-ed (frightened, entertained),* but many have irregular endings, such as *-t* or *-en (burnt, written).*

PRESENT PARTICIPLES	PAST PARTICIPLES
The swaying boxer held his aching head.	Confused, Mary returned to her interrupted conference call.

Like other adjectives, participles answer the question *What kind?* or *Which one?* about the nouns or pronouns they modify.

EXAMPLES   Maggie's **tearing** eyes betrayed her happiness.
(*What kind* of eyes? Answer: *tearing* eyes)

The **broken** door needs to be replaced.
(*Which* door? Answer: *broken* door)

Participles may also have a **present perfect** form.

EXAMPLES   **Having decided**, Christina packed her bags.

Being greeted by the press, the star walked into the awards show.

Verb or Participle? Because **verbs** often have endings such as -*ing* and -*ed,* you may confuse them with **participles.** If a word ending in -*ed* or -*ing* expresses the action of the sentence, it is a verb or part of a verb phrase. If it describes a noun or pronoun, it is a participle.

> A **verb** shows an action, a condition, or the fact that something exists. A **participle** acting as an adjective modifies a noun or a pronoun.

3.1.6
RULE

See Practice 3.1E

ACTING AS VERBS	ACTING AS ADJECTIVES
The cat is crying at the door. (What is the cat doing?)	The crying cat clawed at the door. (Which cat?)
The people were delighted with the new laws. (What delighted the people?)	Delighted, the people approved of the new laws. (What kind of people?)

Participial Phrases
A participle can be expanded by adding modifiers and complements to form a **participial phrase.**

> A **participial phrase** is a participle modified by an adverb or adverbial phrase or accompanied by a complement. The entire participial phrase acts as an adjective.

3.1.7
RULE

The following examples show different ways that participles may be expanded into phrases.

WITH AN ADVERB
Working quickly, we built the house in three weeks.

WITH AN ADVERB PHRASE
Working at a fast pace, we built the house in three weeks.

WITH A COMPLEMENT
Avoiding stops, we built the house in three weeks.

A participial phrase that is nonessential to the basic meaning of a sentence is set off by commas or other forms of punctuation. A participial phrase that is essential is not set off by punctuation.

NONESSENTIAL PHRASES	ESSENTIAL PHRASES
Here is Tina, waiting at the counter .	The girl waiting at the counter is Tina.
Built in 1800 , the bridge was the first in town.	The bridge built in 1800 is the one that needs the most repair.

In the first sentence on the left side of the chart above, *waiting at the counter* merely adds information about Tina, so it is nonessential. In the sentence on the right, however, the same phrase is essential because many different girls might be in view.

In the second sentence on the left, *Built in 1800* is an additional description of *bridge,* so it is nonessential. In the sentence on the right, however, the phrase is essential because it identifies the specific bridge that is being discussed.

RULE 3.1.8

Participial phrases can often be used to combine information from two sentences into one.

TWO SENTENCES
We were exhausted from the ride to California. We rested by the side of the road.

COMBINED
Exhausted by the ride to California , we rested by the side of the road.

TWO SENTENCES
We ate dinner. We shared stories about our day.

COMBINED
Eating dinner , we shared stories about our day.

Notice how part of the verb in one sentence is changed into a participle in the combined sentence.

See Practice 3.1F

PRACTICE 3.1E > Identifying Verbal Phrases

Read each sentence. Then, write the verbal phrase and the word it modifies.

EXAMPLE   Walking quickly, we soon reached our car.

ANSWER   *Walking quickly, we*

1. Searching in the dark, Ann finally found the light switch.

2. The manager, arriving at ten, will unlock the door.

3. The well-known performer, contacted at home, answered all the questions.

4. This tale, first told to me by my mother, has always been my favorite.

5. A dog named Norbert walked across the state to find his family.

6. The highest peak in North America is Mount McKinley, located in Alaska.

7. Exhausted by the rehearsal, the actor took a long nap.

8. Hitting the shelf, I almost knocked over the glass.

9. The contest, lasting all day and night, finally came to an end.

10. Carla, having auditioned yesterday, waited eagerly for the results.

PRACTICE 3.1F > Recognizing Participial Phrases

Read each sentence. Write the participial phrase in each sentence. Then, write *E* for *essential* or *N* for *nonessential*.

EXAMPLE   Chosen by her peers, Natalie was the recipient of the award.

ANSWER   *Chosen by her peers — N*

11. Painting quickly, he completed the mural in less than a month.

12. The puppy shivering with fright wandered through the park.

13. The first important invention made by Edison advanced telegraphy.

14. Winning by a landslide, the team celebrated.

15. The key witness, protected by guards, entered the room.

16. The White House, built on swampland, has sunk one-quarter inch in thirty years.

17. Weighing over one hundred pounds, the pumpkin was sold at auction.

18. The chef, having added olive oil, put the vegetables in the oven.

19. Impeached by the panel, the disgraced politician headed home.

20. I ran to check the mailbox expecting good news.

SPEAKING APPLICATION

With a partner, take turns telling about your favorite after-school activities. Your partner should listen to and identify the verbal phrases that you use.

WRITING APPLICATION

Write three sentences with nonessential phrases and three sentences with essential phrases. Then, rewrite the sentences so that the nonessential phrases become essential phrases and the essential phrases become nonessential phrases.

Gerunds

Many nouns that end in *-ing* are actually **verbals** known as **gerunds.** Gerunds are not difficult to recognize: They always end in *-ing*, and they always function as **nouns.**

3.1.9

A **gerund** is a form of a verb that ends in *-ing* and acts as a **noun.**

FUNCTIONS OF GERUNDS	
Subject	Reading is my favorite pastime.
Direct Object	The Irish people make visiting Ireland a pleasure.
Indirect Object	Mr. Tate's sweet tea makes working a pleasure.
Predicate Nominative	My sister's favorite activity is running.
Object of a Preposition	Their well-behaved horses showed signs of training.
Appositive	Dan's profession, acting, is very competitive.

Verb, Participle, or Gerund? Words ending in *-ing* may be parts of verb phrases, participles acting as adjectives, or gerunds.

3.1.10

Words ending in *-ing* that act as **nouns** are called **gerunds.**
Unlike verbs ending in *-ing,* gerunds do not have helping verbs.
Unlike participles ending in *-ing,* they do not act as adjectives.

VERB	Gabby is **singing** in her seat.
PARTICIPLE	The **singing** girl is very joyful.
GERUND	**Singing** is very soothing.
VERB	My brother was **yelling**, and that upset me.
PARTICIPLE	**Yelling**, my brother upset me.
GERUND	My brother's **yelling** upset me.

Gerund Phrases Like participles, gerunds may be joined by other words to make **gerund phrases.**

> A **gerund phrase** consists of a gerund and one or more modifiers or a complement. These phrases act together as a noun.

3.1.11 RULE

GERUND PHRASES	
With Adjectives	His constant, angry ranting made the commander difficult to tolerate.
With an Adverb	Speaking loudly is not always a good idea.
With a Prepositional Phrase	Many people don't like visitors walking on the grass.
With a Direct Object	Blane was incapable of remembering the speech.
With an Indirect and a Direct Object	The literature professor tried giving her students praise.

Note About Gerunds and Possessive Pronouns: Always use the possessive form of a personal pronoun in front of a gerund.

INCORRECT   We never listen to **him** shouting.

CORRECT   We never listen to **his** shouting.

INCORRECT   **Them** refusing to wear knee pads is dangerous.

See Practice 3.1G   CORRECT   **Their** refusing to wear knee pads is dangerous.

Infinitives

The third kind of verbal is the **infinitive.** Infinitives have many different uses. They can act as nouns, adjectives, or adverbs.

> An **infinitive** is a form of a verb that generally appears with the word *to* in front of it and acts as a noun, an adjective, or an adverb.

3.1.12 RULE

EXAMPLE **The librarian asked the people to speak softly .**

INFINITIVES USED AS NOUNS	
Subject	To understand young children requires practice and patience.
Direct Object	The prisoners decided to rebel .
Predicate Nominative	The girl's only option was to drive home.
Object of a Preposition	Our flight from Washington D.C. was about to leave .
Appositive	You have only one option, to wait .

Unlike gerunds, infinitives can also act as adjectives and adverbs.

INFINITIVES USED AS MODIFIERS	
Adjective	The team showed a willingness to cooperate .
Adverb	Some people were unable to sing .

Prepositional Phrase or Infinitive? Although both **prepositional phrases** and **infinitives** often begin with *to,* you can tell the difference between them by analyzing the words that follow *to.*

3.1.13

> A **prepositional phrase** always ends with a noun or pronoun that acts as the object of the preposition. An **infinitive** always ends with a verb.

PREPOSITIONAL PHRASE	INFINITIVE
The students listened to the instructions .	The purpose of the headmaster is to instruct .
We went to the back of the store.	Make sure to back up your inventory list.

Note About Infinitives Without *to*: Sometimes infinitives do not include the word *to*. When an infinitive follows one of the eight verbs listed below, the *to* is generally omitted. However, it may be understood.

VERBS THAT PRECEDE INFINITIVES WITHOUT *TO*			
dare	help	make	see
hear	let	please	watch

EXAMPLES

He won't dare **[to] go** without a flight plan.

Please help me **[to] reach** the top shelf.

Bob helped Mike **[to] see** the game.

Infinitive Phrases Infinitives also can be joined with other words to form phrases.

> An **infinitive phrase** consists of an infinitive and its modifiers, complements, or subject, all acting together as a single part of speech.

RULE
3.1.14

INFINITIVE PHRASES	
With an Adverb	Tim's family likes to read quietly .
With an Adverb Phrase	To run on the sand is sometimes difficult.
With a Direct Object	Annie hated to leave San Francisco .
With an Indirect and a Direct Object	She promised to show us the video direct object indirect direct object from her soccer game. object
With a Subject and a Complement	I want him to decide his own future . subject complement

See Practice 3.1H

PRACTICE 3.1G Identifying Gerunds and
Gerund Phrases

Read each sentence. Then, write the gerund or
gerund phrase in each sentence.

EXAMPLE   Cooking together is a family
          tradition.

ANSWER   *Cooking together*

1. Sailing has always been Nina's favorite
   activity.

2. He often talks about growing older.

3. Todd enjoys dancing to fast music.

4. Developing a new system is Pablo's dream.

5. I avoid eating too much sugar.

6. I was tired of waiting all day.

7. Working harder is usually the answer.

8. I just finished writing my short story.

9. The performer's best trick was juggling.

10. Ashley spent the afternoon babysitting her
    nephew.

PRACTICE 3.1H Identifying Infinitives and
Infinitive Phrases

Read each sentence. Then, write the infinitive
phrase in each sentence.

EXAMPLE   To win at chess requires skill.

ANSWER   *To win at chess*

11. The magician's best trick was to saw a
    woman in half.

12. Would you like to see the new calves?

13. Nate was practicing daily to improve his
    typing.

14. Jane had hoped to win the contest.

15. To plan an exciting party is no easy task.

16. We would like to see the opera tomorrow.

17. Here are the directions to get to the park.

18. Elaine left to catch her flight to Oregon.

19. His daily goal, to run five miles, is not always
    possible.

20. I bought a new dress to wear to dinner.

SPEAKING APPLICATION

**Take turns with a partner. Say sentences with
gerunds. Your partner should identify each
gerund.**

WRITING APPLICATION

**Write three sentences with infinitive phrases
about what you would like to do when you
graduate.**

3.2 Clauses

Every **clause** contains a subject and a verb. However, not every clause can stand by itself as a complete thought.

> A **clause** is a group of words that contains a subject and a verb.

Independent and Subordinate Clauses

The two basic kinds of clauses are **independent** or **main clauses** and **subordinate clauses.**

> An **independent** or **main clause** can stand by itself as a complete sentence.

Every sentence must contain an independent clause. The independent clause can either stand by itself or be connected to other independent or subordinate clauses.

STANDING ALONE

Mrs. Vera teaches grammar .
  independent clause

WITH ANOTHER INDEPENDENT CLAUSE

Mrs. Vera teaches grammar , and
  independent clause

her friend teaches writing .
  independent clause

WITH A SUBORDINATE CLAUSE

Mrs. Vera teaches grammar , **while her friend**
  independent clause   subordinate clause

teaches writing .

When you subordinate something, you give it less importance.

> A **subordinate clause,** although it has a subject and verb, cannot stand by itself as a complete sentence.

Subordinate clauses can appear before or after an independent clause in a sentence or can even split an independent clause.

LOCATIONS OF SUBORDINATE CLAUSES	
In the Middle of an Independent Clause	The woman to whom I introduced you teaches English.
Preceding an Independent Clause	Unless the flood stops soon , the town will be underwater.
Following an Independent Clause	They asked that they be excused .

See Practice 3.2A

Like phrases, subordinate clauses can function as adjectives, adverbs, or nouns in sentences.

Adjectival Clauses

One way to add description and detail to a sentence is by adding an **adjectival clause.**

> An **adjectival clause** is a subordinate clause that modifies a noun or pronoun in another clause by telling *what kind* or *which one.*

An adjectival clause usually begins with one of the relative pronouns: *that, which, who, whom,* or *whose.* Sometimes, it begins with a relative adverb, such as *before, since, when, where,* or *why.* Each of these words connects the clause to the word it modifies.

> An **adjectival clause** often begins with a **relative pronoun** or a **relative adverb** that links the clause to a noun or pronoun in another clause.

The adjectival clauses in the examples on the next page answer the questions *What kind?* and *Which one?* Each modifies the noun in the independent clause that comes right before the adjectival clause. Notice also that the first two clauses begin with relative pronouns and the last one begins with a relative adverb.

EXAMPLES   I finished reading the magazine **that you loaned me** .

We gave skiing, **which we found challenging** , another try.

In England, we visited the town **where my mother grew up** .

Adjectival clauses can often be used to combine information from two sentences into one. Using adjectival clauses to combine sentences can indicate the relationship between ideas as well as add detail to a sentence.

TWO SENTENCES	COMBINED SENTENCES
The artist set up her easel. The artist is ready to paint.	The artist, who is ready to paint , set up her easel.
My brother won the wrestling match in less than three minutes. He is on the varsity team.	My brother, who is on the varsity team , won the wrestling match in less than three minutes.

Essential and Nonessential Adjectival Clauses Adjectival clauses, like appositives and participial phrases, are set off by punctuation only when they are not essential to the meaning of a sentence. Commas are used to indicate information that is not essential to the meaning of the sentence. When information in an adjectival clause is essential to the sentence, no commas are used.

NONESSENTIAL CLAUSES	ESSENTIAL CLAUSES
One of Dickens's best characters is Pip, who is a main character in *Great Expectations* .	The project that everyone must complete by Wednesday promises to be challenging.
Jenna Vance, who studied every night for a week , passed the test.	A teacher who prepares faithfully usually finds teaching easy.

See Practice 3.2B

Identifying Independent and Subordinate Clauses

Read each sentence. Identify the underlined clause as *independent* or *subordinate*.

EXAMPLE   All the roads will be flooded <u>unless the storm stops soon</u>.

ANSWER   *subordinate*

1. <u>My older sister drives</u>, but my younger one does not.

2. My class has too many students now, but <u>that will change next week</u>.

3. <u>Since I left</u>, the town has changed a lot.

4. <u>As I walked up the stairs</u>, I felt optimistic.

5. <u>Lindsay loved the flowers</u> because they made the room smell sweet.

6. That book was not very good, but <u>I did enjoy the characters</u>.

7. Take the book to the publisher <u>who gives the best compensation</u>.

8. When the holiday season begins, <u>the stores are overflowing with buyers</u>.

9. <u>Whoever wants a ride</u> needs to tell me now.

10. The roast <u>we are having for dinner</u> smells wonderful.

Identifying Adjectival Clauses

Read each sentence. Then, write the adjectival clause in each sentence.

EXAMPLE   The book that you mentioned is sold out.

ANSWER   *that you mentioned*

11. The building, which we visited, is very old.

12. This is the architectural style that I prefer.

13. I bought the painting, which was on sale.

14. The man whom you described is my neighbor.

15. Sophie, who is in my science class, used to live in Singapore.

16. This is the table that I want.

17. The speaker who visited our school was very interesting.

18. I prefer a radio station that plays all types of music.

19. I used the printer that had plenty of ink.

20. The people who live on that street are kind.

SPEAKING APPLICATION

Take turns with a partner. Say three sentences from Practice 3.2A, changing the underlined clauses from subordinate clauses to independent clauses.

WRITING APPLICATION

Write two short sentences that could be combined with an adjectival clause. Exchange papers with a partner, who should combine your sentences with an adjectival clause.

Relative Pronouns **Relative pronouns** help link a subordinate clause to another part of a sentence. They also have a function in the subordinate clause.

> **Relative pronouns** connect adjectival clauses to the words they modify and act as subjects, direct objects, objects of prepositions, or adjectives in the subordinate clauses.

3.2.6 RULE

To tell how a relative pronoun is used within a clause, separate the clause from the rest of the sentence, and find the subject and verb in the clause.

FUNCTIONS OF RELATIVE PRONOUNS IN CLAUSES	
As a Subject	A bridge that is built on a strong foundation is built _subject_ to last.
As a Direct Object	Kevin, whom my brother met in the military, is _direct object_ an officer. (Reworded clause: my brother met *whom* in the military)
As an Object of a Preposition	This is the play about which I heard excellent reviews. _object of a preposition_ (Reworded clause: I heard excellent reviews about *which*)
As an Adjective	The student whose behavior was in question spoke to _adjective_ the principal.

Sometimes in writing and in speech, a relative pronoun is left out of an adjectival clause. However, the missing word, though simply understood, still functions in the sentence.

EXAMPLES   The generals [**whom**] we studied were great
leaders.

See Practice 3.2C

The changes [**that**] they made were successful.

Relative Adverbs Like relative pronouns, **relative adverbs** help link the subordinate clause to another part of a sentence. However, they have only one use within a subordinate clause.

RULE

3.2.7

Relative adverbs connect adjectival clauses to the words they modify and act as adverbs in the clauses.

EXAMPLE   The passenger yearned for the minute **when** she'd be off the ship.

In the example, the adjectival clause is *when she'd be off the ship*. Reword the clause this way to see that *when* functions as an adverb: *she'd be off the ship when*.

Adverbial Clauses

Subordinate clauses may also serve as adverbs in sentences. They are introduced by subordinating conjunctions. Like adverbs, **adverbial clauses** modify verbs, adjectives, or other adverbs.

RULE

3.2.8

Subordinate **adverbial clauses** modify verbs, adjectives, adverbs, or verbals by telling *where, when, in what way, to what extent, under what condition,* or *why.*

An adverbial clause begins with a subordinating conjunction and contains a subject and a verb, although they are not the main subject and verb in the sentence. In the chart that follows, the adverbial clauses are highlighted in orange. Arrows point to the words they modify.

ADVERBIAL CLAUSES	
Modifying a Verb	After you visit Houston, you should begin your report. (Begin *when?*)
Modifying an Adjective	Max seemed peaceful wherever he was. (Peaceful *where?*)
Modifying a Gerund	Driving a car if you have a license is legal. (Driving *under what condition?*)

> **Adverbial clauses** begin with **subordinating conjunctions** and contain subjects and verbs.

EXAMPLE **Whenever** it snows, my dog loves to go
subordinating
conjunction
outside and play.

Recognizing the subordinating conjunctions will help you identify adverbial clauses. The following chart shows some of the most common subordinating conjunctions.

SUBORDINATING CONJUNCTIONS			
after	because	so that	when
although	before	than	whenever
as	even though	though	where
as if	if	unless	wherever
as long as	since	until	while

Whether an adverbial clause appears at the beginning, middle, or end of a sentence can sometimes affect the sentence meaning.

EXAMPLES **Before the year was over**, Tim made plans to visit England.

Tim made plans to visit England **before the year was over**.

Like adjectival clauses, adverbial clauses can be used to combine the information from two sentences into one. The combined sentence shows a close relationship between the ideas.

TWO SENTENCES **It was stormy**. They did not go swimming.

COMBINED **Because** it was stormy, they did not go swimming.
subordinating
conjunction

See Practice 3.2D

PRACTICE 3.2C ▷ Identifying Relative Pronouns and Adjectival Clauses

Read each sentence. Then, write the adjectival clause in each sentence, and underline the relative pronoun that introduces the clause.

EXAMPLE   The contest, which includes a free prize, is open to everyone.

ANSWER   *which includes a free prize*

1. The badge that I earned last summer is in my closet.

2. My sister, whom you met last week, went back to college.

3. The theater, which is twenty miles away, is easily reached by train.

4. The manager who hosted the open house was happy with the large turnout.

5. The recipe that you asked for is in my cookbook.

6. The man who created this game is Irish.

7. The chicken that I roasted was delicious.

8. She is the person who works at the video store.

9. The shirt, which costs only a few dollars, is pink.

10. The cup that holds pencils tipped over.

PRACTICE 3.2D ▷ Recognizing Adverbial Clauses

Read each sentence. Then, write the adverbial clause in each sentence.

EXAMPLE   The principal will make his announcement when classes are over.

ANSWER   *when classes are over*

11. Everyone stopped talking when she walked into the room.

12. I will reply as soon as I get a chance.

13. We will take them swimming so that they can cool off.

14. She is upset when she misses her daily workout.

15. To be able to travel whenever you like is a luxury.

16. She is happy when she hears from you.

17. Because many people were confused, the president explained why we needed to pass the new law.

18. When everyone arrived, we began the presentation.

19. The front of the stage is where the voting will take place.

20. While riding the tram, he took lots of photographs of the scenery.

SPEAKING APPLICATION

Take turns with a partner. Tell about three of your family members or a book you have read recently. Your partner should listen for and identify the relative pronouns that you use that answer *which*, *who*, and *whose*.

WRITING APPLICATION

Write sentences using the relative adverbs *when*, *where*, and *why*.

Elliptical Adverbial Clauses Sometimes, words are omitted in adverbial clauses, especially in those clauses that begin with *as* or *than* and are used to express comparisons. Such clauses are said to be *elliptical.*

> An **elliptical clause** is a clause in which the verb or the subject and verb are understood but not actually stated.

3.2.10 RULE

Even though the subject or the verb (or both) may not appear in an elliptical clause, they make the clause express a complete thought.

In the following examples, the understood words appear in brackets. The sentences are alike, except for the words *she* and *her*. In the first sentence, *she* is a subject of the adverbial clause. In the second sentence, *her* functions as a direct object of the adverbial clause.

VERB UNDERSTOOD	Her brother resembles their father more **than she [does]**.
SUBJECT AND VERB UNDERSTOOD	Her brother resembles their father more **than [he resembles] her**.

See Practice 3.2E

When you read or write elliptical clauses, mentally include the omitted words to clarify the intended meaning.

Noun Clauses

Subordinate clauses can also act as nouns in sentences.

> A **noun clause** is a subordinate clause that acts as a noun.

3.2.11 RULE

A noun clause acts in almost the same way a one-word noun does in a sentence: It tells what or whom the sentence is about.

In a sentence, a noun clause may act as a subject, direct object, indirect object, predicate nominative, object of a preposition, or appositive.

EXAMPLES **Whatever you lost** can be found in the closet.
         subject

My friends remembered **what I wanted to do on my birthday** .
                      direct object

The chart on the next page contains more examples of the functions of noun clauses.

Introductory Words

Noun clauses frequently begin with the words *that, which, who, whom,* or *whose*—the same words that are used to begin adjective clauses. *Whichever, whoever,* or *whomever* may also be used as introductory words in noun clauses. Other noun clauses begin with the words *how, if, what, whatever, where, when, whether,* or *why.*

Introductory words may act as subjects, direct objects, objects of prepositions, adjectives, or adverbs in noun clauses, or they may simply introduce the clauses.

SOME USES OF INTRODUCTORY WORDS IN NOUN CLAUSES	
FUNCTIONS IN CLAUSES	**EXAMPLES**
Adjective	She couldn't decide which dress was her favorite .
Adverb	We want to know how the game is played .
Subject	I want the pattern from whoever knitted that sweater .
Direct Object	Whatever my manager suggested , I did.
No Function	The doctor determined that she had passed .

Note that in the following chart the introductory word *that* in the last example has no function except to introduce the clause.

FUNCTIONS OF NOUN CLAUSES IN SENTENCES	
Acting as a Subject	Whoever is last must turn the lights out.
Acting as a Direct Object	Please tell whomever you want about the good news!
Acting as an Indirect Object	Her joyful personality made whoever met her smile.
Acting as a Predicate Nominative	We don't know whether he will win or lose.
Acting as an Object of a Preposition	Use the DVD for whatever movie you would like.
Acting as an Appositive	The counsel rejected the plea that more money be given away to charity.

Some words that introduce noun clauses also introduce adjectival and adverbial clauses. It is necessary to check the function of the clause in the sentence to determine its type. To check the function, try substituting the words *it, you, fact,* or *thing* for the clause. If the sentence retains its smoothness, you probably replaced a noun clause.

NOUN CLAUSE	I told you **that it was at 6 P.M**.
SUBSTITUTION	I told you.

In the following examples, all three subordinating clauses begin with *where,* but only the first is a noun clause because it functions in the sentence as a direct object.

NOUN CLAUSE	Mr. James told the players **where they would gather for the game**. (Told the players *what?*)
ADJECTIVAL CLAUSE	They took the player to the medical bench, **where a doctor examined his injury**. (*Which* bench?)
ADVERBIAL CLAUSE	She lives **where the weather is cloudy most days**. (Lives *where?*)

Note About Introductory Words: The introductory word *that* is often omitted from a noun clause. In the following examples, the understood word *that* is in brackets.

EXAMPLES	The teacher suggested **[that] I write my name in large print**.
	After her professor chose her for the debate team, Tia knew **[that] she would have a very busy year**.
	She remembered **[that] you wanted to run in the morning**.

See Practice 3.2F

PRACTICE 3.2E > Identifying Elliptical Adverbial Clauses

Read each sentence. Then, write the adverbial clause in each sentence. For the adverbial clauses that are elliptical, add the understood words in parentheses.

EXAMPLE   My handwriting is neater than Julia's handwriting.

ANSWER   *than Julia's handwriting (is)*

1. The length of Mark's arms is shorter than the length of David's arms.

2. My braces will come off sooner than Juanita's braces.

3. Graham's sister is younger than Peter's sister.

4. Don's son is as tall as Don.

5. The cat ran faster than my dog.

6. The sidewalk is hotter than a frying pan.

7. That juice is as sour as a lemon.

8. That color is brighter than neon pink.

9. Nathalia's hair is as smooth as silk is.

10. Alexa plays the piano as well as Drew.

PRACTICE 3.2F > Recognizing Noun Clauses

Read each sentence. Then, write the noun clause and label it *subject, direct object, indirect object, object of a preposition, predicate nominative,* or *appositive*.

EXAMPLE   I wonder how he expects to leave.

ANSWER   *how he expects to leave* — direct object

11. This announcement is exactly what we anticipated.

12. My plan, that the team will practice every night, was rejected.

13. How the animals hunt every night is completely unknown.

14. Do you agree with what they recommend?

15. The repairman will show up on whatever day you indicate.

16. I agree with her idea that we start another project.

17. Whatever time they set is probably too early.

18. A strict exercise routine is what Timothy needs.

19. Brenda gave whoever showed up all the prizes.

20. I think about how I can make them laugh.

SPEAKING APPLICATION

Take turns with a partner. Say sentences that include adverbial clauses. Your partner should listen for and identify each clause.

WRITING APPLICATION

Show that you understand the function of noun clauses. Write four sentences with noun clauses. Then, read your sentences to a partner. Your partner should identify the noun clauses as you speak your sentences.

3.3 The Four Structures of Sentences

Independent and subordinate clauses are the building blocks of sentences. These clauses can be combined in an endless number of ways to form the four basic sentence structures: **simple, compound, complex,** and **compound-complex.**

RULE 3.3.1

A simple sentence contains a single independent or main clause.

Although a simple sentence contains only one main or independent clause, its subject, verb, or both may be compound. A simple sentence may also have modifying phrases and complements. However, it cannot have a subordinate clause.

In the following simple sentences, the subjects are highlighted in yellow, and the verbs are highlighted in orange.

ONE SUBJECT AND VERB
The **athlete** **ran**.

COMPOUND SUBJECT
George and **Tom** **administered** the test.

COMPOUND VERB
The **car** **sputtered** and **stalled**.

COMPOUND SUBJECT AND VERB
Neither the **instructor** nor the **class** **felt** or **heard** the earthquake.

RULE 3.3.2

A compound sentence contains two or more main clauses.

The main clauses in a compound sentence can be joined by a comma and a coordinating conjunction *(and, but, for, nor, or, so, yet)* or by a semicolon (;). Like a simple sentence, a compound sentence contains no subordinate clauses.

EXAMPLE
The **puppy** **carried** his bone into the yard, and **he** **dug** a hole to hide it.

See Practice 3.3A

> A **complex sentence** consists of one independent or main clause and one or more subordinate clauses.

RULE 3.3.3

The independent clause in a complex sentence is often called the main clause to distinguish it from the subordinate clause or clauses. The subject and verb in the independent clause are called the subject of the sentence and the main verb. The second example shows that a subordinate clause may fall between the parts of a main clause. In the examples below, the main clauses are highlighted in blue, and the subordinate clauses are highlighted in pink.

EXAMPLES   No one answered the intercom when it buzzed.

The vase of flowers that the girl placed on the counter doesn't have any tulips.

Note on Complex Sentences With Noun Clauses: The subject of the main clause may sometimes be the subordinate clause itself.

EXAMPLE   That I wanted to leave bothered them.

> A **compound-complex sentence** consists of two or more independent clauses and one or more subordinate clauses.

RULE 3.3.4

In the example below, the independent clauses are highlighted in blue, and the subordinate clause is highlighted in pink.

EXAMPLE   The dog barked when he saw a rabbit, and he ran through the trees after it.

See Practice 3.3B

PRACTICE 3.3A ▶ Distinguishing Between Simple and Compound Sentences

Read each sentence. Then, label each sentence *simple* or *compound*.

EXAMPLE   She will show up, or Don will call her parents.

ANSWER   *compound*

1. My younger brother plays on the tennis team, but my older one is in the band.

2. I am partial to foreign films; my best friend likes horror movies.

3. Have you finished your report on hurricanes?

4. Did Lacy order the shipment today, or will she do it tomorrow?

5. At the end of the cul-de-sac near the mail drop is an abandoned building.

6. In my town, most refuse is buried in a landfill, but the landfill is now in danger of overflowing.

7. The owl serves as a sign of the goddess Athena and wisdom.

8. Stacy and Arturo practice soccer in the morning.

9. I earned every merit badge, so I received an award.

10. You could go to the grocery store, or you could pick up the dry cleaning.

PRACTICE 3.3B ▶ Identifying the Four Structures of Sentences

Read each sentence. Then, label each sentence *simple, compound, complex,* or *compound-complex*.

EXAMPLE   Layla ran into her bedroom.

ANSWER   *simple*

11. All the highways will be covered unless the snow stops soon.

12. I need to go to the library, but I'm feeling too tired to drive.

13. I looked for Dennis and Kenyon at the train station.

14. The audience in the courtroom is large now, but it will get smaller as soon as the case ends.

15. I hope to start my own company, and I want to offer insurance to my employees.

16. Since I started, the processes have changed very little.

17. I enjoy a cup of tea in the morning.

18. You could act like a child, or you could clean up your mess.

19. This is the album that I have been hoping to find.

20. When I start my new job, I will sell my old car, and I will buy another one that is better on gas mileage.

SPEAKING APPLICATION

Take turns with a partner. Tell about your dream jobs. Use both simple and compound sentences. Your partner should listen for and identify each sentence as simple or compound.

WRITING APPLICATION

Write a paragraph about what you think you will be doing ten years from now. Your paragraph should include a variety of correctly structured sentences: simple, compound, complex, and compound-complex.

PRACTICE 1 Identifying Nouns

Read the sentences. Then, label each underlined noun either *concrete* or *abstract*. If the noun is concrete, label it *collective, compound,* or *proper*.

1. The firefighters quickly climbed the fire escape.

2. Sal's greatest wish is to live in Paris.

3. An army would often dig foxholes in which to sleep during World War II.

4. Many onlookers stared in awe at the superstructure before them.

5. The bylaw is up for vote in the legislature this week.

PRACTICE 2 Identifying Pronouns

Read the sentences. Then, label each underlined pronoun *reciprocal, demonstrative, relative, interrogative,* or *indefinite.*

1. What on Earth is that over there?

2. The coach is looking for a student who likes to pitch.

3. Whom should I call?

4. Someone has to know what's going on.

5. Fred and Hal have never met each other.

PRACTICE 3 Classifying Verbs and Verb Phrases

Read the sentences. Then, write the verb or verb phrase in each sentence. Label each either *action verb* or *linking verb.* If the verb is an action verb, label it *transitive* or *intransitive.*

1. The train stopped mere inches from the station.

2. *Dubliners* became my favorite book when I read it last year.

3. The sink appears broken; we need a plumber.

4. My dog Rex can smell anything.

5. Shelly rarely drives after dark.

PRACTICE 4 Identifying Adjectives and Adverbs

Read the sentences. Then, identify the underlined word as an *adjective* or *adverb.* Write the word that is modified.

1. Malcolm plays the banjo quite well.

2. I never shy away from a friendly face.

3. She was disturbed when she heard the news.

4. I never eat before I work out.

5. Manny is looking forward to successfully completing college next year.

PRACTICE 5 Using Conjunctions and Interjections

Read the sentences. Then, write the conjunction or interjection. If there is a conjunction in the sentence, label it *coordinating, correlative,* or *subordinating.*

1. Finally! I can go home.

2. Clarice had to take the subway because her car broke down.

3. The restaurant serves not only Italian food but also Mexican food.

4. Brian doesn't like hot dogs, nor does he like sausages.

5. After Fey left the meeting, she went to get a cup of coffee.

PRACTICE 6 Recognizing Direct and Indirect Objects and Object of a Preposition

Read the sentences. Then, identify the underlined items as *direct object, indirect object,* or *object of a preposition.*

1. Delia mailed her mother a card for Mother's Day.

2. Luke left his jacket in the house.

Continued on next page ▶

3. Helen told <u>Julio</u> and <u>me</u> about the new movie.

4. Jennifer bought <u>Chris</u> a sweater for their <u>anniversary</u>.

5. Each of <u>us</u> will take a <u>number</u> from the hat.

6. Don't give <u>me</u> the <u>news</u> until I'm ready.

7. Ned cleaned and polished the <u>table</u> and the <u>chairs</u>.

8. During the <u>night</u>, our dog Sammy hides under the <u>couch</u>.

9. Bonny will eat her <u>lunch</u> before the one o'clock <u>meeting</u>.

10. Jeremiah showed <u>Alicia</u> and <u>me</u> the rough draft of his short story.

PRACTICE 7 ▷ Identifying Phrases

Write the phrases contained in the following sentences. Identify each phrase as a *prepositional phrase*, *appositive phrase*, *participial phrase*, *gerund phrase*, or *infinitive phrase*.

1. The car quickly disappeared around the corner.

2. Sprinting to the finish line, Terrance felt elated.

3. To ride a bike without a helmet is not safe.

4. The Enlightenment, a fascinating period, influenced many policies of the U.S. Constitution.

5. The bus stopped to let the children cross the street.

6. Darryl, a man of thirty-two, volunteers at the fire department down the street.

7. Swimming laps in a pool is great exercise.

8. When the nurse takes your blood pressure, he slips a cuff around your arm.

9. Amazed by the light show, Joan asked a technician how it was done.

10. Taking a chance, Keith applied for the job after the deadline.

PRACTICE 8 ▷ Recognizing Clauses

Label the underlined clauses in the following sentences *independent* or *subordinate*. Identify any subordinate clause as *adjectival*, *adverbial*, or *noun clause*. Then, label any adjectival clauses as *essential* or *nonessential*.

1. The dog <u>that has a black collar</u> is very well behaved.

2. <u>Sam's baseball crashed through the window</u> to everyone's annoyance.

3. <u>That the road is covered with potholes</u> has been the talk of town hall for months.

4. <u>While the concert was going on</u>, Larry left to answer his cellphone.

5. Mildred likes spiders <u>because they keep pests out of her garden</u>.

6. <u>Oscar, our pet parrot, flew away last week</u> because someone left his cage open.

7. The auto show, <u>which was never well attended</u>, was canceled this year.

8. <u>Even if the stadium were freezing</u>, James would still go to the hockey game.

9. The most fascinating thing about Benjamin Franklin is <u>how he became such a great politician and scientist</u>.

10. The CN Tower, <u>which is in Toronto, Canada</u>, is the tallest tower in North America.

CHAPTER 4

EFFECTIVE SENTENCES

Use sentences of varying lengths and complexities to add dimension to your writing.

WRITE GUY *Jeff Anderson, M.Ed.*

WHAT DO YOU NOTICE?

Observe how the author crafted his sentences as you zoom in on this passage from *Life on the Mississippi* by Mark Twain.

MENTOR TEXT

> Before these events, the day was glorious with expectancy; after them, the day was a dead and empty thing. Not only the boys, but the whole village, felt this.

Now, ask yourself the following questions:

- How does the first sentence reflect the author's use of parallelism?
- What purpose does parallelism serve in this passage?

The prepositional phrases at the beginning of each clause of the first sentence and the parallel clauses *the day was glorious with expectancy* and *the day was a dead and empty thing* are both parallel structures. The author uses parallelism to compare people's feelings before and after certain events, thus showing how important these events are to his characters.

Grammar for Writers Writers use different sentence structures to engage and guide their readers. Start your sentences in different ways to add variety to your writing, and use parallelism to help your readers connect ideas.

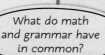

What do math and grammar have in common?

I know—parallel lines!

4.1 The Four Functions of a Sentence

Sentences can be classified according to what they do—that is, whether they state ideas, ask questions, give orders, or express strong emotions.

Declarative sentences are used to declare, or state, facts.

RULE 4.1.1

> A **declarative sentence** states an idea and ends with a period.

DECLARATIVE   Jerusalem is a city in Israel.

To *interrogate* means "to ask." An **interrogative sentence** is a question.

RULE 4.1.2

> An **interrogative sentence** asks a question and ends with a question mark.

INTERROGATIVE   On which continent do elephants live?

Imperative sentences give commands or directions.

RULE 4.1.3

> An **imperative sentence** gives an order or a direction and ends with either a period or an exclamation mark.

EL9

Most imperative sentences start with a verb. In this type of imperative sentence, the subject is understood to be *you*.

IMPERATIVE   Stack the dinner china carefully.

Exclamatory sentences are used to express emotions.

RULE 4.1.4

> An **exclamatory sentence** conveys strong emotion and ends with an exclamation mark.

EXCLAMATORY   That is wonderful!

See Practice 4.1A
See Practice 4.1B

PRACTICE 4.1A ▷ Identifying the Four Types of Sentences

Read each sentence. Then, label each sentence *declarative, interrogative, imperative,* or *exclamatory.*

EXAMPLE   When was your house built?

ANSWER   *interrogative*

1. That was amazing!
2. The upper level is still under construction.
3. How much did you pay for that shirt?
4. Listen closely to me.
5. What is your favorite color?
6. The candidate is someone I trust completely.
7. What a menacing sight!
8. Put on your warmest pair of socks.
9. Who wrote this poem?
10. This was one of the hardest marathons that I've ever run.

PRACTICE 4.1B ▷ Punctuating the Four Types of Sentences

Read each sentence. Then, label each sentence *declarative, interrogative, imperative,* or *exclamatory,* and, in parentheses, write the correct end mark.

EXAMPLE   What a great time we had

ANSWER   *exclamatory (!)*

11. This part of the city gets poor cellphone reception
12. Do you want to arrive Tuesday or Wednesday morning
13. This is baffling
14. My professor does not appreciate tardiness
15. When will my car be ready
16. Turn off the air conditioner when you leave the house
17. I have always wondered what college he attended
18. Ask Ronaldo to hand in his paper
19. Wow, that was exciting
20. Would you hand me the broom, please

SPEAKING APPLICATION

Take turns with a partner. Describe an exciting event that you have experienced. Make sure to use all four sentence types in your description. Your partner should identify each type of sentence in your description.

WRITING APPLICATION

Write a paragraph about your first day of high school. Use at least one declarative, one interrogative, and one imperative sentence in your paragraph.

4.2 Sentence Combining

Too many short sentences can make your writing choppy and disconnected.

One way to avoid the excessive use of short sentences and to achieve variety is to combine sentences.

Sentences can be combined by using a compound subject, a compound verb, or a compound object.

TWO SENTENCES	Kevin enjoyed the concert tonight. Andrew enjoyed the concert tonight.
COMPOUND SUBJECT	Kevin and Andrew enjoyed the concert tonight.
TWO SENTENCES	Jen practiced hard. Jen won the game.
COMPOUND VERB	Jen practiced hard and won the game.
TWO SENTENCES	Joshua saw the plane. Joshua saw the fighter jet.
COMPOUND OBJECT	Joshua saw the plane and the fighter jet.

See Practice 4.2A

Sentences can be combined by joining two main or independent clauses to create a compound sentence.

Use a compound sentence when combining ideas that are related but independent. To join main clauses, use a comma and a coordinating conjunction (*for, and, but, or, nor, yet,* or *so*) or a semicolon.

EXAMPLE	The child was looking for her shoes. She did not notice them outside.
COMPOUND SENTENCE	The child was looking for her shoes, yet she did not notice them outside.

RULE 4.2.3	Sentences can be combined by changing one into a subordinate clause to create a **complex sentence.**

To show the relationship between ideas in which one depends on the other, use a **complex sentence.** The subordinating conjunction will help readers understand the relationship. Some common subordinating conjunctions are *after, although, because, if, since, when,* and *while.*

EXAMPLE	We were tired. We couldn't sleep on the bumpy flight.
COMBINED WITH A SUBORDINATE CLAUSE	We were tired **because we couldn't sleep on the bumpy flight**.

RULE 4.2.4	Sentences can be combined by changing one of them into a **phrase.**

EXAMPLE	My sister will present her paper today. The paper is on insects.
COMBINED WITH PREPOSITIONAL PHRASE	My sister will present her paper **on insects** today.

EXAMPLE	My sister will present her paper on insects today. It is the final paper of the year.
COMBINED WITH APPOSITIVE PHRASE	Today, my sister will present her paper, **the final one of the year**, on insects.

See Practice 4.2B
See Practice 4.2C

Read each set of sentences. Then, combine each set of sentences, using one sentence that contains a compound subject, verb, or object.

EXAMPLE   The team lost the game.
They finished in last place.

ANSWER   *The team lost the game and finished in last place.*

1. Carrie could not sleep last night. She was late for her doctor's appointment.

2. Mars is known as the red planet. Mars is named after the Roman god of war.

3. Aneeta earns impressive grades. She is also a natural leader.

4. Vernon likes to read science fiction novels. Theresa likes to read science fiction novels.

5. Tyler ate breakfast at home. He had lunch at home. He ate dinner at home.

Read each set of sentences. Combine each set by turning one sentence into a phrase that adds detail to the other.

EXAMPLE   The witness spoke to an officer.
He identified the suspect.

ANSWER   *The witness spoke to an officer and identified the suspect.*

6. Percy waited underneath the tree. A friend was with him.

7. Our team captain arrived early. He did warm-up exercises to pass the time.

8. All drivers must navigate the course. The course was designed by professional racers.

9. Stewart Manning is our student body representative. He will speak at tomorrow's pep rally.

10. Many books have been written about time travel. This is a very interesting topic.

SPEAKING APPLICATION

Take turns with a partner. Say two related sentences. Your partner should combine these two sentences into one logical sentence.

WRITING APPLICATION

Write two sentences that relate to each other. Then, combine these two sentences into one. Repeat with two other related sentences.

PRACTICE 4.2C **Combining Sentences by Forming Compound or Complex Sentences**

Read each set of sentences. Then, combine the sentences, using a coordinating or subordinating conjunction. Underline the conjunction that you use and label it *coordinating* or *subordinating*.

EXAMPLE I wanted to sit in the front row. I ordered my tickets early.

ANSWER *I wanted to sit in the front row, <u>so</u> I ordered my tickets early.* — coordinating

1. Julio enjoys reading mystery novels. He has a love for suspense.

2. My brother loves to eat apples. He eats one almost every day.

3. You might not make it to the show on time. The train station is only one block away.

4. Rory and Hanne left early. I did not see them when I arrived at the party.

5. Wendy traveled to Mexico last summer. She did not visit the Pyramid of the Moon.

6. Geoff was able to get on an earlier flight. Geoff's conference ended early.

7. Yusef really enjoys listening to jazz music. His girlfriend prefers classical music.

8. Bears hibernate during winter. Butterflies migrate south.

9. I waited in line to buy the album. I read the last chapter of my book.

10. Scientists have learned much about the universe. Scientists still send craft into outer space to gather more information.

SPEAKING APPLICATION

Take turns with a partner. Describe a memorable event. Be sure to include at least four complex or compound sentences that contain coordinating or subordinating conjunctions.

WRITING APPLICATION

Write a paragraph about a favorite relative. Use compound and complex sentences with coordinating and subordinating conjunctions in your paragraph.

4.3 Varying Sentences

Vary your sentences to develop a rhythm, to achieve an effect, or to emphasize the connections between ideas. There are several ways you can vary your sentences.

Varying Sentence Length

To emphasize a point or surprise a reader, include a short, direct sentence to interrupt the flow of long sentences. Notice the effect of the last sentence in the following paragraph.

EXAMPLE   The Jacobites derived their name from *Jacobus,* the Latin name for King James II of England, who was dethroned in 1688 by William of Orange during the Glorious Revolution. Unpopular because of his Catholicism and autocratic ruling style, James fled to France to seek the aid of King Louis XIV. In 1690, James, along with a small body of French troops, landed in Ireland in an attempt to regain his throne. His hopes ended at the Battle of the Boyne.

Some sentences contain only one idea and can't be broken. It may be possible, however, to state the idea in a shorter sentence. Other sentences contain two or more ideas and might be shortened by breaking up the ideas.

LONGER SENTENCE   Many of James II's predecessors were able to avoid major economic problems, but James had serious economic problems.

MORE DIRECT   Unlike many of his predecessors, James II was unable to avoid major economic problems.

LONGER SENTENCE   James tried to work with Parliament to develop a plan of taxation that would be fair and reasonable, but members of Parliament rejected his efforts, and James dissolved the Parliament.

SHORTER SENTENCES   James tried to work with Parliament to develop a fair and reasonable taxation plan. However, because members of Parliament rejected his efforts, James dissolved the Parliament.

Varying Sentence Beginnings

Another way to create sentence variety is to start sentences with different parts of speech.

WAYS TO VARY SENTENCE BEGINNINGS	
Start With a Noun	Houses are difficult to build.
Start With an Adverb	Naturally, houses are difficult to build.
Start With an Adverbial Phrase	Because of their complexity, houses are difficult to build.
Start With a Participial Phrase	Having tried to build several houses, I know how hard it is.
Start With a Prepositional Phrase	For the average person, houses are very difficult to build.
Start With an Infinitive Phrase	To build a safe and durable house was my goal.

See Practice 4.3A

Using Inverted Word Order

You can also vary sentence beginnings by reversing the traditional subject–verb order to create verb–subject order. You can reverse order by starting the sentence with a **participial phrase** or a **prepositional phrase.** You can also move a complement to the beginning of the sentence.

SUBJECT–VERB ORDER

The soldier waited for the command to leave.

The soldier drove the tank into the desert.

The sound of tanks filled the air.

The light was blinding.

VERB–SUBJECT ORDER

Waiting for the command to leave was the
                         participial phrase
soldier.

Into the desert drove the soldier.
    prepositional phrase

Filling the air was the sound of tanks.
    participial phrase

Blinding was the light.
  predicate adjective

See Practice 4.3B

PRACTICE 4.3A ▷ **Revising to Vary Sentence Beginnings**

Read each sentence. Rewrite each sentence to begin with the part of speech or phrase indicated in parentheses. You may need to add a word or phrase.

EXAMPLE   Certain types of diseases have recurred throughout history. (prepositional phrase)

ANSWER   *Throughout history, certain types of diseases have recurred.*

1. Lidia accepted the invitation. (adverb)
2. Search the Internet. (infinitive phrase)
3. Some cities are using street-cars to reduce pollution. (infinitive phrase)
4. Cheering fans threw confetti onto the field. (prepositional phrase)
5. The president did many great things. (prepositional phrase)
6. We finally reached camp. (participial phrase)
7. The wind blew violently through the trees. (adverb)
8. Lots of acorns tumbled out of the trees. (adverb)
9. Many sets of twins were born on that day. (prepositional phrase)
10. Michael stood at the foot of the stairs. (prepositional phrase)

PRACTICE 4.3B ▷ **Inverting Sentences to Vary Subject-Verb Order**

Read each sentence. Rewrite each sentence by inverting subject-verb order to verb-subject order.

EXAMPLE   The baby slept in a crib.

ANSWER   *In a crib slept the baby.*

11. The bird flew over my head, high in the sky.
12. The pigeons headed homeward after they were released.
13. Bertha's brother announced, "I will pay the airfare for the trip."
14. The Texas Revolution ended at the Battle of San Jacinto.
15. Nancy read the scary story.
16. Percy dived into the pool.
17. I have broken six dishes while practicing for my balancing act.
18. Lots of fans crowded the room.
19. Julius Caesar was born on July 12, 100 BC.
20. Your paper will be improved by reorganizing the last few paragraphs.

SPEAKING APPLICATION

Take turns with a partner. Read three sentences from Practice 4.3A, but change the directive in parentheses. Your partner should follow the directive to revise how the sentence begins.

WRITING APPLICATION

Write three sentences about your morning routine. Then, exchange papers with a partner. Your partner should invert the order of your sentences from subject–verb order to verb–subject order to vary the beginnings.

4.4 Avoid Fragments and Run-ons

Hasty writers sometimes omit crucial words, punctuate awkwardly, or leave their thoughts unfinished, causing two common sentence errors: **fragments** and **run-ons**.

Recognizing Fragments

Although some writers use them for stylistic effect, **fragments** are generally considered errors in standard English.

> **Do not capitalize and punctuate phrases, subordinate clauses, or words in a series as if they were complete sentences.**

Reading your work aloud to listen for natural pauses and stops should help you avoid fragments. Sometimes, you can repair a fragment by connecting it to words that come before or after it.

> **One way to correct a fragment is to connect it to the words in a nearby sentence.**

PARTICIPIAL FRAGMENT	inspired by the talent of the singer
ADDED TO A NEARBY SENTENCE	**Inspired by the talent of the singer**, Deb went to the concert twice.
PREPOSITIONAL FRAGMENT	before their band
ADDED TO A NEARBY SENTENCE	The trio of singers came on stage **before their band**.
PRONOUN AND PARTICIPIAL FRAGMENT	the one on the bed
ADDED TO NEARBY SENTENCE	The warm woolen blanket I want is **the one on the bed**.

Another way to correct a fragment is to add any sentence part that is needed to make the fragment a complete sentence.

Remember that every complete sentence must have both a subject and a verb and express a complete thought. Check to see that each of your sentences contains all of the parts necessary to be complete.

NOUN FRAGMENT

the team of young soccer players

COMPLETED SENTENCES

The team of young soccer players
subject

ran **across the field.**
verb

We **excitedly** **watched**
subject   verb

the team of young soccer players .
direct object

Notice what missing sentence parts must be added to the following types of phrase fragments to make them complete.

	FRAGMENTS	COMPLETED SENTENCES
Noun Fragment With Participial Phrase	the fruit eaten by us	The fruit was eaten by us.
Verb Fragment	will be at the conference tomorrow	I will be at the conference tomorrow.
Prepositional Fragment	in the bathroom closet	I put the towels in the bathroom closet.
Participial Fragment	found under the table	The magazines found under the table are mine .
Gerund Fragment	teaching children to swim	Teaching children to swim is exciting .
Infinitive Fragment	to meet the new instructor	I expect to meet the new instructor.

You may need to attach a **subordinate clause** to a main clause to correct a fragment.

A **subordinate clause** contains a subject and a verb but does not express a complete thought and cannot stand alone as a sentence. Link it to a main clause to make the sentence complete.

ADJECTIVAL CLAUSE FRAGMENT	which was being read inside
COMPLETED SENTENCE	I planned on hearing the author's excerpt, **which was being read inside the store** .

ADVERBIAL CLAUSE FRAGMENT	after she read the first book
COMPLETED SENTENCE	**After she read the first book** , she was ready for the sequel.

NOUN CLAUSE FRAGMENT	whatever movie we see in this theater
COMPLETED SENTENCE	We always enjoy **whatever movie we see in this theater** .

Series Fragments A fragment is not always short. A long series of words still needs to have a subject and a verb and express a complete thought. It may be a long fragment masquerading as a sentence.

SERIES FRAGMENT	COMPLETE SENTENCE
after reading Shakespeare's play, with its probing look at love and family, in the style so typical of this well-known playwright	After reading Shakespeare's play, with its probing look at love and family, in the style so typical of this well-known playwright, I was able to form an interesting character assessment .

See Practice 4.4A

Avoiding Run-on Sentences

A **run-on** sentence is two or more sentences capitalized and punctuated as if they were a single sentence.

RULE
4.4.5

> **Use punctuation and conjunctions to correctly join or separate parts of a run-on sentence.**

There are two kinds of **run-ons: fused sentences**, which are two or more sentences joined with no punctuation, and **comma splices**, which have two or more sentences separated only by commas rather than by commas and conjunctions.

FUSED SENTENCE	The student studied every day she was the valedictorian of the class.
COMMA SPLICE	Only one check arrived in the mail, the other checks never came.

As with fragments, proofreading or reading your work aloud will help you find run-ons. Once found, they can be corrected by adding punctuation and conjunctions or by rewording the sentences.

FOUR WAYS TO CORRECT RUN-ONS		
	RUN-ON	CORRECTION
With End Marks and Capitals	The storm hit with full force in the basement the family was huddled together.	The storm hit with full force. In the basement, the family was huddled together.
With Commas and Conjunctions	The food needed to be cooked we could not locate the pans.	The food needed to be cooked, but we could not locate the pans.
With Semicolons	We have many colleges around the country, for example, Pennsylvania is sometimes called the college state.	We have many colleges around the country; for example, Pennsylvania is sometimes called the college state.
By Rewriting	The movie began late, the projector wasn't working.	The movie began late because the projector wasn't working.

See Practice 4.4B

PRACTICE 4.4A ▷ **Identifying and Correcting Fragments**

Read each sentence. If an item contains a fragment, rewrite it to make a complete sentence. If an item contains a complete sentence, write *correct*.

EXAMPLE   Reluctantly chose to lead the team.

ANSWER   *Reluctantly, he chose to lead the team.*

1. A strong wind blowing from the south.

2. An invasion from Mars was the movie's theme.

3. Coming around the next bend.

4. Raised her hand eagerly.

5. Listen to me, please.

6. Sitting quietly, reading a book.

7. Safe drivers always watch.

8. Acted without a thought for his own safety.

9. We went down the hill.

10. Unless it is refrigerated.

PRACTICE 4.4B ▷ **Revising to Eliminate Run-on Sentences**

Read each sentence. Correct each run-on by correctly joining or separating the sentence parts.

EXAMPLE   Mrs. Ladner spoke softly I listened carefully.

ANSWER   *Mrs. Ladner spoke softly, so I listened carefully.*

11. We opened the box it contained dishes.

12. This is my answer I won't change my mind.

13. The trains are quicker the buses are cheaper.

14. The electricity went out I looked for the flashlight.

15. What time is the play, will you come and get me?

16. I ran after him however he had already driven away.

17. I lost the first wrestling match I won the second.

18. Is this your paper it's really well-written.

19. My cousin collects baseball cards I collect seashells.

20. I waved, Raisa waved back.

SPEAKING APPLICATION

Take turns with a partner. Use different words to make the fragments in Practice 4.4A into complete sentences.

WRITING APPLICATION

Write four run-on sentences. Then, exchange papers with a partner, and correct your partner's run-on sentences.

4.5 Misplaced and Dangling Modifiers

Careful writers put modifiers as close as possible to the words they modify. When modifiers are misplaced or left dangling in a sentence, the result may be illogical or confusing.

Recognizing Misplaced Modifiers

A **misplaced modifier** is placed too far from the modified word and appears to modify the wrong word or words.

RULE 4.5.1

> A **misplaced modifier** seems to modify the wrong word in the sentence.

MISPLACED MODIFIER
The boy tripped over the curb **walking on the sidewalk**.

CORRECTION
The boy **walking on the sidewalk** tripped over the curb.

MISPLACED MODIFIER
We heard the dog barking **while sitting outside**.

CORRECTION
While sitting outside, we heard the dog barking.

Recognizing Dangling Modifiers

With **dangling modifiers,** the word that should be modified is missing from the sentence. Dangling modifiers usually come at the beginning of a sentence and are followed by a comma. The subject being modified should come right after the comma.

RULE 4.5.2

> A **dangling modifier** seems to modify the wrong word or no word at all because the word it should modify has been omitted from the sentence.

See Practice 4.5A

DANGLING PARTICIPIAL PHRASE
Measuring carefully, the gap in the floor was closed accurately.
(*Who* did the measuring?)

CORRECTED SENTENCE
Measuring carefully, **the carpenter** accurately closed the gap in the floor.

Dangling participial phrases are corrected by adding missing words and making other needed changes.

Dangling infinitive phrases and elliptical clauses can be corrected in the same way. First, identify the subject of the sentence. Then, make sure each subject is clearly stated. You may also need to change the form of the verb.

DANGLING INFINITIVE PHRASE
To cross the river, the bridge must be used.
(*Who* is crossing?)

CORRECTED SENTENCE
To cross the river, **hikers** must use the bridge.

DANGLING ELLIPTICAL CLAUSE
While hiking in the mountains, a black bear was sighted.
(*Who* was hiking and sighted the bear?)

CORRECTED SENTENCE
While hiking in the mountains, **we** saw a black bear.

EL8

A dangling adverbial clause may also occur when the antecedent of a pronoun is not clear.

DANGLING ADVERBIAL CLAUSE
When she was thirty years old, Kate's mother planned a party near the water.
(*Who* is thirty, Kate or her mother?)

CORRECTED SENTENCE
When Kate was thirty years old, her mother planned a party near the water.

See Practice 4.5B

PRACTICE 4.5A > Identifying and Correcting Misplaced Modifiers

Read each sentence. Then, rewrite each sentence, putting the misplaced modifier closer to the words it should modify. If a sentence is correct, write *correct*.

EXAMPLE   The conductor gave instructions with his baton in hand.

ANSWER   *The conductor, with his baton in hand, gave instructions.*

1. The store is having a sale that just opened.
2. The book won an award with many colorful illustrations.
3. The treasure chest was buried filled with jewels.
4. The shirt that you want will cost thirty dollars.
5. The team won with stronger swimmers.
6. The man asked for help holding a heavy object.
7. The room with a fireplace has been rented.
8. Vanessa reminded me to bring my notebook twice.
9. The pianist played a new composition sitting on the piano bench.
10. Cranky and tired, I put the baby down for a nap.

PRACTICE 4.5B > Identifying and Correcting Dangling Modifiers

Read each sentence. Then, rewrite the sentences, correcting any dangling modifiers by supplying missing words or ideas.

EXAMPLE   Walking to school, her notebook was lost.

ANSWER   *Walking to school, she lost her notebook.*

11. To enter the race, a form must be completed.
12. To knit a hat, all the yarn must be bought at once.
13. Having solved the problem, liftoff could take place.
14. To get the job, references must be verified.
15. While taking inventory, the store was closed.
16. Cutting out all the wordiness, the essay was improved.
17. When not talking, the room was filled with silence.
18. After examining the evidence, the accused was released.
19. Wrapped in my blanket, the cold was no problem.
20. After washing the clothes, the clothes needed to be folded.

SPEAKING APPLICATION

Take turns with a partner. Tell about an exciting experience that you have had. Use modifiers in your sentences. Your partner should listen for and identify the modifiers and tell whether they are correctly placed.

WRITING APPLICATION

Use sentences 18, 19, and 20 as models to write similar sentences with dangling modifiers. Then, rewrite each sentence to correct the dangling modifiers.

4.6 Faulty Parallelism

Good writers try to present a series of ideas in similar grammatical structures so the ideas will read smoothly. If one element in a series is not parallel with the others, the result may be jarring or confusing.

Recognizing the Correct Use of Parallelism

To present a series of ideas of equal importance, you should use parallel grammatical structures.

4.6.1 RULE

> **Parallelism** involves presenting equal ideas in words, phrases, clauses, or sentences of similar types.

PARALLEL WORDS	The dancer looked **graceful**, **fit**, and **agile**.
PARALLEL PHRASES	The greatest feeling I know is **to dance on the stage flawlessly** and **to have the audience and all my friends applaud graciously**.
PARALLEL CLAUSES	The ballet slippers **that you recommended** and **that my daughter wants** are on sale.
PARALLEL SENTENCES	**It couldn't be**, of course. **It could never, never be**. –Dorothy Parker

Correcting Faulty Parallelism

Faulty parallelism occurs when a writer uses unequal grammatical structures to express related ideas.

4.6.2 RULE

> Correct a sentence containing faulty parallelism by rewriting it so that each parallel idea is expressed in the same grammatical structure.

Faulty parallelism can involve words, phrases, and clauses in a series or in comparisons.

Nonparallel Words, Phrases, and Clauses in a Series
Always check for parallelism when your writing contains items in
a series.

Correcting Faulty Parallelism in a Series

NONPARALLEL STRUCTURES

Planning , **filming** , and **edit** are all steps in
   gerund   gerund   noun
the movie process.

CORRECTION

Planning , **filming** , and **editing** are all steps
   gerund   gerund   gerund
in the movie process.

NONPARALLEL STRUCTURES

I could not wait **to see the new show** ,
                     infinitive phrase
to get dressed up , and **visiting the theatre** .
   infinitive phrase   participial phrase

CORRECTION

I could not wait **to see the new show** , **to get**
                     infinitive phrase
dressed up , and **to visit the theater** .
  infinitive phrase   infinitive phrase

NONPARALLEL STRUCTURE

Some experts feel **that cheering is not a**
                 noun clause
contact sport , but **it requires caution and**
               independent clause
athleticism .

CORRECTION

Some experts feel **that cheering is not a**
                 noun clause
contact sport but **that it requires caution**
               noun clause
and athleticism .

Another potential problem involves correlative conjunctions, such
as *both ... and* or *not only ... but also.* Though these conjunctions
connect two related items, writers sometimes misplace or split
the first part of the conjunction. The result is faulty parallelism.

NONPARALLEL	Anne **not only** won the gymnastics championship **but also** the national title.
PARALLEL	Anne won **not only** the gymnastics championship **but also** the national title.

Nonparallel Words, Phrases, and Clauses in Comparisons
As the saying goes, you cannot compare apples with oranges. In writing comparisons, you generally should compare a phrase with the same type of phrase and a clause with the same type of clause.

Correcting Faulty Parallelism in Comparisons

NONPARALLEL
STRUCTURES

Many people prefer **potatoes** to **eating**
                   noun   gerund phrase
broccoli .

CORRECTION

Many people prefer **potatoes** to **broccoli** .
             noun   noun

NONPARALLEL
STRUCTURES

I left my office **at 9:00 P.M.** rather than
                  prepositional phrase
stopping work at 4:30 P.M.
           participial phrase

CORRECTION

I left my office **at 9:00 P.M.** rather than
                  prepositional phrase
at the usual 4:30 P.M.
       prepositional phrase

NONPARALLEL
STRUCTURES

Jenny delights **in snowy days** as much as
subject   prepositional phrase
sunny **days** delight other **people** .
   subject   direct object

CORRECTION

Jenny delights **in snowy days** as much as
subject   prepositional phrase
other **people** delight **in sunny days** .
   subject   prepositional phrase

See Practice 4.6A

4.7 Faulty Coordination

When two or more independent clauses of unequal importance are joined by *and*, the result can be faulty **coordination**.

Recognizing Faulty Coordination

To *coordinate* means to "place side by side in equal rank." Two independent clauses that are joined by the coordinating conjunction *and*, therefore, should have equal rank.

RULE 4.7.1

> **Use *and* or other coordinating conjunctions only to connect ideas of equal importance.**

CORRECT COORDINATION

Tim designed a ship, **and** Jake built it.

Sometimes, however, writers carelessly use *and* to join main clauses that either should not be joined or should be joined in another way so that the real relationship between the clauses is clear. Faulty coordination puts all the ideas on the same level of importance, even though logically they should not be.

FAULTY COORDINATION

Demand for computers accelerated in the twenty-first century, **and** the computer became an important factor in offices.

I don't feel well, **and** the trip was very long.

The road was bumpy, **and** it was winding and making me sick.

Occasionally, writers will also string together so many ideas with *and's* that the reader is left breathless.

STRINGY SENTENCE

The helicopter that flew over the city did a few dips and turns, **and** the people on the ground craned their necks to watch, **and** everyone laughed and cheered.

Correcting Faulty Coordination

Faulty coordination can be corrected in several ways.

> **One way to correct faulty coordination is to put unrelated ideas into separate sentences.**

When faulty coordination occurs in a sentence in which the main clauses are not closely related, separate the clauses and omit the coordinating conjunction.

FAULTY COORDINATION	Demand for computers accelerated in the twenty-first century, **and** the computer became an important factor in offices.
CORRECTION	Demand for computers accelerated in the twenty-first century. The computer became an important factor in offices.

> **You can correct faulty coordination by putting less important ideas into subordinate clauses or phrases.**

If one main clause is less important than, or subordinate to, the other, turn it into a subordinate clause. You can also reduce a less important idea to a phrase.

FAULTY COORDINATION	I didn't do well, **and** the run was easy.
CORRECTION	I didn't do well, **even though** the run was easy.
FAULTY COORDINATION	The road was bumpy, **and** it made me feel sick.
CORRECTION	I was feeling sick, because the road was bumpy.

Stringy sentences should be broken up and revised using any of the three methods just described. Following is one way that the stringy sentence on the previous page can be revised.

REVISION OF A STRINGY SENTENCE	The helicopter that flew over the city did a few dips and turns. Craning their necks to watch, the people on the ground laughed and cheered.

See Practice 4.6B

Revising to Eliminate Faulty Parallelism

Read each sentence. Then, rewrite each sentence to correct any nonparallel structures.

EXAMPLE   I left work tired, cold, and wanting a meal.

ANSWER   *I left work tired, cold, and hungry.*

1. Today, I have classes to attend, a meeting to lead, and cleaning my room.

2. I like my little sister because she is smart, funny, and I like to play cards with her.

3. Theresa will stay overnight and cooking breakfast in the morning.

4. Kent did a poor job washing the car more because he was rushed than that he did not know how to do it.

5. I prefer Greek mythology to reading nonfiction.

6. I will not go to the play because I would have to buy a ticket, and you have to dress up.

7. The story that Dad told about me was funny, interesting, and I was entertained.

8. I have a dog, Ning has a cat, but a goldfish is Roger's only pet.

9. The ice skater landed her jumps but makes other mistakes.

10. I both cleaned my room and the garage.

Revising to Eliminate Faulty Coordination

Read each sentence. Then, rewrite each sentence to correct the faulty coordination.

EXAMPLE   The waiter brought the main course, and it is lasagna.

ANSWER   *The waiter brought the main course, lasagna.*

11. The Carlsbad Caverns are in New Mexico, and we visited them last year.

12. The students were ready at 11:00, and arriving at 4:00 were their parents.

13. Misty is a talented singer, and people like to hear her perform.

14. Bijou found a kitten, and it is white.

15. Amy is afraid of honeybees, and they are necessary for cross-pollination.

16. Albert Einstein was a brilliant scientist, and he left Germany before World War II.

17. I jogged in the park, and crowds filled the paths there.

18. Our bags were packed, and we left for home.

19. Jim was searching for a job, and he had graduated from college last week.

20. The alarm clock woke me this morning, and it was still dark.

SPEAKING APPLICATION

Take turns with a partner. Tell about something you plan to do with your family or friends. Try to include two or three activities in each sentence. Your partner should listen for and correct any faulty parallelism.

WRITING APPLICATION

Use sentences 18, 19, and 20 as models to write three similar sentences that contain faulty coordination. Exchange papers with a partner, and correct each other's work.

CHAPTER 5

VERB USAGE

Use verbs strategically to shape how you present the events in your writing.

WRITE GUY *Jeff Anderson, M.Ed.*

WHAT DO YOU NOTICE?

Size up the verbs as you zoom in on these sentences from the inaugural address of President John F. Kennedy.

MENTOR TEXT

> In your hands, my fellow citizens, more than in mine, will rest the final success or failure of our course. Since this country was founded, each generation of Americans has been summoned to give testimony to its national loyalty.

Now, ask yourself the following questions:

- Is the first sentence written in the active voice or passive voice?
- In the second sentence, which voice is used in each of the two clauses, and what might be the reason for using this voice?

The first sentence is written in the active voice, or tense, because the subject *success or failure* performs the action of the verb *will rest*. The second sentence is written in the passive voice, or tense, because the subject of each clause does not perform the action of the verb. The passive verbs are *was founded* and *has been summoned*. The passive voice is used here because the speaker is focused on the future, not on who founded the country or who summoned the people.

Grammar for Writers When you have a choice between active and passive voice, you should usually choose the active voice. Because it is more direct, the active voice makes your writing more vibrant and powerful.

The song was sung by the singer, and she was accompanied by the band.

Hmm . . . and the concert was enjoyed by all?

5.1 Verb Tenses

Besides expressing actions or conditions, verbs have different **tenses** to indicate when the action or condition occurred.

A tense is the form of a verb that shows the time of an action or a condition.

EL5

The Six Verb Tenses

There are six tenses that indicate when an action or a condition of a verb is, was, or will be in effect. Each of these six tenses has at least two forms.

Each tense has a basic and a progressive form.

The chart that follows shows examples of the six tenses.

THE BASIC FORMS OF THE SIX TENSES	
Present	Bill writes for magazines.
Past	He wrote about the economy for news magazines.
Future	He will write about new economic trends.
Present Perfect	He has written for many newspapers, too.
Past Perfect	He had written for his school newspaper when he was in college.
Future Perfect	He will have written about many subjects during his writing career.
Present	Marie runs track.
Past	She ran track last year.
Future	She will run in this week's meet.
Present Perfect	She has run in every meet this year.
Past Perfect	She had run relay races, too.
Future Perfect	She will have run throughout high school.

See Practice 5.1A

Basic Verb Forms or Tenses

Verb tenses are identified simply by their tense names. The **progressive tenses,** however, are identified by their tense names plus the word *progressive*. Progressive tenses show that an action is or was happening for a period of time.

The chart below shows examples of the six tenses in their progressive form or tense. Note that all of these progressive tenses end in *-ing*. (See the section on verb conjugation later in this chapter for more about the progressive tense.)

THE PROGRESSIVE TENSES	
Present Progressive	Mark is writing about history.
Past Progressive	He was writing in the library.
Future Progressive	He will be writing at home tonight.
Present Perfect Progressive	He has been writing since he was in elementary school.
Past Perfect Progressive	He had been writing about sports before he began writing about history.
Future Perfect Progressive	Next year, he will have been writing for magazines for a decade.

The Emphatic Form

There is also a third form or tense, the **emphatic,** which exists only for the present and past tenses. The **present emphatic** is formed with the helping verbs *do* or *does,* depending on the subject. The **past emphatic** is formed with *did.* The purpose of the emphatic tense is to put more emphasis on, or to stress, the action of the verb.

THE EMPHATIC TENSES OF THE PRESENT AND THE PAST	
Present Emphatic	Our team does play better defense than Central's team. Most of my family does like to go to the shore during the summer.
Past Emphatic	I did exercise last night to work on my endurance. Mona did wonder what had happened to her backpack.

See Practice 5.1B

PRACTICE 5.1A **Identifying Verb Tenses**

Read each sentence. Then, write the tense of the underlined verb in each sentence.

EXAMPLE   Liz <u>has balanced</u> perfectly on the beam many times.

ANSWER   *present perfect*

1. We did not know the team <u>practiced</u> yesterday afternoon.

2. We hope the honeybees <u>will make</u> more honey by next spring.

3. Ben <u>takes</u> algebra this year.

4. Blanca <u>had left</u> for the day.

5. Sam <u>will learn</u> to play the piano.

6. Dan <u>takes</u> swimming lessons at the town pool.

7. Mary <u>will have sung</u> in the shower this morning.

8. I <u>will join</u> the choir next semester.

9. My father <u>has worked</u> very hard at his job.

10. I <u>will have gone</u> to college.

PRACTICE 5.1B **Recognizing Tenses or Forms of Verbs**

Read each sentence. Then, write the verb and the tense of the verb.

EXAMPLE   I was mowing the lawn all day yesterday.

ANSWER   *was mowing* — past progressive

11. Sasha will have been watching television in the evening.

12. Matthew will be playing for a different team next spring.

13. The teacher did return our tests before the bell rang.

14. It had been snowing since 1:00 P.M.

15. I did tell my sister the truth.

16. Latoya and her friends will have been studying.

17. The play will have been over by 8:00 P.M.

18. The blue paint does look better than the green.

19. I will be ordering lunch for you.

20. Miguel is taking karate classes after school.

SPEAKING APPLICATION

Take turns with a partner. Tell what you did yesterday and what you plan to do today. Use past, present, and future forms of verb tenses. Your partner should listen for and identify each verb tense that you use.

WRITING APPLICATION

Write your own sentences, using different verb tenses. Then, underline the verb or verb phrase in each sentence, and write the tense of each verb.

The Four Principal Parts of Verbs

Every verb in the English language has four **principal parts** from which all of the tenses are formed.

> A verb has four principal parts: the **present**, the **present participle**, the **past**, and the **past participle**.

5.1.3 RULE

The chart below shows the principal parts of the verbs *wait*, *laugh*, and *run*.

THE FOUR PRINCIPAL PARTS			
PRESENT	PRESENT PARTICIPLE	PAST	PAST PARTICIPLE
wait	waiting	waited	(have) waited
laugh	laughing	laughed	(have) laughed
run	running	ran	(have) run

The first principal part, the present, is used for the basic forms of the present and future tenses, as well as for the emphatic forms or tenses. The present tense is formed by adding an -*s* or -*es* when the subject is *he, she, it,* or a singular noun. The future tense is formed with the helping verb *will*. *(I will wait. Mary will laugh. Carl will run.)* The present emphatic is formed with the helping verb *do* or *does*. *(I do wait. Mary does laugh. Carl does run.)* The past emphatic is formed with the helping verb *did*. *(I did wait. Mary did laugh. Carl did run.)*

EL6

The second principal part, the present participle, is used with helping verbs for all of the progressive forms. *(I am waiting. Mary is laughing. Carl is running.)*

The third principal part, the past, is used to form the past tense. *(I waited. Mary laughed. Carl ran.)* As in the example *ran*, the past tense of a verb can change its spelling. (See the next section for more information.)

See Practice 5.1C
See Practice 5.1D

The fourth principal part, the past participle, is used with helping verbs to create the perfect tenses. *(I have waited. Mary had laughed. Carl had run.)*

Recognizing the Four Principal Parts of Verbs

Read each sentence. Then, write the principal part and label as *present, present participle, past,* or *past participle.*

EXAMPLE   We were just walking past the school.

ANSWER   *walking* — *present participle*

1. Sue and Eric wash the dishes after dinner.
2. Liam is reading in bed for a while.
3. The team practiced soccer for several hours.
4. I had quoted that profound speech.
5. It is raining lightly.
6. Jing and Grace reached the end of the trail.
7. The storm had flooded the streets.
8. Jen had better grades than Seth.
9. I drove you home after practice.
10. Taylor is taking world history this semester.

PRACTICE 5.1D **Identifying the Four Principal Parts of Verbs**

Read each sentence. Then, identify the principal part used to form each verb.

EXAMPLE   They are playing chess.

ANSWER   *present participle*

11. I fell on the slippery path.
12. They have read a play by William Shakespeare.
13. The glass vase shattered.
14. I believe in miracles.
15. She is smiling happily.
16. He is running to the library.
17. I promised earnestly.
18. She is forgetting about the dinner party.
19. They arrived on time.
20. You are leading the procession.

SPEAKING APPLICATION

Take turns with a partner. Tell about a place that you have visited. Your partner should listen for and identify the principal parts that you use.

WRITING APPLICATION

Write four sentences that use each of the four principal parts. Then, circle the principal part in each sentence, and write the name of that principal part.

Regular and Irregular Verbs

The way the past and past participle forms of a verb are formed determines whether the verb is **regular** or **irregular.**

Regular Verbs The majority of verbs are regular. Regular verbs form their past and past participles according to a predictable pattern.

> A **regular verb** is one for which the past and past participle are formed by adding *-ed* or *-d* to the present form.

5.1.4 RULE

In the chart below, notice that a final consonant is sometimes doubled to form the present participle, the past, and the past participle. A final *e* may also be dropped to form the participle.

See Practice 5.1E
See Practice 5.1F

PRINCIPAL PARTS OF REGULAR VERBS			
PRESENT	PRESENT PARTICIPLE	PAST	PAST PARTICIPLE
manage	managing	managed	(have) managed
describe	describing	described	(have) described
slip	slipping	slipped	(have) slipped

Irregular Verbs Although most verbs are regular, many of the most common verbs are irregular. Irregular verbs do not use a predictable pattern to form their past and past participles.

> An **irregular verb** is one whose past and past participle are *not* formed by adding *-ed* or *-d* to the present form.

5.1.5 RULE

Usage Problems Remembering the principal parts of irregular verbs can help you avoid usage problems. One common usage problem is using a principal part that is not standard.

INCORRECT   Kim **sleeped** late this morning.

CORRECT   Kim **slept** late this morning.

A second usage problem is confusing the past and past participle when they have different forms.

INCORRECT Tamara **done** her research in the library.

CORRECT Tamara **did** her research in the library.

Some common irregular verbs are shown in the charts that follow.
Use a dictionary if you are not sure how to form the principal
parts of an irregular verb.

IRREGULAR VERBS WITH THE SAME PRESENT, PAST, AND PAST PARTICIPLE			
PRESENT	PRESENT PARTICIPLE	PAST	PAST PARTICIPLE
burst	bursting	burst	(have) burst
cost	costing	cost	(have) cost
cut	cutting	cut	(have) cut
hit	hitting	hit	(have) hit
hurt	hurting	hurt	(have) hurt
let	letting	let	(have) let
put	putting	put	(have) put
set	setting	set	(have) set
shut	shutting	shut	(have) shut
split	splitting	split	(have) split
spread	spreading	spread	(have) spread

Note About *Be: Be* is one of the most irregular of all of the verbs.
The present participle of *be* is *being*. The past participle is *been*.
The present and the past depend on the subject and tense of the
verb.

CONJUGATION OF *BE*		
	SINGULAR	PLURAL
Present	I am. You are. He, she, or it is.	We are. You are. They are.
Past	I was. You were. He, she, or it was.	We were. You were. They were.
Future	I will be. You will be. He, she, or it will be.	We will be. You will be. They will be.

IRREGULAR VERBS WITH THE SAME PAST AND PAST PARTICIPLE

PRESENT	PRESENT PARTICIPLE	PAST	PAST PARTICIPLE
bring	bringing	brought	(have) brought
build	building	built	(have) built
buy	buying	bought	(have) bought
catch	catching	caught	(have) caught
fight	fighting	fought	(have) fought
find	finding	found	(have) found
get	getting	got	(have) got or (have) gotten
hold	holding	held	(have) held
keep	keeping	kept	(have) kept
lay	laying	laid	(have) laid
lead	leading	led	(have) led
leave	leaving	left	(have) left
lose	losing	lost	(have) lost
pay	paying	paid	(have) paid
say	saying	said	(have) said
sell	selling	sold	(have) sold
send	sending	sent	(have) sent
shine	shining	shone or shined	(have) shone or (have) shined
sit	sitting	sat	(have) sat
sleep	sleeping	slept	(have) slept
spend	spending	spent	(have) spent
stand	standing	stood	(have) stood
stick	sticking	stuck	(have) stuck
sting	stinging	stung	(have) stung
strike	striking	struck	(have) struck
swing	swinging	swung	(have) swung
teach	teaching	taught	(have) taught
win	winning	won	(have) won
wind	winding	wound	(have) wound

IRREGULAR VERBS THAT CHANGE IN OTHER WAYS

PRESENT	PRESENT PARTICIPLE	PAST	PAST PARTICIPLE
arise	arising	arose	(have) arisen
become	becoming	became	(have) become
begin	beginning	began	(have) begun
bite	biting	bit	(have) bitten
break	breaking	broke	(have) broken
choose	choosing	chose	(have) chosen
come	coming	came	(have) come
do	doing	did	(have) done
draw	drawing	drew	(have) drawn
drink	drinking	drank	(have) drunk
drive	driving	drove	(have) driven
eat	eating	ate	(have) eaten
fall	falling	fell	(have) fallen
fly	flying	flew	(have) flown
give	giving	gave	(have) given
go	going	went	(have) gone
grow	growing	grew	(have) grown
know	knowing	knew	(have) known
lie	lying	lay	(have) lain
ride	riding	rode	(have) ridden
ring	ringing	rang	(have) rung
rise	rising	rose	(have) risen
run	running	ran	(have) run
see	seeing	saw	(have) seen
sing	singing	sang	(have) sung
sink	sinking	sank	(have) sunk
speak	speaking	spoke	(have) spoken
swim	swimming	swam	(have) swum
take	taking	took	(have) taken
tear	tearing	tore	(have) torn
throw	throwing	threw	(have) thrown
wear	wearing	wore	(have) worn
write	writing	wrote	(have) written

See Practice 5.1G
See Practice 5.1H

PRACTICE 5.1E > **Recognizing Principal Parts of Regular Verbs**

Read each regular verb. Then, add the missing principal parts. The order of the parts should be present, present participle, past, and past participle.

EXAMPLE   _____ _____ cluttered _____

ANSWER   *clutter*
cluttering
cluttered
(have) cluttered

1. _____ applauding _____ _____

2. measure _____ _____ _____

3. produce _____ _____ _____

4. _____ _____ replaced _____

5. _____ smelling _____ _____

6. _____ _____ _____ (have) cheated

7. _____ embarrassing _____ _____

8. improve _____ _____ _____

9. _____ _____ _____ (have) squeezed

10. _____ _____ noticed _____

PRACTICE 5.1F > **Using the Correct Form of Regular Verbs**

Read each sentence. Then, fill in each blank by choosing the correct verb form from those given in parentheses.

EXAMPLE   I _____ you were not in attendance at the meeting. (realizing, realized)

ANSWER   *realized*

11. Vic _____ for a salad. (opt, opted)

12. Yesterday, I _____ Ling that she could come over after school today. (promise, promised)

13. The cheerleaders _____ chants during the football games. (shouting, shout)

14. I _____ that we should be allowed to leave books in our lockers. (agreeing, agree)

15. The ball _____ high. (bounced, bouncing)

16. The hurricane _____ an evacuation of the city. (has forced, forcing)

17. Please _____ me for dinner. (join, joined)

18. Mr. Turner is _____ the food and clothing drive. (managing, managed)

19. Mia _____ the award more times than any other student. (earning, has earned)

20. I _____ the furniture. (kept, keeping)

SPEAKING APPLICATION

Take turns with a partner. Tell about something you did last summer. Use a different principal part in each of your sentences. Your partner should listen for and identify the principal parts in your sentences.

WRITING APPLICATION

Use your completion of sentence 20 as a model to write three sentences of your own. Replace the verb in sentence 20 with other participle forms of regular verbs.

PRACTICE 5.1G > **Recognizing Principal Parts of Irregular Verbs**

Read each word. Then, write the present participle, the past, and the past participle of each verb.

EXAMPLE   awake

ANSWER   *awaking, awoke, (have) awoken*

1. bring _____
2. fly _____
3. put _____
4. make _____
5. draw _____
6. hear _____
7. sing _____
8. break _____
9. tear _____
10. sit _____

PRACTICE 5.1H > **Supplying the Correct Form of Irregular Verbs**

Read each sentence. Then, write the appropriate form of each irregular verb indicated in parentheses.

EXAMPLE   NASA (understand) _____ the risks involved with a mission to the Moon.

ANSWER   *understood*

11. The first steps on the Moon were _____ by Neil Armstrong on July 20, 1969. (take)

12. He _____ the first man to walk on the surface of the Moon. (become)

13. Armstrong _____ his way out of the *Eagle* and onto the Moon. (make)

14. He later said that the ground _____ like powdered charcoal. (feel)

15. Armstrong _____ his first few minutes on the Moon taking photographs. (spend)

16. He then _____ an American flag into the Moon's surface. (stick)

17. Millions of Americans _____ the landing on their television screens. (see)

18. They _____ Armstrong speak from the Moon. (hear).

19. Armstrong _____, "That's one small step for man, one giant leap for mankind." (say)

20. The United States had _____ the space race against the Soviet Union. (win)

SPEAKING APPLICATION

Take turns with a partner. Say the present form of five irregular verbs. Your partner should tell the present participle, past, and past participle of each verb.

WRITING APPLICATION

Write three sentences about what you think of the first moon landing. Include the correct form of at least three irregular verbs in your writing.

Verb Conjugation

The **conjugation** of a verb displays all of its different forms.

> A **conjugation** is a complete list of the singular and plural forms of a verb in a particular tense.

The singular forms of a verb correspond to the singular personal pronouns (*I, you, he, she, it*), and the plural forms correspond to the plural personal pronouns (*we, you, they*).

To conjugate a verb, you need the four principal parts: the present (*pay*), the present participle (*paying*), the past (*paid*), and the past participle (*paid*). You also need various helping verbs, such as *has, have,* or *will*.

Notice that only three principal parts—the present, the past, and the past participle—are used to conjugate all six of the basic forms.

CONJUGATION OF THE BASIC FORMS OF *PAY*		SINGULAR	PLURAL
Present	First Person Second Person Third Person	I pay. You pay. He, she, or it pays.	We pay. You pay. They pay.
Past	First Person Second Person Third Person	I paid. You paid. He, she, or it paid.	We paid. You paid. They paid.
Future	First Person Second Person Third Person	I will pay. You will pay. He, she, or it will pay.	We will pay. You will pay. They will pay.
Present Perfect	First Person Second Person Third Person	I have paid. You have paid. He, she, or it has paid.	We have paid. You have paid. They have paid.
Past Perfect	First Person Second Person Third Person	I had paid. You had paid. He, she, or it had paid.	We had paid. You had paid. They had paid.
Future Perfect	First Person Second Person Third Person	I will have paid. You will have paid. He, she, or it will have paid.	We will have paid. You will have paid. They will have paid.

See Practice 5.1I

Conjugating the Progressive Tense With *Be*

As you learned earlier, the **progressive tense** shows an ongoing action or condition. To form the progressive tense, use the present participle form of the verb (the *-ing* form) with a form of the verb *be*.

CONJUGATION OF THE PROGRESSIVE FORMS OF *PAY*		SINGULAR	PLURAL
Present Progressive	First Person Second Person Third Person	I am paying. You are paying. He, she, or it is paying.	We are paying. You are paying. They are paying.
Past Progressive	First Person Second Person Third Person	I was paying. You were paying. He, she, or it was paying.	We were paying. You were paying. They were paying.
Future Progressive	First Person Second Person Third Person	I will be paying. You will be paying. He, she, or it will be paying.	We will be paying. You will be paying. They will be paying.
Present Perfect Progressive	First Person Second Person Third Person	I have been paying. You have been paying. He, she, or it has been paying.	We have been paying. You have been paying. They have been paying.
Past Perfect Progressive	First Person Second Person Third Person	I had been paying. You had been paying. He, she, or it had been paying.	We had been paying. You had been paying. They had been paying.
Future Perfect Progressive	First Person Second Person Third Person	I will have been paying. You will have been paying. He, she, or it will have been paying.	We will have been paying. You will have been paying. They will have been paying.

See Practice 5.1J

PRACTICE 5.1I ▷ **Conjugating the Basic Forms of Verbs**

Read each verb. Then, complete the conjugations for all six basic forms of the verb, using the subject indicated in parentheses.

EXAMPLE run (I)

ANSWER *I run, I ran, I will run, I have run, I had run, I will have run*

1. sing (I) _____
2. jump (you) _____
3. see (she) _____
4. prepare (we) _____
5. think (they) _____
6. believe (he) _____
7. control (I) _____
8. fight (we) _____
9. laugh (she) _____
10. inspire (you) _____

PRACTICE 5.1J ▷ **Conjugating the Progressive Forms of Verbs**

Read each verb. Then, complete the conjugations for all six progressive forms of the verb, using the subject indicated in parentheses.

EXAMPLE run (I)

ANSWER *I am running, I was running, I will be running, I have been running, I had been running, I will have been running*

11. watch (they) _____
12. join (we) _____
13. kick (you) _____
14. collect (she) _____
15. wish (I) _____
16. choose (they) _____
17. learn (he) _____
18. cheer (we) _____
19. smile (you) _____
20. blush (she) _____

SPEAKING APPLICATION

Choose six verbs not used in Practice 5.1I. With a partner, take turns conjugating each verb for all six basic forms.

WRITING APPLICATION

Choose three verbs not used in Practice 5.1J. Conjugate each verb for all six progressive forms.

5.2 The Correct Use of Tenses

The basic, progressive, and emphatic forms of the six tenses show time within one of three general categories: **present, past,** and **future.** This section will explain how each verb form has a specific use that distinguishes it from the other forms.

Present, Past, and Future Tense

Good usage depends on an understanding of how each form works within its general category of time to express meaning.

Uses of Tense in Present Time
Three different forms can be used to express present time.

RULE

5.2.1

> The three forms of the **present tense** show present actions or conditions as well as various continuing actions or conditions.

EXPRESSING PRESENT TENSE	
Present	I study .
Present Progressive	I am studying .
Present Emphatic	I do study .

The main uses of the basic form of the present tense are shown in the chart below.

EXPRESSING PRESENT TENSE	
Present Action	Emma is swimming in a meet.
Present Condition	She wants to win.
Regularly Occurring Action	She practices every afternoon.
Regularly Occurring Condition	She is a strong swimmer.
Constant Action	People swim in pools all year.
Constant Condition	Some pools are open to the public.

See Practice 5.2A

Historical Present The present tense may also be used to express historical events. This use of the present, called the **historical present tense,** is occasionally used in narration to make past actions or conditions sound more lively.

THE HISTORICAL PRESENT TENSE	
Past Actions Expressed in Historical Present Tense	The Union soldier crawls up the hill and looks for enemy soldiers.
Past Condition Expressed in Historical Present Tense	The armies of the North and the South are at war with one another during the Civil War.

The **critical present tense** is most often used to discuss deceased authors and their literary achievements.

THE CRITICAL PRESENT TENSE	
Action Expressed in Critical Present	Walt Whitman writes about exploring the natural world.
Condition Expressed in Critical Present	In addition, Whitman is the author of several volumes of poetry.

The **present progressive tense** is used to show a continuing action or condition of a long or short duration.

USES OF THE PRESENT PROGRESSIVE TENSE	
Long Continuing Action	Keisha is working at the store.
Short Continuing Action	She is learning how to work the cash register.
Continuing Condition	She is enjoying her job.

USES OF THE PRESENT EMPHATIC TENSE	
Emphasizing a Statement	Peter does like to cook meals.
Denying a Contrary Assertion	No, he does not like to clean up after cooking.
Asking a Question	Did he try your recipe for spaghetti?
Making a Sentence Negative	He does not have a sauce recipe he likes.

See Practice 5.2B

PRACTICE 5.2A ▷ **Identifying the Tense in Present Time**

Read each sentence. Then, label the form of the underlined verb *present*, *present progressive*, or *present emphatic*.

EXAMPLE   My mother is making dinner in the kitchen.

ANSWER   *present progressive*

1. That flight <u>leaves</u> daily from Gate B at 3:00 P.M.

2. Many businesses <u>are offering</u> deals to fight the competition.

3. The shuttle bus <u>waits</u> to transport passengers.

4. The doctor's office <u>is</u> always busy.

5. A letter of congratulations <u>does seem</u> appropriate.

6. Dan <u>anticipates</u> a lengthy involvement.

7. I <u>notice</u> a new ship in the harbor.

8. John Williams <u>composes</u> with an attention to detail.

9. My brothers <u>are playing</u> video games in the den.

10. Professors <u>are</u> usually experts on their subjects.

PRACTICE 5.2B ▷ **Supplying Verbs in Present Time**

Read each sentence. Then, complete each sentence with an appropriate verb in the present tense.

EXAMPLE   First thing in the morning, Pete usually _____ his teeth.

ANSWER   *brushes*

11. Every afternoon after school, Jaya _____ her homework at the kitchen table.

12. The president of the United States _____ in the White House.

13. Connor _____ his teacher he will succeed in science class.

14. Stella, Jen, and Maria _____ to remain best friends forever.

15. Doug _____ his grandfather to the supermarket every Saturday morning.

16. Marcus _____ to his favorite radio station while eating breakfast every morning.

17. Jamie _____ his lunch to school instead of buying it in the cafeteria.

18. Jose and his brother _____ groceries after school.

19. Cara _____ to the National Honor Society at her high school.

20. Raj _____ the winning serve for the volleyball team.

SPEAKING APPLICATION

Take turns with a partner. Tell about things that happen in your school community. Your partner should listen for and name the use of present-tense verbs in your sentences.

WRITING APPLICATION

Write five sentences that use verbs in the present tense. Underline the verbs in your sentences.

Uses of the Past Tense

There are seven verb forms that express past actions or conditions.

> The seven forms that express **past tense** show actions and conditions that began at some time in the past.

FORMS EXPRESSING PAST TENSE	
Past	I drew.
Present Perfect	I have drawn.
Past Perfect	I had drawn.
Past Progressive	I was drawing.
Present Perfect Progressive	I have been drawing.
Past Perfect Progressive	I had been drawing.
Past Emphatic	I did draw.

The uses of the most common form, the past, are shown below.

USES OF THE PAST TENSE	
Completed Action	Kate edited Bob's paper.
Completed Condition	She was careful to catch Bob's errors.

Notice in the chart above that the time of the action or the condition could be changed from indefinite to definite if such words as *last week* or *yesterday* were added to the sentences.

See Practice 5.2C

Present Perfect The **present perfect tense** always expresses indefinite time. Use it to show actions or conditions continuing from the past to the present.

USES OF THE PRESENT PERFECT TENSE	
Completed Action (Indefinite Time)	They have rehearsed their parts.
Completed Condition (Indefinite Time)	They have been in this theater.
Action Continuing to Present	The tickets have sold well.
Condition Continuing to Present	I have hoped people enjoy the play.

Past Perfect The **past perfect tense** expresses an action that took place before another action.

USES OF THE PAST PERFECT TENSE	
Action Completed Before Another Action	My teacher had created the final exam before she gave us study guidelines.
Condition Completed Before Another Condition	She had been sure that we would be successful on the test.

These charts show the **past progressive** and **emphatic tenses.**

USES OF THE PROGRESSIVE TENSE TO EXPRESS PAST TIME	
Past Progressive	**LONG CONTINUING ACTION** We were going to the seaside resort. **SHORT CONTINUING ACTION** We were planning to try surfing. **CONTINUOUS CONDITION** It was exciting to surf, but also a bit scary.
Present Perfect Progressive	**CONTINUING ACTION** We have been swimming all winter to increase our endurance.
Past Perfect Progressive	**CONTINUING ACTION INTERRUPTED** We had been dreaming of big waves, but then we decided that small ones would be fine.

USES OF THE PAST EMPHATIC TENSE	
Emphasizing a Statement	My guitar playing did improve after I tried your technique.
Denying a Contrary Assertion	Yes, I did practice the chords!
Asking a Question	Where did you learn how to play so well?
Making a Sentence Negative	I did not appreciate how hard it was to play the guitar.

See Practice 5.2D

PRACTICE 5.2C > Identifying Tense in Past Time

Read each sentence. Then, write the verb in each sentence that shows past time and identify the tense form.

EXAMPLE   The police officer rerouted all traffic.

ANSWER   *rerouted* — *past*

1. The visitor had left after knocking on the door for several minutes.

2. We played Central High's basketball team twice this season.

3. We did follow all of the rules of the game.

4. I have been in a great mood all week.

5. The first settlers lived a much simpler life.

6. After a few days, we had adjusted to the new schedule.

7. A small crowd was gathering in the courtyard.

8. My first class started at 8:00 A.M.

9. We had finished reviewing our notes just before the fire drill.

10. The class officers have been meeting about the theme for the spring dance.

PRACTICE 5.2D > Supplying Verbs in Past Time

Read each sentence. Then, write the form of each verb indicated in parentheses.

EXAMPLE   We _____ the Vatican during our trip to Rome. (visit; past progressive)

ANSWER   *were visiting*

11. I _____ the test long before the time was up. (complete; past perfect)

12. The baby _____ through the night. (sleep; past perfect progressive)

13. I was happy to see that it _____ during the night. (snow; past perfect progressive)

14. We _____ years for the eclipse to reoccur. (wait; past perfect progressive)

15. It _____ unusually cold out when I left my house this morning. (be; past perfect)

16. The new movie theater in town _____. (open; past perfect)

17. The game _____ when we got to the arena. (start; past progressive)

18. I _____ at the student council assembly yesterday. (speak; past emphatic)

19. Frank worried that he _____ to a hasty conclusion. (jump; past perfect)

20. We _____ in the library for hours. (study; past emphatic)

SPEAKING APPLICATION

Take turns with a partner. Identify the use of the past-tense verbs in the sentences in Practice 5.2C.

WRITING APPLICATION

Use your correction of sentence 20 as a model to write three sentences of your own. Replace the verb in your corrected sentence with other past progressive forms of verbs.

Uses of the Future Tense

The **future tense** shows actions or conditions that will happen at a later date.

RULE 5.2.3

> The future tense expresses actions or conditions that have not yet occurred.

FORMS EXPRESSING FUTURE TENSE	
Future	I will drive.
Future Perfect	I will have driven.
Future Progressive	I will be driving.
Future Perfect Progressive	I will have been driving.

USES OF THE FUTURE AND THE FUTURE PERFECT TENSE	
Future	I will jog every afternoon. I will take different routes.
Future Perfect	I will have jogged ten miles every day this week. At the end of this month, I will have jogged for four years.

Notice in the next chart that the **future progressive** and the **future perfect progressive tenses** express only future actions.

USES OF THE PROGRESSIVE TENSE TO EXPRESS FUTURE TIME	
Future Progressive	Janice will be playing tennis today.
Future Perfect Progressive	When she graduates, she will have been playing for four years on the high school team.

The basic forms of the present and the present progressive tense are often used with other words to express future time.

EXAMPLES   The movie **opens** downtown next week.

My friends **are waiting** to see it.

See Practice 5.2E
See Practice 5.2F

PRACTICE 5.2E > **Identifying Tense in Future Time**

Read each sentence. Then, write the future-tense verbs in each sentence and identify the form of the tense.

EXAMPLE   The train will be arriving shortly.

ANSWER   *will be arriving — future progressive*

1. The convention will have continued for another five days.

2. The play will be running for ten years.

3. They will have played the other team by then.

4. We will be traveling over Pike's Peak.

5. This will have been my first airplane ride.

6. Tomorrow night we will adjust our clocks.

7. We will be at the beach soon.

8. He will have been working at the ranch.

9. The guests will have arrived at the party by noon.

10. Susan will compete in the swim meet on Saturday.

PRACTICE 5.2F > **Supplying Verbs in Future Time**

Read each sentence. Then, rewrite each sentence, filling in the blank with the future tense of the verb indicated in parentheses.

EXAMPLE   The children _____ outside tonight. (sleep, future)

ANSWER   *The children will sleep outside tonight.*

11. The paint _____ by tomorrow. (dry, future progressive)

12. She _____ to Europe. (travel, future perfect)

13. The doctor said that she _____ before next week. (heal, future perfect)

14. The school day _____ at 3:00. (end, future)

15. Caitlyn _____ home by 5:00 P.M. (walk, future perfect)

16. Tonight, I _____ the entire house. (clean, future progressive)

17. The cast _____ all day today. (practice, future)

18. By the end of the year, I _____ at the same job for four years. (work, future perfect progressive)

19. He _____ his paper after school. (write, future progressive)

20. The clowns _____ at the rodeo by this weekend. (perform, future perfect progressive)

SPEAKING APPLICATION

Take turns with a partner. Tell about your career plans or what you hope to be doing in ten years. Use future-tense verbs in your sentences. Your partner should listen for and name the future-tense verbs that you use.

WRITING APPLICATION

Rewrite your corrections for sentences 11, 12, and 13, changing the verbs to include other future-tense verbs. Make sure your sentences still make sense.

Sequence of Tenses

A sentence with more than one verb must be consistent in its time sequence.

When showing a sequence of events, do not shift tenses unnecessarily.

EXAMPLES   Jim **will wait** for me, then we **will walk** home.

My dog **has brought** me her ball and **has gotten** her leash.

I **swam** all afternoon and **slept** all night.

Sometimes, however, it is necessary to shift tenses, especially when a sentence is complex or compound-complex. The tense of the main verb often determines the tense of the verb in the subordinate clause. Moreover, the form of the participle or infinitive often depends on the tense of the verb in the main clause.

Verbs in Subordinate Clauses It is frequently necessary to look at the tense of the main verb in a sentence before choosing the tense of the verb in the subordinate clause.

The tense of a verb in a subordinate clause should follow logically from the tense of the main verb.

INCORRECT   I **will think** that Marta **went** downtown.

CORRECT   I **think** that Marta **went** downtown.

As you study the combinations of tenses in the charts on the next pages, notice that the choice of tenses affects the logical relationship between the events being expressed. Some combinations indicate that the events are **simultaneous**—meaning that they occur at the same time. Other combinations indicate that the events are **sequential**—meaning that one event occurs before or after the other.

SEQUENCE OF EVENTS		
MAIN VERB	**SUBORDINATE VERB**	**MEANING**
MAIN VERB IN PRESENT TENSE		
I understand...	**PRESENT** that she cooks delicious meals. **PRESENT PROGRESSIVE** that she is cooking delicious meals. **PRESENT EMPHATIC** that she does cook delicious meals.	Simultaneous events: All events occur in present time.
I understand...	**PAST** that she cooked delicious meals. **PRESENT PERFECT** that she has cooked delicious meals. **PAST PERFECT** that she had cooked delicious meals. **PAST PROGRESSIVE** that she was cooking delicious meals. **PRESENT PERFECT PROGRESSIVE** that she has been cooking delicious meals. **PAST PERFECT PROGRESSIVE** that she had been cooking delicious meals. **PAST EMPHATIC** that she did cook delicious meals.	Sequential events: The cooking comes before the understanding.
I understand...	**FUTURE** that she will cook delicious meals. **FUTURE PERFECT** that she will have cooked delicious meals. **FUTURE PROGRESSIVE** that she will be cooking delicious meals. **FUTURE PERFECT PROGRESSIVE** that she will have been cooking delicious meals.	Sequential events: The understanding comes before the cooking.

SEQUENCE OF EVENTS		
MAIN VERB	**SUBORDINATE VERB**	**MEANING**
MAIN VERB IN PAST TENSE		
I understood…	**PAST** that she cooked delicious meals. **PAST PROGRESSIVE** that she was cooking delicious meals. **PAST EMPHATIC** that she did cook delicious meals.	Simultaneous events: All events take place in the past.
I understood…	**PAST PERFECT** that she had cooked delicious meals. **PAST PERFECT PROGRESSIVE** that she had been cooking delicious meals.	Sequential events: The cooking came before the understanding.
MAIN VERB IN FUTURE TENSE		
I will understand…	**PRESENT** if she cooks delicious meals. **PRESENT PROGRESSIVE** if she is cooking delicious meals. **PRESENT EMPHATIC** if she does cook delicious meals.	Simultaneous events: All events take place in future time.
I will understand…	**PAST** if she cooked delicious meals. **PRESENT PERFECT** if she has cooked delicious meals. **PRESENT PERFECT PROGRESSIVE** if she has been cooking delicious meals. **PAST EMPHATIC** if she did cook delicious meals.	Sequential events: The cooking comes before the understanding.

Time Sequence With Participles and Infinitives Frequently, the form of a participle or infinitive determines whether the events are simultaneous or sequential. Participles can be present (*watching*), past (*watched*), or perfect (*having watched*). Infinitives can be present (*to watch*) or perfect (*to have watched*).

> **The form of a participle or an infinitive should logically relate to the verb in the same clause or sentence.**

5.2.6 RULE

To show simultaneous events, you will generally need to use the present participle or the present infinitive, whether the main verb is present, past, or future.

Simultaneous Events

IN PRESENT TIME **Watching** the movie, she **cries**.
     present   present

IN PAST TIME **Watching** the movie, she **cried**.
     present   past

IN FUTURE TIME **Watching** the movie, she **will cry**.
     present   future

To show sequential events, use the perfect form of the participle and infinitive, regardless of the tense of the main verb.

Sequential Events

IN PRESENT TIME **Having watched** the movie, she **is crying**.
     perfect   present progressive
(She watched *before* she cried.)

IN PAST TIME **Having watched** the movie, she **cried**.
     perfect   past
(She watched *before* she cried.)

SPANNING PAST AND FUTURE TIME **Having watched** the movie, she **will cry**.
     perfect   future
(She will cry *after* watching.)

See Practice 5.2G
See Practice 5.2H

PRACTICE 5.2G Identifying the Time Sequence in Sentences With More Than One Verb

Read each sentence. Then, write the verb of the event that happens second in each sentence.

EXAMPLE   Even though the alarm clock rings, I roll over in my bed.

ANSWER   *roll*

1. She had been working on the project for two years before she made her first discovery.

2. In the past, most people wanted big cars, but now many drive small ones.

3. I wanted a big minivan, but I will be getting a small sedan instead.

4. Most children learn to talk after they have learned to walk.

5. Greg likes to reminisce about the fish that he caught last summer.

6. Astronomers predict that the sun will stop giving off energy in about ten billion years.

7. When the crew saw land, they cheered.

8. People will buy homes when interest rates are lowered.

9. Students will get their prizes after we verify their scores.

10. I start my summer job as soon as I finish orientation.

PRACTICE 5.2H Recognizing and Correcting Errors in Tense Sequence

Read each sentence. Then, if a sentence has an error in tense sequence, rewrite it to correct the error. If a sentence is correct, write *correct*.

EXAMPLE   The river flows down the valley and emptied into the lake.

ANSWER   *The river flows down the valley and empties into the lake.*

11. The wind changed directions and became stronger.

12. The volcano erupted and destroys the tiny island.

13. A robin catches worms and fed her young.

14. The nurses checked on their patients and give them their medicine.

15. All of the students studied hard and learn the material.

16. The puppets sang and dance to the music.

17. One of the horses kicked down the fence and ran toward the woods.

18. The skier turns and came to a stop on the slope.

19. The kitten hides under the bed and slept.

20. The rider got off her horse and removes the saddle.

SPEAKING APPLICATION

Take turns with a partner. Tell about something fun you like to do. Use two verbs in each of your sentences. Your partner should listen for and identify the sequence of events in all of your sentences.

WRITING APPLICATION

Use sentences 11, 13, and 15 as models to write your own sentences with incorrect tense sequence. Then, exchange papers with a partner. Your partner should rewrite your sentences, using the correct sequence in tense.

Modifiers That Help Clarify Tense

The time expressed by a verb can often be clarified by adverbs such as *often*, *sometimes*, *always*, or *frequently* and phrases such as *once in a while*, *within a week*, *last week*, or *now and then*.

> **Use modifiers when they can help clarify tense.**

5.2.7 RULE

In the examples below, the modifiers that help clarify the tense of the verb are highlighted in orange. Think about how the sentences would read without the modifiers. Modifiers help to make your writing more precise and interesting.

EXAMPLES Dogs **like** to run **every day**.

My dog **goes** to the park **once a day**.

My dog **goes** to the park **now and then**.
(These two sentences have very different meanings.)

Occasionally, I **walk** my dog all the way to the dog run.

She **always loves** to play with other dogs.

By tomorrow, we **will have gone** to the dog run three times this week.

My dog also **likes** to walk **twice a day**.

Playing catch **is now** one of her favorite sports.

Sometimes, she **attempts** to catch the ball before I throw it.

She **always pants** hard **after** she **plays** catch.

See Practice 5.2I
See Practice 5.2J

PRACTICE 5.2I ▷ Identifying Modifiers That Help Clarify Tense

Read each sentence. Then, write the modifier in each sentence that helps clarify the verb tense.

EXAMPLE   This morning, they cooked breakfast for the whole family.

ANSWER   *This morning*

1. Chad always has trouble getting up early.
2. Every morning, Shoshana makes her bed.
3. I never want to see another tragic drama again.
4. We finally finished our project at midnight.
5. He occasionally helps his mother in her garden.
6. I practice my karate movements every day.
7. My mother always includes a note in my lunch box.
8. It is just now time for dinner.
9. Suddenly, the door burst open.
10. My sister vacuums the house every week.

PRACTICE 5.2J ▷ Supplying Modifiers to Clarify Meaning

Read each sentence. Then, fill in the blank with a modifier that will clarify the meaning of each sentence.

EXAMPLE   _____, the bus departs at 9:15 A.M.

ANSWER   *Daily*

11. I _____ see a plane in the sky.
12. _____, the phone began to ring.
13. The little ducks jumped into the pond _____.
14. Keshaun _____ decided to return my phone call.
15. My father _____ wants to eat liver and onions.
16. _____, we watch movies and eat out on Friday nights.
17. Skyler goes to swim practice _____.
18. It is _____ time to put the turkey in the oven.
19. We _____ prepare a healthy meal for one another.
20. _____, my mother lets me stay up late.

SPEAKING APPLICATION

Take turns with a partner. Tell about trips that you have taken. Use modifiers that help clarify tense in your sentences. Your partner should listen for and identify the modifiers in your sentences.

WRITING APPLICATION

Use your corrections for sentences 11, 13, and 19 as models to write your own sentences. Rewrite the sentences to include different modifiers that clarify meaning.

5.3 The Subjunctive Mood

There are three **moods,** or ways in which a verb can express an action or condition: **indicative, imperative,** and **subjunctive.** The **indicative** mood, which is the most common, is used to make factual statements (*Karl is helpful.*) and to ask questions (*Is Karl helpful?*). The **imperative** mood is used to give orders or directions (*Be helpful.*).

Using the Subjunctive Mood

There are two important differences between verbs in the **subjunctive** mood and those in the indicative mood. First, in the present tense, third-person singular verbs in the subjunctive mood do not have the usual -*s* or -*es* ending. Second, the subjunctive mood of *be* in the present tense is *be;* in the past tense, it is *were,* regardless of the subject.

INDICATIVE MOOD	SUBJUNCTIVE MOOD
He practices his music.	I suggest that he practice every day.
We are here to perform.	We insist that everyone be ready to perform.
We are prepared.	If we were not prepared, we would not perform well.

> Use the subjunctive mood (1) in clauses beginning with *if* or *that* to express an idea that is contrary to fact or (2) in clauses beginning with *that* to express a request, a demand, or a proposal.

RULE 5.3.1

Expressing Ideas Contrary to Fact Ideas that are contrary to fact are commonly expressed as wishes or conditions. Using the subjunctive mood in these situations shows that the idea expressed is not true now and may never be true.

EXAMPLES Emma wishes that the sun **were** shining.

She wished that she **were** able to go to the beach.

She could have had more fun if the weather **were** clear.

Some *if* clauses do not take a subjunctive verb. If the idea expressed may be true, an indicative form is used.

EXAMPLES I told my little brother that **if** the sun **was** shining, we'd go to the park.

If we **want** to get a swing, we'll have to leave soon.

Expressing Requests, Demands, and Proposals Verbs that request, demand, or propose are often followed by a *that* clause containing a verb in the subjunctive mood.

REQUEST The instructor requests that the student **drive** carefully.

DEMAND It is required that the student **drive** carefully.

PROPOSAL He proposed that the student **drive** carefully.

See Practice 5.3A

Auxiliary Verbs That Express the Subjunctive Mood

EL7

Because certain helping verbs suggest conditions contrary to fact, they can often be used in place of the subjunctive mood.

Could, would, or *should* can be used with a verb to express the subjunctive mood.

The sentences on the left in the chart below have the usual subjunctive form of the verb *be: were.* The sentences on the right have been reworded with *could, would,* and *should.*

THE SUBJUNCTIVE MOOD WITH AUXILIARY VERBS	
WITH FORMS OF *BE*	WITH *COULD, WOULD,* OR *SHOULD*
If the sky were clear, we'd go out.	If the sky could be clear, we'd go out.
If she were to win the scholarship, she'd be happy.	If she could win the scholarship, she'd be happy.
If I were to write to you, would you answer me?	If I should write to you, would you answer me?

See Practice 5.3B

Identifying Mood (Indicative, Imperative, Subjunctive)

Read each sentence. Then, identify whether each sentence expresses the *indicative, imperative,* or *subjunctive* mood.

EXAMPLE   If I were you, I would buy some land.

ANSWER   *subjunctive*

1. Sheila may demand a refund for the damaged goods.

2. Gary will bring flashlights on the company trip.

3. If I were tired, I would take a nap.

4. Julio was there at the park.

5. Do you recommend reading *The Grapes of Wrath?*

6. It is best that John and Jagger work together.

7. I need to leave soon.

8. Give me a hand with this leaking faucet.

9. It is necessary to keep an emergency kit in your car.

10. Be home by 9:00.

Supplying Auxiliary Verbs to Express the Subjunctive Mood

Read each sentence. Then, rewrite each sentence, completing it by supplying an auxiliary verb to express the subjunctive mood.

EXAMPLE   If there was a concert tonight, we _____ go.

ANSWER   *If there was a concert tonight, we would go.*

11. John _____ prefer that his son go hiking.

12. I _____ suggest that you check with your mother first.

13. If it was possible to help him, I _____ do it.

14. We really _____ be supportive if he comes home early.

15. I _____ go to the game if the weather were better.

16. What _____ she do about the dance tonight?

17. If I were you, I _____ keep doing that.

18. It _____ help the cause if you donated your old, gently worn coats.

19. If this were Friday, we _____ be finished with our tests.

20. If your brother were a year or two older, he _____ join our team.

SPEAKING APPLICATION

With a partner, take turns saying sentences that express the indicative, imperative, and subjunctive moods. Your partner should listen for and identify which mood each sentence expresses.

WRITING APPLICATION

Use the auxiliary verbs that you used to rewrite sentences 15, 16, and 17 to write your own sentences. Make sure that your sentences express the subjunctive mood.

5.4 Voice

This section discusses a characteristic of verbs called **voice.**

Voice or tense is the form of a verb that shows whether the subject is performing the action or is being acted upon.

In English, there are two voices: **active** and **passive.** Only action verbs can indicate the active voice; linking verbs cannot.

Active and Passive Voice or Tense

If the subject of a verb performs the action, the verb is active; if the subject receives the action, the verb is passive.

Active Voice Any action verb can be used in the active voice. The action verb may be transitive (that is, it may have a direct object) or intransitive (without a direct object).

A verb is active if its subject performs the action.

In the examples below, the subject performs the action. In the first example, the verb *telephoned* is transitive; *team* is the direct object, which receives the action. In the second example, the verb *developed* is transitive; *pictures* is the direct object. In the third example, the verb *gathered* is intransitive; it has no direct object. In the last example, the verb *worked* is intransitive and has no direct object.

ACTIVE
VOICE

The captain **telephoned** the **team**.
            transitive verb   direct object

Bill **developed** twenty-five **pictures** of the ocean.
     transitive verb   direct object

Telephone messages **gathered** on the desk while
                    intransitive verb
she was away.

Bill **worked** quickly.
     intransitive verb

See Practice 5.4A
See Practice 5.4B

EL6

Passive Voice Most action verbs can also be used in the passive voice.

> A verb is passive if its action is performed upon the subject.

RULE 5.4.3

In the following examples, the subjects are the receivers of the action. The first example names the performer, the captain, as the object of the preposition *by* instead of the subject. In the second example, no performer of the action is mentioned.

PASSIVE VOICE

The **team** **was telephoned** by the captain.
   receiver of action   verb

The **messages** **were gathered** into neat piles.
   receiver of action   verb

> A passive verb is always a verb phrase made from a form of *be* plus the past participle of a verb. The tense of the helping verb *be* determines the tense of the passive verb.

RULE 5.2.4

The chart below provides a conjugation in the passive voice of the verb *choose* in the three moods. Notice that there are only two progressive forms and no emphatic form.

THE VERB *CHOOSE* IN THE PASSIVE VOICE	
Present Indicative	He is chosen.
Past Indicative	He was chosen.
Future Indicative	He will be chosen.
Present Perfect Indicative	He has been chosen.
Past Perfect Indicative	He had been chosen.
Future Perfect Indicative	He will have been chosen.
Present Progressive Indicative	He is being chosen.
Past Progressive Indicative	He was being chosen.
Present Imperative	(You) be chosen.
Present Subjunctive	(if) he be chosen
Past Subjunctive	(if) he were chosen

See Practice 5.2C

Using Active and Passive Voice

Writing that uses the active voice tends to be much more lively than writing that uses the passive voice. The active voice is usually more direct and economical. That is because active voice shows someone doing something.

Use the active voice whenever possible.

ACTIVE VOICE   Anthony **won** the trophy.

PASSIVE VOICE   The trophy **was won** by Anthony.

The passive voice has two uses in English.

Use the passive voice when you want to emphasize the receiver of an action rather than the performer of an action.

EXAMPLE   Joe **was selected** to represent our school.

Use the passive voice to point out the receiver of an action whenever the performer is not important or not easily identified.

EXAMPLE   The boat **was rocked** by the ocean, and it felt like the boat might capsize.

The active voice lends more excitement to writing, making it more interesting to readers. In the example below, notice how the sentence you just read has been revised to show someone doing something, rather than something just happening.

EXAMPLE   The ocean **rocked** the boat, and it felt like the boat might capsize.

(*What* rocked the boat and made it feel like it might capsize?)   See Practice 5.4D

PRACTICE 5.4A > **Recognizing Active Voice (Active Tense)**

Read each sentence. Then, write the active verb(s) in each sentence.

EXAMPLE   The storm battered and damaged the oak tree.

ANSWER   *battered, damaged*

1. My mother painted that picture and framed it herself.

2. The delivery person left a package on the front porch.

3. The detective examined and documented the evidence.

4. The airliner landed safely.

5. My aunt taught me the game of tennis.

6. The sanctuary houses and protects wild animals.

7. The two astronauts floated in space.

8. The man slowly opened the front door and then let the dog out.

9. A famous architect designed that building.

10. I planned and prepared tonight's meal with care.

PRACTICE 5.4B > **Using Active Verbs**

Read each item. Then, write different sentences, using each item as an active verb or verbs.

EXAMPLE   informed

ANSWER   *Cherie informed me about the quiz.*

11. cancels

12. journeyed

13. swarmed

14. smelled, ate

15. climbed, saw

16. sings, watches

17. returned

18. fishing, caught

19. paid, walked

20. spotted

SPEAKING APPLICATION

Take turns with a partner. Say sentences in the active voice. Your partner should listen for and identify the active verbs in each of your sentences.

WRITING APPLICATION

Write two sentences in the active voice, using more than one active verb in each sentence.

PRACTICE 5.4C ▷ Forming the Tenses of Passive Verbs

Read each verb. Then, using the subject indicated in parentheses, conjugate each verb in the passive voice for the present indicative, past indicative, future indicative, present perfect indicative, and future perfect indicative.

EXAMPLE   bite (it)

ANSWER   *it is bitten, it was bitten, it will be bitten, it has been bitten, it had been bitten, it will have been bitten*

1. interrupt (he)

2. open (it)

3. select (she)

4. use (it)

5. alarm (we)

6. choose (he)

7. stop (she)

8. win (it)

9. sell (it)

10. convince (you)

PRACTICE 5.4D ▷ Supplying Verbs in the Active Voice (Active Tense)

Read each sentence. Then, complete each sentence by supplying a verb in the active voice.

EXAMPLE   The San Antonio Spurs _____ the championship.

ANSWER   *won*

11. Georgia _____ the paper.

12. The students _____ the reports.

13. The quarterback _____ the football for more than forty yards.

14. Thousands of fans _____ the concert.

15. The people in the restaurant _____ the chef's special.

16. Vincent van Gogh _____ the picture.

17. The children's librarian _____ the story with great expression.

18. Jorge and I _____ the gifts.

19. The hungry children _____ the meal.

20. A famous author _____ the book.

SPEAKING APPLICATION

Take turns with a partner. Say active verbs. Your partner should say the basic forms of each verb in the passive voice.

WRITING APPLICATION

Choose five of the verbs that you supplied for Practice 5.4D. Write a new sentence for each verb. Be sure to use the active voice in your sentences.

CHAPTER 6

PRONOUN USAGE

Use pronouns correctly to craft sentences that readers can follow with ease.

WRITE GUY *Jeff Anderson, M.Ed.*

WHAT DO YOU NOTICE?

Track down the pronouns as you zoom in on these lines from the poem "The Negro Speaks of Rivers" by Langston Hughes.

MENTOR TEXT

> I heard the singing of the Mississippi when Abe Lincoln
> went down to New Orleans, and I've seen its muddy
> bosom turn all golden in the sunset.

Now, ask yourself the following questions:

- Why is the pronoun *I* used in the two places in which it appears?
- To which word does the pronoun *its* refer?

I is used because it is the subject performing the action in both the phrase *I heard the singing* and the phrase *I've seen its muddy bosom*. The pronoun *I* also shows that the speaker is telling about his or her own experiences. The pronoun *its* refers to the Mississippi River and shows ownership of the noun *bosom*.

Grammar for Writers Writers who understand important pronoun usage rules avoid common mistakes. For example, confusing *its* and *it's* is avoidable if you know that *its* is a possessive pronoun, whereas *it's* is a contraction that stands for the words *it is* or *it has*.

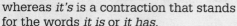

Is this book *yours*?

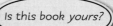

Yes, *it's* mine. And *its* sequel also belongs to *me*.

6.1 Case

Nouns and pronouns are the only parts of speech that have **case.**

6.1.1

Case is the form of a noun or a pronoun that shows how it is used in a sentence.

The Three Cases

Nouns and pronouns have three cases, each of which has its own distinctive uses.

6.1.2

The three cases of nouns and pronouns are the **nominative,** the **objective,** and the **possessive.**

CASE	USE IN SENTENCE
Nominative	As the Subject of a Verb, Predicate Nominative, or Nominative Absolute
Objective	As the Direct Object, Indirect Object, Object of a Preposition, Object of a Verbal, or Subject of an Infinitive
Possessive	To Show Ownership

Case in Nouns

The case, or form, of a noun changes only to show possession.

NOMINATIVE
The **box** had been hidden for months.

(*Box* is the subject of the verb *had been hidden*.)

OBJECTIVE
We tried to find the **box** .
(*Box* is the object of the infinitive *to find.*)

POSSESSIVE
The **box's** location could not be determined.
(The form changes when *'s* is added to show possession.)

Case in Pronouns

Personal pronouns often have different forms for all three cases. The pronoun that you use depends on its function in a sentence.

NOMINATIVE	OBJECTIVE	POSSESSIVE
I	*me*	*my, mine*
you	*you*	*your, yours*
he, she, it	*him, her, it*	*his, her, hers, its*
we, they	*us, them*	*our, ours*
		their, theirs

EXAMPLES   **I** watched the documentary about planes.

Ben sent the camera to **me**.

See Practice 6.1A   The documentary about planes is **mine**.

The Nominative Case in Pronouns

The **nominative case** is used when a personal pronoun acts in one of three ways.

> Use the **nominative case** when a pronoun is the subject of a verb, the subject of a predicate nominative, or the subject of a pronoun in a nominative absolute.

6.1.3 RULE

A **nominative absolute** consists of a noun or nominative pronoun followed by a participial phrase. It functions independently from the rest of the sentence.

EXAMPLE   **We having entered the kitchen,** the chef began

to cook according to the recipe.

NOMINATIVE PRONOUNS	
As the Subject of a Verb	I will consult the directions while she asks for help.
As a Predicate Nominative	The winners were he and she.
In a Nominative Absolute	We having landed on time, the flight attendant opened the cabin door.

Nominative Pronouns in Compounds

When you use a pronoun in a compound subject or predicate nominative, check the case either by mentally crossing out the other part of the compound or by inverting the sentence.

COMPOUND SUBJECT

The lawyer and **I** inspected the contracts.

(**I** inspected the contracts.)

She and her mother went shopping.

(**She** went shopping.)

COMPOUND PREDICATE NOMINATIVE

The best cooks were Emily and **she**.

(Emily and **she** were the best cooks.)

The instructors were Bon and **I**.

(Bon and **I** were the instructors.)

Nominative Pronouns With Appositives

When an appositive follows a pronoun that is being used as a subject or predicate nominative, the pronoun should stay in the nominative case. To check that you have used the correct case, either mentally cross out the appositive or isolate the subject and verb.

SUBJECT

We scientists use microscopes.

(**We** use microscopes.)

PREDICATE NOMINATIVE

The champions were **we** Tigers.

(**We** were the champions.)

APPOSITIVE AFTER NOUN

The hikers, who were **he** and **I**, climbed the mountain.

(**He** and **I** climbed the mountain.)

See Practice 6.1B

PRACTICE 6.1A > Identifying Case

Read each sentence. Then, label the underlined pronoun in each sentence *nominative*, *objective*, or *possessive*.

EXAMPLE   Are these blueberries <u>yours</u>?

ANSWER   *possessive*

1. Our teacher explained the problem to <u>me</u>.

2. That jacket with the silk lining is <u>mine</u>.

3. <u>She</u> should have followed his advice.

4. Please tell <u>me</u> the truth.

5. We bought <u>him</u> some flowers.

6. Why are <u>they</u> always in a hurry?

7. This is <u>your</u> seat for the show.

8. You can buy strawberries or pick <u>them</u>.

9. By law, the land should be <u>hers</u>.

10. The man in that picture is <u>he</u>.

PRACTICE 6.1B > Supplying Pronouns in the Nominative Case

Read each sentence. Then, write the correct pronoun from the choices in parentheses to complete each sentence.

EXAMPLE   When Jenny left the store, (she, her) forgot her keys.

ANSWER   *she*

11. (He, him) told the class about his cruise.

12. When (her, she) woke up, Heather's papers were scattered around the room.

13. I can't believe Shaun and (he, him) traveled all the way from another country.

14. (Them, They) are searching for information about their ancestors.

15. The first girl chosen was (she, her).

16. The treasure hunters, (he and her, he and she), were interviewed by reporters.

17. When the storm reached Texas, (it, its) intensified.

18. (Us, We) finished plowing our part of the field first.

19. While Tricia was there, (her, she) took advantage of the sunny weather.

20. Mike and (she, her) are leaving tomorrow.

SPEAKING APPLICATION

Take turns with a partner. Describe a fun time that you have had with friends or family members. Use sentences that contain one or more pronouns. Your partner should identify the case of each pronoun that you use.

WRITING APPLICATION

Write five sentences. Each sentence should contain a nominative pronoun in a compound subject.

The Objective Case

Objective pronouns are used for any kind of object in a sentence as well as for the subject of an infinitive.

RULE 6.1.4

Use the **objective case** for the object of any verb, preposition, or verbal or for the subject of an Infinitive.

OBJECTIVE PRONOUNS	
Direct Object	The tennis ball hit her on the foot.
Indirect Object	My grandmother sent me a bracelet from Nepal.
Object of Preposition	The conductor stood in front of us on the stage in the Opera House.
Object of Participle	The lion stalking them hid in the brush and didn't move.
Object of Gerund	Seeing them after all this time will be a relief.
Object of Infinitive	I promised to help him study this weekend.
Subject of Infinitive	The police chief wanted him to work tonight.

Objective Pronouns in Compounds

As with the nominative case, errors with objective pronouns most often occur in compounds. To find the correct case, mentally cross out the other part of the compound.

EXAMPLES   The threatening floods alarmed Ray and **her**.
(Threatening floods alarmed **her**.)

Bob wrote Jim and **me** instructions for the game.
(Bob wrote **me** instructions.)

Note About *Between*: Be sure to use the objective case after the preposition *between*.

INCORRECT   This conversation is between you and **I**.

CORRECT   This conversation is between you and **me**.

Objective Pronouns With Appositives

Use the objective case when a pronoun that is used as an object or as the subject of an infinitive is followed by an appositive.

EXAMPLES   The biology test intimidated **us** students.

My aunt brought **us** nephews baseball tickets.

See Practice 6.1C

Our mother asked **us** children to be quiet.

The Possessive Case

One use for the **possessive case** is before gerunds. A **gerund** is a verbal form ending in *-ing* that is used as a noun.

> **Use the possessive case before gerunds.**

6.1.5   RULE

EXAMPLES   **Your** cooking was the best I've ever had.

We disagreed with **his** assuming that we were late.

Jon supports **our** deciding to leave.

Common Errors in the Possessive Case

Be sure not to use an apostrophe with a possessive pronoun because possessives already show ownership. Spellings such as *her's, our's, their's,* and *your's* are incorrect.

In addition, be sure not to confuse possessive pronouns and contractions that sound alike. *It's* (with an apostrophe) is the contraction for *it is* or *it has. Its* (without the apostrophe) is a possessive pronoun that means "belonging to it." *You're* is a contraction of *you are;* the possessive form of *you* is *your.*

POSSESSIVE
PRONOUNS
The plan had served **its** purpose.

Don't forget **your** banner.

CONTRACTIONS   **It's** possible we will go out tonight.

You're the one who wouldn't stop and ask for

See Practice 6.1D

directions.

PRACTICE 6.1C › Supplying Pronouns in the Objective Case

Read each sentence. Then, write an objective pronoun to complete each sentence.

EXAMPLE   We all want _____ to win the prize.

ANSWER   *her*

1. We would like to talk to _____.

2. Paula gave _____ that recipe.

3. Will you send _____ that article today?

4. The heavy rain has Omar and _____ worried about flooding.

5. We got _____ a gift certificate.

6. I had trouble choosing among _____.

7. Julio asked _____ to fix dinner.

8. Mrs. Hernandez asked Tanya and _____ to distribute the books.

9. Thank you for helping _____ with the task.

10. The conversation was between you and _____.

PRACTICE 6.1D › Recognizing Pronouns in the Possessive Case

Read each sentence. Then, write the correct pronoun from the choices in parentheses to complete each sentence.

EXAMPLE   I am happy with (my, mine) decision.

ANSWER   *my*

11. (Her, She) singing made everyone happy.

12. The boy could not prove that the mitt was (his, him).

13. (They, Their) umbrellas were blown by the wind.

14. The dog licked (its, it) paws.

15. Rai thought (she, her) painting was the best.

16. I don't know if it's (her, she) book that I found on the chair.

17. (Us, Our) volunteering resulted in getting a commendation from the mayor.

18. The plate with the rose decoration is (my, mine).

19. The town council is unlikely to approve (they, their) request.

20. That jacket could only be (her, hers).

SPEAKING APPLICATION

Take turns with a partner. Read each sentence in Practice 6.1C, omitting the objective pronoun. Your partner should complete each sentence, using a correct objective pronoun.

WRITING APPLICATION

Write a paragraph about something you own. Underline all the possessive pronouns in your paragraph.

6.2 Special Problems With Pronouns

Choosing the correct case is not always a matter of choosing the form that "sounds correct," because writing is usually more formal than speech. For example, it would be incorrect to say, "John is smarter than *me*." because the verb is understood in the sentence: "John is smarter than *I [am]*."

Using *Who* and *Whom* Correctly

In order to decide when to use *who* or *whom* and the related forms *whoever* and *whomever*, you need to know how the pronoun is used in a sentence and what case is appropriate.

> ***Who*** is used for the nominative case. ***Whom*** is used for the objective case.

6.2.1 RULE

CASE	PRONOUNS	USE IN SENTENCES
Nominative	*who* *whoever*	As the Subject of a Verb or Predicate Nominative
Objective	*whom* *whomever*	As the Direct Object, Object of a Verbal, Object of a Preposition, or Subject of an Infinitive
Possessive	*whose* *whosever*	To Show Ownership

EXAMPLES

I know **who** has a new house.

Jon brought **whoever** was home Chinese food for dinner.

Anne did not know **whom** the director chose.

Whose shoes are sitting in the hallway?

The nominative and objective cases are the source of certain problems. Pronoun problems can appear in two kinds of sentences: direct questions and complex sentences.

In Direct Questions

Who is the correct form when the pronoun is the subject of a simple question. *Whom* is the correct form when the pronoun is the direct object, object of a verbal, or object of a preposition.

Questions in subject–verb word order always begin with *who*. However, questions in inverted order never correctly begin with *who*. To see if you should use *who* or *whom*, reword the question as a statement in subject–verb word order.

EXAMPLES	**Who** wants to have lunch at the deli?
	Whom did you ask to the party?
	(You did ask **whom** to the party.)

In Complex Sentences

Follow these steps to see if the case of a pronoun in a subordinate clause is correct. First, find the subordinate clause. If the complex sentence is a question, rearrange it in subject–verb order. Second, if the subordinate clause is inverted, rearrange the words in subject–verb word order. Finally, determine how the pronoun is used in the subordinate clause.

EXAMPLE	**Who**, may I ask, has seen the documentary?
REARRANGED	I may ask **who** has seen the documentary.
USE OF PRONOUN	(subject of the verb *has seen*)

EXAMPLE	Is the captain the one **whom** they chose?
REARRANGED	They chose **whom** to be captain.
USE OF PRONOUN	(object of the verb *chose*)

Note About *Whose*: The word *whose* is a possessive pronoun; the contraction *who's* means "who is" or "who has."

POSSESSIVE PRONOUN	**Whose** DVD is this?
CONTRACTION	**Who's** [who has] taken my DVD?

See Practice 6.2A

Pronouns in Elliptical Clauses

An **elliptical clause** is one in which some words are omitted but still understood. Errors in pronoun usage can easily be made when an elliptical clause that begins with *than* or *as* is used to make a comparison.

> In **elliptical clauses** beginning with *than* or *as*, use the form of the pronoun that you would use if the clause were fully stated.

6.2.2 RULE

The case of the pronoun is determined by whether the omitted words fall before or after the pronoun. The omitted words in the examples below are shown in brackets.

WORDS OMITTED BEFORE PRONOUN

You bought Ben more than **me** .

(You bought Ben more than [you bought] **me** .)

WORDS OMITTED AFTER PRONOUN

Anna is as hardworking as **she** .

(Anna is as hardworking as **she** [is].)

Mentally add the missing words. If they come *before* the pronoun, choose the objective case. If they come *after* the pronoun, choose the nominative case.

CHOOSING A PRONOUN IN ELLIPTICAL CLAUSES
1. Consider the choices of pronouns: nominative or objective.
2. Mentally complete the elliptical clause.
3. Base your choice on what you find.

The case of the pronoun can sometimes change the entire meaning of the sentence.

NOMINATIVE PRONOUN

He liked dogs more than **I** .

He liked dogs more than **I** [did].

OBJECTIVE PRONOUN

He liked dogs more than **me** .

He liked dogs more than [he liked] **me** .

See Practice 6.2B

PRACTICE 6.2A ▷ **Choosing *Who* or *Whom*
Correctly**

Read each sentence. Then, write *who* or *whom*
to complete each sentence.

EXAMPLE _____ is the president of your class?

ANSWER *Who*

1. There are several drummers _____ the
conductor has not heard.

2. Anyone _____ saw the play agrees it was
great.

3. The quarterback _____ we supported won the
game.

4. Carl is a boy _____ knows how to sing.

5. Are you aware of _____ the teacher selected?

6. _____, in your opinion, is the best qualified?

7. The jury has acquitted the man _____ was
accused of stealing.

8. To _____ did you report the robbery?

9. _____ was there with you?

10. With _____ did you have dinner last night?

PRACTICE 6.2B ▷ **Identifying the Correct
Pronoun in Elliptical Clauses**

Read each sentence. Then, complete each
elliptical clause by choosing the correct pronoun
in parentheses and adding the missing words in
brackets.

EXAMPLE Tammi is a better skier than (I, me).

ANSWER *Tammi is a better skier than
I [am].*

11. He was as surprised as (I, me).

12. That waiter gave Damian more change than
(I, me).

13. This painter has better style than (she, her).

14. You are a better player than (he, him).

15. She was as close to the stage as (I, me).

16. Jordan spoke to Emmanuel longer than to
(him, he).

17. We are farther along than (they, them).

18. My sister has fewer pets than (she, her).

19. You are less experienced than (she, her).

20. Because Uncle Roy travels for work, he has
visited many more cities than (I, me).

SPEAKING APPLICATION

**Take turns with a partner. Ask questions that
use the word *who* or *whom*. Your partner
should respond by also using *who* and *whom*
correctly in his or her response.**

WRITING APPLICATION

**Write five sentences that contain elliptical
clauses. Then, underline the pronoun in each
elliptical clause and add the missing words in
brackets.**

CHAPTER 7

AGREEMENT

Knowing how to relate subjects and verbs and nouns and pronouns will help you to write expert sentences.

WRITE GUY *Jeff Anderson, M.Ed.*

WHAT DO YOU NOTICE?

Focus on agreement as you zoom in on this sentence from the story "Winter Dreams" by F. Scott Fitzgerald.

MENTOR TEXT

> He was a favorite caddy, and the thirty dollars a month he earned through the summer were not to be made elsewhere around the lake.

Now, ask yourself the following questions:

- To which noun does the second pronoun *he* refer?
- What is the subject and verb of the clause that comes after the comma and conjunction *and*? How do they agree?

The second pronoun *he* is the same favorite caddy to which the first pronoun *he* refers. In the second main, or independent, clause, the subject is the plural noun *dollars,* which agrees in number with the plural verb *were.* The intervening clause *he earned through the summer* does not affect the agreement of the subject and verb.

Grammar for Writers Writers use a variety of sentences to make their writing more interesting. When crafting complex sentences, writers should check that their verbs agree with their subjects and that their pronouns have clear antecedents.

Do you always make your subject agree with your verb?

Of course! They know who's boss.

7.1 Subject–Verb Agreement

For a subject and a verb to agree, both must be singular, or both must be plural. In this section, you will learn how to make sure singular and plural subjects and verbs agree.

Number in Nouns, Pronouns, and Verbs

In grammar, **number** indicates whether a word is singular or plural. Only three parts of speech have different forms that indicate number: nouns, pronouns, and verbs.

RULE 7.1.1

> **Number** shows whether a noun, pronoun, or verb is singular or plural.

Recognizing the number of most nouns is seldom a problem because most form their plurals by adding *-s* or *-es*. Some, such as *mouse* or *ox,* form their plurals irregularly: *mice, oxen.*

Pronouns, however, have different forms to indicate their number. The chart below shows the different forms of personal pronouns in the nominative case, the case that is used for subjects.

PERSONAL PRONOUNS		
SINGULAR	PLURAL	SINGULAR OR PLURAL
I	*we*	*you*
he, she, it	*they*	

The grammatical number of verbs is sometimes difficult to determine. That is because the form of many verbs can be either singular or plural, and they may form plurals in different ways.

SINGULAR She **thinks** .

She **has thought** .

PLURAL We **think** .

We **have thought** .

Some verb forms can be only singular. The personal pronouns *he*, *she*, and *it* and all singular nouns call for singular verbs in the present and the present perfect tense.

ALWAYS SINGULAR

She **paints**.

She **has painted**.

Kate **paints**.

Kris **has painted**.

She **walks**.

She **has walked**.

The verb *be* in the present tense has special forms to agree with singular subjects. The pronoun *I* has its own singular form of *be*; so do *he*, *she*, *it*, and singular nouns.

ALWAYS SINGULAR

I **am** working out.

He **is** fun.

Bette **is** early.

He **is** coming.

All singular subjects except *you* share the same past tense verb form of *be*.

ALWAYS SINGULAR

I **was** going shopping.

She **was** editor in chief.

Christina **was** early to dinner.

He **was** boarding the airplane.

See Practice 7.1A

A verb form will always be singular if it has had an *-s* or *-es* added to it or if it includes the words *has*, *am*, *is*, or *was*. The number of any other verb depends on its subject.

The chart on the next page shows verb forms that are always singular and those that can be singular or plural.

VERBS THAT ARE ALWAYS SINGULAR	VERBS THAT CAN BE SINGULAR OR PLURAL
(he, she, Jane) sees	(I, you, we, they) see
(he, she, Jane) has seen	(I, you, we, they) have seen
(I) am	(you, we, they) are
(he, she, Jane) is	(you, we, they) were
(I, he, she, Jane) was	

Singular and Plural Subjects

When making a verb agree with its subject, be sure to identify the subject and determine its number.

RULE 7.1.2 **A singular subject must have a singular verb. A plural subject must have a plural verb.**

SINGULAR SUBJECT AND VERB	PLURAL SUBJECT AND VERB
The English teacher works in China.	These English teachers work in China.
He was being mysterious about their anniversary dinner.	They were being mysterious about their anniversary dinner.
Daphne looks through an encyclopedia for term-paper topics.	Daphne and Dan look through an encyclopedia for term-paper topics.
Israel is a small country in the Middle East.	Israel and Jordan are small countries in the Middle East.
Halley takes American literature.	Halley and Rachael take American literature.
Michael is planning a vacation to the Grand Canyon.	Michael and Alan are planning a vacation to the Grand Canyon.
Jennifer plays trumpet in the school band.	Jennifer and Jess play in the school band.
He looks through the magazines.	They look through the magazines.
Amanda has been studying how to garden successfully.	They have been studying how to garden successfully.

See Practice 7.1B

PRACTICE 7.1A **Identifying Number in Nouns, Pronouns, and Verbs**

Read each word or group of words. Write whether the word or words are *singular*, *plural*, or *both*.

EXAMPLE   lunch

ANSWER   *singular*

1. they
2. learns
3. have seen
4. you understand
5. fish
6. computers
7. rummages
8. we
9. man
10. he

PRACTICE 7.1B **Identifying Singular and Plural Subjects and Verbs**

Read each sentence. Then, write the subject and verb in each sentence, and label them *plural* or *singular*.

EXAMPLE   My dog never eats food from the table.

ANSWER   subject: *dog*; verb: *eats* — singular

11. Air conditioning makes the room cool and inviting.
12. I reject the idea of passing up the challenge.
13. These luxurious rugs never go out of style.
14. Despite advances in technology, tornadoes are still difficult to predict.
15. The student body president is running for re-election.
16. Our science fair project is on volcanic activity in Hawaii.
17. The teams in this year's competition are very talented.
18. The sisters join the choir every year.
19. I am making a four-course meal for my family reunion.
20. The pages of this book are beginning to fade.

SPEAKING APPLICATION

Take turns with a partner. Tell about what you want to do after graduating from high school. Your partner should listen for and name the plural and singular nouns and verbs that you use.

WRITING APPLICATION

Use sentences 12, 16, and 18 as a model to write three similar sentences. Exchange papers with a partner. Your partner should change the subject from singular to plural or plural to singular, making sure that the verbs agree with the new subjects.

Intervening Phrases and Clauses

When you check for agreement, mentally cross out any words that separate the subject and verb.

RULE 7.1.3

> **A phrase or clause that interrupts a subject and its verb does not affect subject–verb agreement.**

In the first example below, the singular subject *discovery* agrees with the singular verb *interests* despite the intervening prepositional phrase *of the clay pots,* which contains a plural noun.

EXAMPLES   The **discovery** of the clay pots **interests** many people.

The **scientists** , whose testing is nearly finished, **require** more funding.

Intervening parenthetical expressions—such as those beginning with *as well as, in addition to, in spite of,* or *including*—also have no effect on the agreement of the subject and verb.

EXAMPLES   Your **information** , in addition to your eyewitness testimony, **is helping** to solve the crimes.

Angelina's **trip** , including visits to Italy and Greece, **is lasting** twelve months.

See Practice 7.1C

Relative Pronouns as Subjects

When *who, which,* or *that* acts as a subject of a subordinate clause, its verb will be singular or plural depending on the number of the antecedent.

RULE 7.1.4

> **The antecedent of a relative pronoun determines its agreement with a verb.**

EXAMPLES   She is the only **one** of the doctors **who** **has** experience working in pediatrics.

(The antecedent of *who* is *one*.)

She is the only one of several **doctors** **who** **have** experience working in pediatrics.

(The antecedent of *who* is *doctors*.)

Compound Subjects

A **compound subject** has two or more simple subjects, which are usually joined by *or* or *and*. Use the following rules when making compound subjects agree with verbs.

Subjects Joined by *And*

Only one rule applies to compound subjects connected by *and:* The verb is usually plural, whether the parts of the compound subject are all singular, all plural, or mixed.

> **A compound subject joined by *and* is generally plural and must have a plural verb.**

7.1.5 RULE

TWO SINGULAR SUBJECTS	A **hurricane** and a **rainstorm hit** the city.
TWO PLURAL SUBJECTS	**Tomatoes** and **carrots cover** the top of the salad.
A SINGULAR SUBJECT AND A PLURAL SUBJECT	A slice of **tomato** and several **slices of onion go** on each sandwich.

There are two exceptions to this rule. The verb is singular if the parts of a compound subject are thought of as one item or if the word *every* or *each* precedes the compound subject.

EXAMPLES **Macaroni and cheese was** all he could cook.

Every weather center and emergency network in the United States issues warnings for severe weather.

Singular Subjects Joined by *Or* or *Nor*
When both parts of a compound subject connected by *or* or *nor* are singular, a singular verb is required.

RULE 7.1.6

Two or more singular subjects joined by *or* or *nor* must have a singular verb.

EXAMPLE A **banana** or a **carrot is** a healthy snack.

Plural Subjects Joined by *Or* or *Nor*
When both parts of a compound subject connected by *or* or *nor* are plural, a plural verb is required.

RULE 7.1.7

Two or more plural subjects joined by *or* or *nor* must have a plural verb.

EXAMPLE Neither **apples** nor **bananas are** as delicious as pears.

Subjects of Mixed Number Joined by *Or* or *Nor*
If one part of a compound subject is singular and the other is plural, the verb agrees with the subject that is closer to it.

RULE 7.1.8

If one or more singular subjects are joined to one or more plural subjects by *or* or *nor*, the subject closest to the verb determines agreement.

EXAMPLES Neither **Bridgette** nor my **friends are ready**.

Neither my **friends** nor **Bridgette is ready**.

See Practice 7.1D

PRACTICE 7.1C > **Identifying Intervening Phrases and Clauses**

Read each sentence. Then, write the intervening phrase or clause between the subject and the verb.

EXAMPLE   Winter, my favorite of all seasons, is finally here.

ANSWER   *my favorite of all seasons*

1. Allan, along with his sisters, enjoys going to the movies.

2. These magazines in the doctor's office are outdated.

3. A pharmacist, a person who dispenses medicine, lives in our neighborhood.

4. This watch, unlike that one, is not expensive.

5. Lakes formed from craters in the earth are not very common around here.

6. Jane, accompanied by Lisa, has gone to see her first foreign film.

7. Tomorrow, the first student who answers a question correctly will receive extra credit.

8. The clock, which is digital, is brand new.

9. The coach of the team will soon retire.

10. A bicyclist, by law, must wear a helmet.

PRACTICE 7.1D > **Making Verbs Agree With Singular and Compound Subjects**

Read each sentence. Then, for each sentence, choose the form of the verb given in parentheses that agrees with the subject.

EXAMPLE   Some water or juice (is, are) what you need to feel hydrated.

ANSWER   *is*

11. Carrots and peas (go, goes) well together.

12. School and state office buildings (shut, shuts) down when there is a snowstorm.

13. Neither he nor they (are, is) busy.

14. Two sandwiches and two drinks (is, are) needed for the field trip.

15. Meatballs (were, was) my favorite homemade dish.

16. My sister and her family (live, lives) in South Carolina.

17. Mom or Dad (picks, pick) me up after school.

18. Neither the bus nor the train (travels, travel) near our house.

19. Cotton and silk (are, is) the most comfortable fabrics.

20. Keeping a notepad and pencil by the phone (make, makes) a lot of sense.

SPEAKING APPLICATION

Take turns with a partner. Tell about a time when you were very happy about something. Use sentences with intervening clauses. Your partner should identify the intervening clauses in your sentences.

WRITING APPLICATION

Reread sentences 11 through 20. Write whether the subject in each sentence is *singular* or *compound*.

Confusing Subjects

Some kinds of subjects have special agreement problems.

Hard-to-Find Subjects and Inverted Sentences

Subjects that appear after verbs are said to be **inverted.**
Subject–verb order is usually inverted in questions. To find out
whether to use a singular or plural verb, mentally rearrange the
sentence into subject–verb order.

> A verb must still agree in number with a subject that comes
> after it.

EXAMPLE	On the deck **are** two lounge **chairs**.
REARRANGED IN SUBJECT–VERB ORDER	Two lounge **chairs are** on the deck.

The words *there* and *here* often signal an inverted sentence.
These words never function as the subject of a sentence.

EXAMPLES	There **are** the group **photos**.
	Here **is** the revised **itinerary**.

Note About *There's* and *Here's*: Both of these contractions
contain the singular verb *is: there is* and *here is*. They should be
used only with singular subjects.

CORRECT	**There's** only one **family** expected.
	Here's a pink **T-shirt** to try on.

See Practice 7.1E

Subjects With Linking Verbs

Subjects with linking verbs may also cause agreement problems.

> A linking verb must agree with its subject, regardless of the
> number of its predicate nominative.

EXAMPLES   The **coaches are** all here.

One **reason** we expect a heat wave **is** that the temperature is already 90!

In the first example, the plural verb *are* agrees with the plural subject *coaches*. In the next example, the singular subject *reason* takes the singular verb *is*.

Collective Nouns

Collective nouns name groups of people or things. Examples include *audience, class, club,* and *committee.*

> A collective noun takes a singular verb when the group it names acts as a single unit. A collective noun takes a plural verb when the group acts as individuals.

SINGULAR   The freshman **class graduates** in 2012.

(The members act as a unit.)

PLURAL   The senior **class were going** to different colleges.

(The members act individually.)

Nouns That Look Like Plurals

Some nouns that end in *-s* are actually singular. For example, nouns that name branches of knowledge, such as *civics,* and those that name single units, such as *mumps,* take singular verbs.

> Use singular verbs to agree with nouns that are plural in form but singular in meaning.

SINGULAR   **Gymnastics is** very difficult.

When words such as *ethics* and *politics* do not name branches of knowledge but indicate characteristics, their meanings are plural. Similarly, such words as *eyeglasses, pants,* and *scissors* generally take plural verbs.

PLURAL Jack's **eyeglasses are** on the table.

Indefinite Pronouns

Some indefinite pronouns are always singular, some are always plural, and some may be either singular or plural. Prepositional phrases do not affect subject–verb agreement.

RULE 7.1.13

Singular indefinite pronouns take singular verbs. Plural indefinite pronouns take plural verbs.

SINGULAR *anybody, anyone, anything, each, either, everybody, everyone, everything, neither, nobody, no one, nothing, somebody, someone, something*

PLURAL *both, few, many, others, several*

SINGULAR **Everyone** on the tour bus **has exited**.

PLURAL **Many** of the houses **were painted** today.

RULE 7.1.14

The pronouns *all, any, more, most, none,* and *some* usually take a singular verb if the antecedent is singular, and a plural verb if it is plural.

SINGULAR **Some** of the building **was painted** by Monday.

PLURAL **Some** of the people **are** waiting in the conference room.

Titles of Creative Works and Names of Organizations

Plural words in the title of a creative work or in the name of an organization do not affect subject–verb agreement.

RULE 7.1.15

A title of a creative work or name of an organization is singular and must have a singular verb.

EXAMPLES **The Centers for Disease Control and Prevention is** a helpful organization.
(organization)

Haystacks by Claude Monet **is** a famous series of art.
(creative work)

Amounts and Measurements

Although they appear to be plural, most amounts and measurements actually express single units or ideas.

> **A noun expressing an amount or measurement is usually singular and requires a singular verb.**

7.1.16 RULE

EXAMPLES **Ten thousand dollars is** the cost in property taxes for the house.

(*Ten thousand dollars is one sum of money.*)

Six miles was our distance from the nearest camping site.

(*Six miles is a single distance.*)

Three quarters of the town **attends** the Spring Planting Fair.

(*Three quarters is one part of the town.*)

Half of the branches **were broken**.

(*Half* refers to a number of individual branches, and not part of an individual branch, so it is plural.)

See Practice 7.1F

> **PRACTICE 7.1E** **Identifying Subjects and Verbs in Inverted Sentences**

Read each sentence. Then, identify the subject and verb in each sentence.

EXAMPLE   Here are your books.

ANSWER   subject: *books*; verb: *are*

1. On the ground lie many colorful leaves.
2. There are no disagreements among the students.
3. Behind the fence grows a hodge podge of wild flowers.
4. Under our feet is the lush, thick lawn.
5. On the wall hangs the patchwork quilt.
6. There are three new students in our class.
7. At the end of the school year is our annual party.
8. Standing behind you were the principal and assistant principal.
9. Here is an updated version of that software.
10. At the top of the hill stood the lone oak tree.

> **PRACTICE 7.1F** **Making Verbs Agree With Confusing Subjects**

Read each sentence. Then, write the correct verb from the choices in parentheses to complete each sentence.

EXAMPLE   Two thirds of the movie (was, were) suspenseful.

ANSWER   *was*

11. The poetry series (end, ends) this week.
12. *The Lord of the Rings* (was, were) an outstanding trilogy.
13. The panel (deliberates, deliberate) on the proposal.
14. Half of my money (was, were) put into a savings account.
15. Civics (was, were) the class in which I got the highest grade.
16. Forty-four dollars (is, are) enough to pay for the train ticket.
17. The pair of gloves (is, are) too big for my hands.
18. The congressman's politics (help, helps) him get re-elected.
19. Everyone at the party (has, have) been dancing.
20. Most of the contestants (were, was) not familiar with the rules of the game.

SPEAKING APPLICATION

Take turns with a partner. Describe an interesting scene from a book that you've read, using some inverted sentences. Your partner should identify the subjects and verbs in your inverted sentences.

WRITING APPLICATION

Write three sentences that include confusing subjects. Then, underline the subject in each of your sentences and make sure the subjects and verbs in your sentences agree.

7.2 Pronoun–Antecedent Agreement

Like a subject and its verb, a pronoun and its antecedent must agree. An **antecedent** is the word or group of words for which the pronoun stands.

Agreement Between Personal Pronouns and Antecedents

While a subject and verb must agree only in number, a personal pronoun and its antecedent must agree in three ways.

> A personal pronoun must agree with its antecedent in number, person, and gender.

7.2.1 RULE

The **number** of a pronoun indicates whether it is singular or plural. **Person** refers to a pronoun's ability to indicate either the person speaking (first person), the person spoken to (second person), or the person, place, or thing spoken about (third person). **Gender** is the characteristic of nouns and pronouns that indicates whether the word is *masculine* (referring to males), *feminine* (referring to females), or *neuter* (referring to neither males nor females).

The only pronouns that indicate gender are third-person singular personal pronouns.

GENDER OF THIRD-PERSON SINGULAR PRONOUNS	
Masculine	*he, him, his*
Feminine	*she, her, hers*
Neuter	*it, its*

In the example below, the pronoun *his* agrees with the antecedent *Prince of Wales* in number (both are singular), in person (both are third person), and in gender (both are masculine).

EXAMPLE   The Prince of Wales has shared **his** memories with the reporter.

Agreement in Number

There are three rules to keep in mind to determine the number of compound antecedents.

Use a singular personal pronoun when two or more singular antecedents are joined by *or* or *nor*.

EXAMPLES Either Blane **or** Ben will bring **his** outline of a proposal to the meeting.

Neither Chase **nor** Kevin will eat **his** new power bar.

Use a plural personal pronoun when two or more antecedents are joined by *and*.

EXAMPLE Kate **and** I are baking for **our** fundraiser.

An exception occurs when a distinction must be made between individual and joint ownership. If individual ownership is intended, use a singular pronoun to refer to a compound antecedent. If joint ownership is intended, use a plural pronoun.

SINGULAR **Benjamin and Carrie** played **his** drum set.

PLURAL **Benjamin and Carrie** paid for **their** drum set.

SINGULAR Neither **Amy nor Beth** let me ride **her** bike.

PLURAL Neither **Amy nor Beth** let me ride **their** bike.

The third rule applies to compound antecedents whose parts are mixed in number.

Use a plural personal pronoun if any part of a compound antecedent joined by *or* or *nor* is plural.

184 Agreement

See Practice 7.2A

EXAMPLE If either the **congressman** or the
reporters arrive, take **them** to the office.

Agreement in Person and Gender Avoid shifts in person or gender of pronouns.

> As part of pronoun–antecedent agreement, take care not to shift either person or gender.

7.2.5 RULE

SHIFT IN PERSON **Katherine** is planning to visit Paris, France, because **you** can see how the French live.

CORRECT **Katherine** is planning to visit Paris, France, because **she** wants to see how the French live.

SHIFT IN GENDER The **cat** threw **its** head up in the air and jumped in **his** spot.

CORRECT The **cat** threw **its** head up in the air and jumped in **its** spot.

Generic Masculine Pronouns Traditionally, a masculine pronoun has been used to refer to a singular antecedent whose gender is unknown. Such use is called *generic* because it applies to both masculine and feminine genders. Many writers now prefer to use *his or her, he or she, him or her,* or to rephrase a sentence to eliminate the situation.

> When gender is not specified, either use *his or her* or rewrite the sentence.

7.2.6 RULE

EXAMPLES Each **student** chose a famous author about which to write **his or her report**.

Students chose famous authors about which to write **their reports**.

See Practice 7.2B

Pronoun–Antecedent Agreement

PRACTICE 7.2A > Making Personal Pronouns Agree With Their Antecedents

Read each sentence. Then, for each sentence, choose the personal pronoun in parentheses that agrees with the antecedent.

EXAMPLE   Dawn and I started a newsletter in (her, our) school.

ANSWER   *our*

1. Cecil was proud of (his, their) dogs' tricks.
2. Neither Karen nor her brothers like (her, their) soup too hot.
3. Andy or Donald will wait by (their, his) car.
4. Sandra let the hamsters out of (their, her) cages.
5. Neither Edith nor Sally brought (her, their) book to read on the bus.
6. The dog or the cat left (their, its) toy under the chair.
7. Mark hangs up his shirts and pants because (they, he) doesn't want them to get wrinkled.
8. Amy or Laura will lend you (her, their) notes.
9. The audience clapped (their, its) hands.
10. Each of the lions circled (its, their) prey.

PRACTICE 7.2B > Revising for Agreement in Person and Gender

Read each sentence. Then, revise each sentence so that the pronoun agrees with the antecedent.

EXAMPLE   The dog is chasing his tail.

ANSWER   *The dog is chasing its tail.*

11. All citizens must pay her taxes.
12. The captain wears a band around their arm.
13. Kramer reads in bed because he believes that it helps you to sleep.
14. Both of my brothers gave his gently used clothes to the shelter.
15. Each person placed their ballot into the box.
16. The male part of the flower will fertilize the plant with his pollen.
17. The mailbox has flowers on her.
18. The children read his or her books.
19. Each manager has her own office.
20. The famous actress responds to all of her e-mails because she believes that you should keep in touch with your fans.

SPEAKING APPLICATION

Take turns with a partner. Tell about members of your family. Use several different pronouns in your sentences. Your partner should name the pronouns that you use and tell whether they agree with their antecedents.

WRITING APPLICATION

Use Sentences 14, 15, and 19 as models to write similar sentences. Then, exchange papers with a partner. Your partner should revise each sentence to make the personal pronoun agree with the antecedent.

Agreement With Indefinite Pronouns

When an indefinite pronoun, such as *each, all,* or *most,* is used
with a personal pronoun, the pronouns must agree.

> **Use a plural personal pronoun when the antecedent is a plural
> indefinite pronoun.**

7.2.7 RULE

EXAMPLES **Many** of the children were excited about **their**
camping trip.

All the students forgot to bring **their** homework.

When both pronouns are singular, a similar rule applies.

> **Use a singular personal pronoun when the antecedent is a
> singular indefinite pronoun.**

7.2.8 RULE

In the first example, the personal pronoun *her* agrees in number
with the singular indefinite pronoun *one.* The gender (feminine) is
determined by the word *girls.*

EXAMPLES Only **one** of the girls practiced **her** clarinet.

One of the girls remembered to bring **her**
clarinet.

If other words in the sentence do not indicate a gender, you may
use *him or her, he or she, his or her,* or rephrase the sentence.

EXAMPLES **Each** of the playwrights read **his or her** lines.

The **playwrights** practiced **their** lines.

For indefinite pronouns that can be either singular or plural, such
as *all, any, more, most, none,* and *some,* agreement depends on
the antecedent of the indefinite pronoun.

EXAMPLES **Most** of the park had lost **its** enjoyment.
(The antecedent of *most* is *park,* which is singular.)

Most of the students wanted **their** scores posted.
(The antecedent of *most is students,* which is plural.)

Some of the milk **was** too sour to drink.
(The antecedent of *some is milk,* which is singular.)

All of the plates **were** on the kitchen table.
(The antecedent of *all is plates,* which is plural.)

In some situations, strict grammatical agreement may be illogical. In these situations, either let the meaning of the sentence determine the number of the personal pronoun, or reword the sentence.

ILLOGICAL When **each of the cellphones buzzed** ,
I answered **it** as quickly as possible.

MORE LOGICAL When **each of the cellphones buzzed** ,
I answered **them** as quickly as possible.

MORE LOGICAL When **all of the cellphones buzzed** ,
I answered **them** as quickly as possible.   See Practice 7.2C

Agreement With Reflexive Pronouns

Reflexive pronouns, which end in *-self* or *-selves,* should only refer to a word earlier in the same sentence.

RULE 7.2.9

A reflexive pronoun must agree with an antecedent that is clearly stated.

EXAMPLES **Katherine** made breakfast for **herself** .

You should tell **yourself** to be happy.

Professional **comedians** enjoy making fun
of **themselves** .   See Practice 7.2D

PRACTICE 7.2C > Supplying Indefinite Pronouns

Read each sentence. Then, fill in the blank with an appropriate indefinite pronoun that agrees with the antecedent.

EXAMPLE   _____ of the boys could deliver his lines.

ANSWER   *None*

1. Only _____ of the girls remembered their locker numbers.

2. _____ of the yard has weeds covering it.

3. _____ of my friends take their younger siblings with them to the park.

4. _____ house has its own backyard.

5. _____ of the shirts already had tags on them.

6. _____ of the students have finished choosing their research topic.

7. I liked the food, but _____ of it had too much garlic.

8. I think _____ of these books have landscape pictures in them.

9. _____ of the pasta was eaten.

10. _____ of the players on the girls' soccer team provide their own uniform.

PRACTICE 7.2D > Supplying Reflexive Pronouns

Read each sentence. Then, rewrite each sentence, filling in the blank with the correct reflexive pronoun that agrees with the antecedent.

EXAMPLE   Can you imagine _____ in a meadow full of colorful flowers?

ANSWER   *Can you imagine yourself in a meadow full of colorful flowers?*

11. I made _____ scrambled eggs for breakfast.

12. What are you planning to do with _____ on a day off from school?

13. I think I will treat _____ to frozen yogurt today.

14. Perhaps we'll buy _____ new boots.

15. Rosie will go to the game by _____.

16. I think we can finish the job by _____.

17. You owe _____ some alone time.

18. That silly dog is chasing _____ around in a circle.

19. Fortunately, Jessica did not injure _____ when she fell off the chair.

20. They told _____ they would never do that again.

SPEAKING APPLICATION

Take turns with a partner. Say sentences with indefinite pronouns that agree with their antecedents. Your partner should repeat each of your sentences, substituting another indefinite pronoun that makes sense in the sentence.

WRITING APPLICATION

Use sentences 11, 12, and 16 as models to write similar sentences. Then, exchange papers with a partner. Your partner should rewrite each of your sentences, using the correct reflexive pronoun that agrees with the antecedent.

7.3 Special Problems With Pronoun Agreement

This section will show you how to avoid some common errors that can obscure the meaning of your sentences.

Vague Pronoun References

One basic rule governs all of the rules for pronoun reference.

> **To avoid confusion, a pronoun requires an antecedent that is either stated or clearly understood.**

The pronouns *which, this, that,* and *these* should not be used to refer to a vague or overly general idea.

In the following example, it is impossible to determine exactly what the pronoun *these* stands for because it may refer to three different groups of words.

VAGUE REFERENCE   Chris was exhausted, the children were hungry, and the heater was broken. **These** made our trip to the ski lodge unbearable.

This vague reference can be corrected in two ways. One way is to change the pronoun to an adjective that modifies a specific noun. The second way is to revise the sentence so that the pronoun *these* is eliminated.

CORRECT   Chris was exhausted, the children were hungry, and the heater was broken. **These misfortunes** made our trip to the ski lodge unbearable.

CORRECT   Chris's exhaustion, the children's hunger, and the broken heater made our trip to the ski lodge unbearable.

> **The personal pronouns *it, they,* and *you* should always have a clear antecedent.**

In the next example, the pronoun *it* has no clearly stated antecedent.

VAGUE
REFERENCE   Halley is planning to travel next year.

It should be very eye-opening.

Again, there are two methods of correction. The first method is to replace the personal pronoun with a specific noun. The second method is to revise the sentence entirely in order to make the whole idea clear.

CORRECT   Halley is planning to travel next year.

The experience should be very eye-opening.

CORRECT   **Halley's plan** to travel next year should be

very eye-opening.

In the next example, the pronoun *they* is used without an accurate antecedent.

VAGUE
REFERENCE   I enjoyed directing the show, but **they** never

indicated which scenes were the best.

CORRECT   I enjoyed directing the show, but **the audience**

never indicated which scenes were the best.

VAGUE
REFERENCE   When we arrived at the theater, **they** told us

which actors and actresses were running late.

CORRECT   When we arrived at the theater, **the usher** told us

which actors and actresses were running late.

RULE 7.3.3

> Use *you* only when the reference is truly to the reader or listener.

VAGUE REFERENCE **You** couldn't understand a word the officer said.

CORRECT **We** couldn't understand a word the officer said.

VAGUE REFERENCE In the company my father worked for, **you** were expected to work long hours every day.

CORRECT In the company my father worked for, **employees** were expected to work long hours every day.

Note About *It:* In many idiomatic expressions, the personal pronoun *it* has no specific antecedent. In statements such as "It is late," *it* is an idiom that is accepted as standard English.

See Practice 7.3A

Ambiguous Pronoun References

A pronoun is **ambiguous** if it can refer to more than one antecedent.

RULE 7.3.4

> A pronoun should never refer to more than one antecedent.

In the following sentence, *she* is confusing because it can refer to either *Sally* or *Jane*. Revise such a sentence by changing the pronoun to a noun or rephrasing the sentence entirely.

AMBIGUOUS REFERENCE Sally told Jane about the play **she** wanted to be in.

CORRECT Sally told Jane about the play **Jane** wanted to be in.

(Sally knew about the play.)

RULE 7.3.5

> Do not repeat a personal pronoun in a sentence if it can refer to a different antecedent each time.

192 Agreement

AMBIGUOUS REPETITION   When Brent asked his father if **he** could borrow the truck, **he** said that **he** needed it.

CLEAR   When Brent asked his father if **he** could borrow the truck, **Brent** said that **he** needed it.

CLEAR   When Brent asked his father if **he** could borrow the truck, his **father** said that **he** needed it **himself**.

Notice that in the first sentence above, it is unclear whether *he* is referring to Brent or to his father. To eliminate the confusion, Brent's name was used in the second sentence. In the third sentence, the reflexive pronoun *himself* helps to clarify the meaning.

Avoiding Distant Pronoun References

A pronoun should be placed close to its antecedent.

> **A personal pronoun should always be close enough to its antecedent to prevent confusion.**

7.3.6 **RULE**

A distant pronoun reference can be corrected by moving the pronoun closer to its antecedent or by changing the pronoun to a noun. In the example below, *it* is too far from the antecedent *ankle*.

DISTANT REFERENCE   Anne shifted her weight from her injured ankle. A week ago, she had fallen in ballet class, hurting herself on the wood floor. Now **it** was wrapped with bandages.

CORRECT   Anne shifted her weight from her injured ankle. A week ago, she had fallen in ballet class, hurting herself on the wood floor. Now her **ankle** was wrapped with bandages.

See Practice 7.3B   (*Ankle* replaces the pronoun *it*.)

PRACTICE 7.3A Correcting Vague Pronouns

Read each sentence. Then, rewrite each sentence to correct the use of vague pronouns.

EXAMPLE   They said that it was going to be sunny today.

ANSWER   *The weather person said that it was going to be sunny today.*

1. The gate is held closed with a latch, but it has rusted.

2. In Mexico, you must be a citizen to own beachside property.

3. Katrina saw the dress in the picture window and thought it was very nice.

4. The good news spread throughout the town, and it was well-received.

5. You can't buy tickets until the gate opens.

6. Jason has a great imagination, and this makes me eager to hear his stories.

7. The movie was confusing because they cut too many important scenes.

8. Many poets use vague references, and this confuses readers.

9. There were too many twists in the movie's plot and this upset the audience.

10. From where my cousin lives, you can see the ocean.

PRACTICE 7.3B Recognizing Ambiguous Pronouns

Read each sentence. Then, rewrite each sentence to avoid the use of ambiguous pronouns.

EXAMPLE   Steve told Jesse that he might lose his job.

ANSWER   *Steve told Jesse that Jesse might lose his job.*

11. Tim asked his father if he could go to a movie, but he said no.

12. When my uncle takes my cousin to the park, he is very happy.

13. Audrey told Marni that she was being given a raise.

14. When Tyra looked into the microscope to see the specimen, it seemed hazy.

15. I gave David a shirt and tie for his birthday, but it did not please him.

16. Before leaving Tatiana with Grandma, we should tell her where we're going.

17. Donna explained to Jane the story she just read.

18. After Nick told his father about the new job, he wished him luck.

19. Betsy told Nancy that her cat's health was improving.

20. When Kendra told Alexa that she was moving to Texas, she said she would miss her.

SPEAKING APPLICATION

Take turns with a partner. Say sentences that contain vague pronouns. Your partner should correct your sentences.

WRITING APPLICATION

Use sentences 11, 13, and 15 as models to write similar sentences. Then, exchange papers with a partner. Your partner should rewrite each sentence, correcting the ambiguous pronoun references.

CHAPTER 8

USING MODIFIERS

Understanding the degrees of adjectives and adverbs will help you make effective comparisons.

WRITE GUY *Jeff Anderson, M.Ed.*

WHAT DO YOU NOTICE?

Find the modifier that is used to compare as you zoom in on this sentence from the story "The Fall of the House of Usher" by Edgar Allan Poe.

MENTOR TEXT

> I shudder at the thought of any, even the most trivial, incident, which may operate upon this intolerable agitation of soul.

Now, ask yourself the following questions:

- Which degree of comparison is the adjective that modifies *incident*?
- Why did the author use this degree of comparison?

The phrase *most trivial* that modifies the noun *incident* is in the superlative degree. *Most* is used because the word *trivial* has three syllables, and adding the ending *-est* would sound awkward. The author used the superlative degree to show that even an incident that is more trivial than any other possible incident has a terrible effect on the narrator.

Grammar for Writers By using degrees of comparison, writers can help readers better understand ideas and visualize images. To craft clear comparisons, check whether you should use the endings *-er* or *-est* or the words *more* or *most*.

Why can't I say *beautifuler* instead of *more beautiful*?

Because *beautifuler* is awkward. You wouldn't want to be *more awkward* than others, right?

8.1 Degrees of Comparison

In the English language, there are three degrees, or forms, of most adjectives and adverbs that are used in comparisons.

Recognizing Degrees of Comparison

In order to write effective comparisons, you first need to know the three degrees.

> The three degrees of comparison are the **positive**, the **comparative**, and the **superlative**.

The following chart shows adjectives and adverbs in each of the three degrees. Notice the three different ways that modifiers are changed to show degree: (1) by adding -er or -est, (2) by adding more or most, and (3) by using entirely different words.

DEGREES OF ADJECTIVES		
POSITIVE	**COMPARATIVE**	**SUPERLATIVE**
simple	simpler	simplest
impressive	more impressive	most impressive
good	better	best
DEGREES OF ADVERBS		
soon	sooner	soonest
impressively	more impressively	most impressively
well	better	best

See Practice 8.1A

Regular Forms

Adjectives and adverbs can be either **regular** or **irregular,** depending on how their comparative and superlative degrees are formed. The degrees of most adjectives and adverbs are formed regularly. The number of syllables in regular modifiers determines how their degrees are formed.

> Use -er or more to form the comparative degree and -est or most to form the superlative degree of most one- and two-syllable modifiers.

EXAMPLES	loud	louder	loudest
	spiteful	more spiteful	most spiteful

> **All adverbs that end in -ly form their comparative and superlative degrees with *more* and *most*.**

EXAMPLES	importantly	more importantly	most importantly
	hopefully	more hopefully	most hopefully

> **Use *more* and *most* to form the comparative and superlative degrees of all modifiers with three or more syllables.**

EXAMPLES	difficult	more difficult	most difficult
	ambitious	more ambitious	most ambitious

Note About Comparisons With *Less* and *Least*: *Less* and *least* can be used to form another version of the comparative and superlative degrees of most modifiers.

EXAMPLES	difficult	less difficult	least difficult
	ambitious	less ambitious	least ambitious

See Practice 8.1B

Irregular Forms

The comparative and superlative degrees of a few commonly used adjectives and adverbs are formed in unpredictable ways.

> **The irregular comparative and superlative forms of certain adjectives and adverbs must be memorized.**

In the chart on the following page, the form of some irregular modifiers differs only in the positive degree. The modifiers *bad*, *badly*, and *ill*, for example, all have the same comparative and superlative degrees *(worse, worst)*.

IRREGULAR MODIFIERS		
POSITIVE	COMPARATIVE	SUPERLATIVE
bad, badly, ill	worse	worst
far (distance)	farther	farthest
far (extent)	further	furthest
good, well	better	best
late	later	last or latest
little (amount)	less	least
many, much	more	most

RULE 8.1.6

Bad is an adjective. Do not use it to modify an action verb. *Badly* is an adverb. Use it after an action verb but not after a linking verb.

INCORRECT Some seniors treated the younger students **bad**.

CORRECT Some seniors treated the younger students **badly**.

INCORRECT Jennifer feels **badly** about losing the election.

CORRECT Jennifer feels **bad** about losing the election.

Note About *Good* and *Well*: *Good* is always an adjective and cannot be used as an adverb after an action verb. It can, however, be used as a predicate adjective after a linking verb.

INCORRECT The band played their instruments **good** today.

CORRECT The band sounded **good** today.

Well is generally an adverb. However, when *well* means "healthy," it is an adjective and can be used after a linking verb.

CORRECT Marta kicks a soccer ball **well**.

CORRECT Marta should be **well** soon.

See Practice 8.1C
See Practice 8.1D

PRACTICE 8.1A ▷ **Recognizing Positive, Comparative, and Superlative Degrees of Comparison**

Read each sentence. Then, identify the degree of comparison of the underlined word or words as *positive*, *comparative*, or *superlative*.

EXAMPLE   Harrison might find it <u>harder</u> to see than Jesse.

ANSWER   *comparative*

1. Larry has the <u>fastest</u> horse on the team.
2. There have been <u>fewer</u> cases of chickenpox this year than last.
3. Mickey brought home an <u>excellent</u> report card today.
4. Last night I had the <u>weirdest</u> dream.
5. Leo began his speech <u>nervously</u>.
6. This is the <u>warmest</u> February I can remember.
7. Goldman will surely be named <u>most valuable</u> player this year.
8. Jenny will be <u>more cautious</u> on her next camping trip.
9. Jose ate his meal <u>hungrily</u>.
10. The patient seemed <u>more alert</u> after the medicine had worn off.

PRACTICE 8.1B ▷ **Forming Regular Comparative and Superlative Degrees of Comparison**

Read each sentence. Then, rewrite each sentence with the correct comparative or superlative degree of the modifier indicated in parentheses.

EXAMPLE   The problem was _____ than I expected. (difficult)

ANSWER   *The problem was more difficult than I expected.*

11. The _____ thing to do is to wait until we know all our options. (wise)
12. Their furniture is _____ than mine. (dark)
13. This pillow is _____ than that one. (soft)
14. Melanie is the _____ person in her family. (artistic)
15. She responded to the treatment _____ than he did. (quickly)
16. His opinion is _____ to understand than hers. (difficult)
17. That hard rock is the _____ place to sit on. (comfortable)
18. The marathon will be _____ to complete if you train for it. (easy)
19. She is the candidate's _____ supporter. (eager)
20. The music was _____ than I expected. (loud)

SPEAKING APPLICATION

Take turns with a partner. Describe items found in your classroom. Use comparative, superlative, and positive degrees of comparison. Your partner should listen for and identify which degree of comparison you are using in each of your descriptions.

WRITING APPLICATION

Rewrite sentences 14, 15, and 17, changing the modifiers in parentheses. Then, exchange papers with a partner. Your partner should write the correct degree of the modifiers in your sentences.

PRACTICE 8.1C ▷ Supplying Irregular Comparative and Superlative Forms

Read each modifier. Then, write its irregular comparative and superlative forms.

EXAMPLE good

ANSWER *better, best*

1. far (distance)
2. far (extent)
3. little (amount)
4. bad
5. late
6. ill
7. well
8. badly
9. much
10. many

PRACTICE 8.1D ▷ Supplying Irregular Modifiers

Read each sentence. Then, fill in the blank with the form of the modifier indicated in parentheses that best completes each sentence.

EXAMPLE I was the _____ person to vote. (late)

ANSWER *last*

11. Despite taking the medicine, I still felt _____ than before. (ill)
12. The moderator would not allow any _____ debate on the subject. (far)
13. Even the _____ change in temperature can affect plant growth. (little)
14. Because of the cliffhanger, _____ people tuned in to the show than ever before. (many)
15. How much _____ do we have to go before we can rest? (far)
16. Global warming can have the _____ impact in the polar regions. (much)
17. In my opinion, the _____ cotton comes from Texas. (good)
18. Our team played much _____ during the second half of the game. (well)
19. Hervé was the _____ person to leave the show. (late)
20. I had the _____ grade in the entire class. (good)

SPEAKING APPLICATION

Take turns with a partner. Say sentences with irregular comparative and superlative forms. Your partner should indicate if incorrect forms have been used and suggest corrections.

WRITING APPLICATION

Write pairs of sentences using each of these modifiers correctly: *less* and *least*, *more* and *most*, *farthest* and *furthest*, *bad* and *badly*.

8.2 Making Clear Comparisons

The comparative and superlative degrees help you make comparisons that are clear and logical.

Using Comparative and Superlative Degrees

One basic rule that has two parts covers the correct use of comparative and superlative forms.

> Use the **comparative degree** to compare two persons, places, or things. Use the **superlative degree** to compare three or more persons, places, or things.

8.2.1 RULE

The context of a sentence should indicate whether two items or more than two items are being compared.

COMPARATIVE   His part is **harder** to learn than mine.

My costume is **more colorful** than hers.

Sandy has **less** time on stage than Marco.

SUPERLATIVE   His part is the **hardest** one to learn.

My costume is the **most colorful** one in the cast.

Sandy has the **least** time on stage of anyone.

In informal writing, the superlative degree is sometimes used just for emphasis, without any specific comparison.

EXAMPLE   Emily sang **most beautifully**!

Note About Double Comparisons: A double comparison is caused by using both *-er* and *more* or both *-est* and *most* to form a regular modifier or by adding an extra comparison form to an irregular modifier.

INCORRECT   His sailboat is **more** **faster** than mine.

CORRECT   His sailboat is **faster** than mine.

See Practice 8.2A
See Practice 8.2B

| PRACTICE 8.2A | **Supplying the Comparative and Superlative Degrees of Modifiers** |

Read each sentence. Then, fill in the blank with the correct form of the underlined modifier.

EXAMPLE   This restaurant is <u>good</u>, but that one is even _____.

ANSWER   *better*

1. Candyce played <u>badly</u> on the soccer field, but Susan played even _____.

2. All of the salespeople are <u>successful</u>, but Jeanine is _____.

3. I still feel <u>ill</u>, but yesterday I felt _____.

4. George looks <u>good</u> in blue, but he looks _____ in green.

5. Randolph lives <u>farther</u> from school than Rick, but Cece lives the _____.

6. I have <u>little</u> interest in movies and even _____ in plays.

7. I have homework in English, <u>more</u> homework in science, and the _____ in French.

8. We drove quite <u>far</u> today, but we must drive _____ tomorrow.

9. There was <u>much</u> commotion in the hall, but inside the room there was even _____ commotion.

10. Gwen has a <u>better</u> record than Louis, but Kate has the _____ record of the three.

| PRACTICE 8.2B | **Revising Sentences to Correct Errors in Modifier Usage** |

Read each sentence. Then, rewrite each sentence, correcting any errors in the usage of modifiers to make comparisons. If a sentence contains no errors, write *correct*.

EXAMPLE   Delia's recent babysitting experience was far best than the one before.

ANSWER   *Delia's recent babysitting experience was far better than the one before.*

11. Kenny is the more interesting person at the party.

12. Gary is funniest than his brother David.

13. She is the younger person to win the prize.

14. Which of the two towns is farthest from here?

15. The book is least suspenseful now that I've figured out what happens.

16. Marta is best at acting than her twin sister.

17. I was more impressed than you were.

18. Were you the stronger member of the wrestling team?

19. Which of the twins dances best?

20. Linda is the fastest runner on the track team.

SPEAKING APPLICATION

Take turns with a partner. Compare three books, using comparative and superlative degrees of modifiers. Your partner should listen for and identify your comparisons.

WRITING APPLICATION

Write three sentences with errors in modifier usage. Then, exchange papers with a partner. Your partner should correct your sentences.

Using Logical Comparisons

Two common usage problems are the comparison of unrelated items and the comparison of something with itself.

Balanced Comparisons
Be certain that things being compared in a sentence are similar.

> **Your sentences should only compare items of a similar kind.**

The following unbalanced sentences illogically compare dissimilar things.

UNBALANCED **Mike's statue** is taller than **Gina**.

CORRECT **Mike's statue** is taller than **Gina's**.

UNBALANCED The **height of the fence** is greater than the **dog can jump**.

CORRECT The **height of the fence** is greater than the **height the dog can jump**.

Note About *Other* and *Else* in Comparisons
Another illogical comparison results when something is inadvertently compared with itself.

> **When comparing one of a group with the rest of the group, make sure that your sentence contains the word *other* or the word *else*.**

8.2.3 RULE

Adding *other* or *else* when comparing one person or thing with a group will make the comparison clear and logical.

ILLOGICAL His paintings are more beautiful than any paintings.
> (His paintings cannot be more beautiful than themselves.)

LOGICAL His paintings are more beautiful than any **other** paintings.

See Practice 8.2C
See Practice 8.2D

PRACTICE 8.2C > Revising to Make Comparisons Balanced and Logical

Read each sentence. Then, rewrite each sentence, correcting the unbalanced or illogical comparison.

EXAMPLE This year's team looks stronger than last year.

ANSWER *This year's team looks stronger than last year's.*

1. Rita's den is larger than Mike.
2. Our school has a better team than any school in town.
3. Al's bike is newer than Levi.
4. Amiri's artistic ability is greater than Andy.
5. My sister handles pressure better than any member of our family.
6. Today's temperature is colder than yesterday.
7. Jane worked harder than any person on the nominating committee.
8. The instructions for baking a pie are easier than cake.
9. Leslie's SAT scores were higher than her sister.
10. Frannie's project had fewer diagrams than Donna.

PRACTICE 8.2D > Writing Clear Comparisons

Read each sentence. Then, rewrite each sentence, filling in the blanks to make a comparison that is clear and logical.

EXAMPLE Your sculpture was better than _____.

ANSWER *Your sculpture was better than any other sculpture in the class.*

11. Mary's speech was more interesting than _____.
12. The tail of a beaver is broader and flatter than _____.
13. Aunt Winnie's homemade jelly is sweeter than _____.
14. The mileage we get in this car is better than _____.
15. A stroll in the garden is less invigorating than _____.
16. The grade on Kemau's paper is better than _____.
17. The egg of an ostrich is bigger than _____.
18. Replacing all four tires on a car will be more expensive than _____.
19. Today's weather is warmer than _____.
20. These directions for assembling a bicycle are less complicated than _____.

SPEAKING APPLICATION

Take turns with a partner. Say sentences that have unbalanced or illogical comparisons. Your partner should restate the sentences, using balanced and logical comparisons.

WRITING APPLICATION

Use sentences 11, 13, and 15 as models to write similar sentences. Then, exchange papers with a partner. Your partner should fill in the blanks to make the comparison in each sentence clear and logical.

Avoiding Comparisons With Absolute Modifiers

Some modifiers cannot be used logically to make comparisons because their meanings are *absolute*—that is, their meanings are entirely contained in the positive degree. For example, if a line is *vertical*, another line cannot be *more* vertical. Some other common absolute modifiers are *dead, entirely, fatal, final, identical, infinite, opposite, perfect, right, straight,* and *unique.*

> **Avoid using absolute modifiers illogically in comparisons.**

8.2.4 RULE

INCORRECT	The exam is the **most final** one before vacation.
CORRECT	The exam is the **final** one before vacation.

Often, it is not only the word *more* or *most* that makes an absolute modifier illogical; sometimes it is best to replace the absolute modifier with one that expresses the intended meaning more precisely.

ILLOGICAL	Your thesis is **more unique** than anyone else's.
CORRECT	Your thesis is **more original** than anyone else's.

Sometimes an absolute modifier may overstate the meaning that you want.

ILLOGICAL	That research paper caused the **most fatal** damage to my average this year.
CORRECT	That research paper caused the **most severe** damage to my average this year.

See Practice 8.2E
See Practice 8.2F

In the preceding example, *most fatal* is illogical because something is either fatal or it is not. However, even *fatal* is an overstatement. *Most severe* better conveys the intended meaning.

PRACTICE 8.2E > Revising Sentences to Correct Comparisons Using Absolute Modifiers

Read each sentence. Then, correct each illogical comparison by replacing the absolute modifier with more precise words.

EXAMPLE   That painter has the most unique style of any other artist.

ANSWER   *That painter's style is unique among artists.*

1. His answer was more final than we expected.

2. Of all the children, Joanne looks most identical to her mother.

3. Carlo's answers are more right than Frank's.

4. Now that he is in the second grade, Jamison draws rounder circles than he once did.

5. He threw the ball straighter than an arrow.

6. I have never seen a deader plant than that fern.

7. The challenger's position is more opposite of mine than the incumbent's.

8. After the hike, he was more entirely exhausted than I was.

9. Her second novel was more perfect than her first.

10. The names of the most final contestants were announced.

PRACTICE 8.2F > Revising Overstated Absolute Modifiers

Read each sentence. Then, rewrite each sentence, revising the overstated absolute modifier.

EXAMPLE   His love for her is extremely everlasting.

ANSWER   *His love for her is everlasting.*

11. Joe's diagram is more perfect than Maura's.

12. A decision passed by the Supreme Court is the most absolute.

13. The plants in the garden are completely dead.

14. A fish is more mortal than a whale.

15. Funding for sports should be given more equally.

16. Of the pups in the litter, the black one is the most alive.

17. The captain's orders are more final than the first mate's.

18. Winning a gold medal is Tristan's most ultimate goal.

19. The trees by the river were slightly destroyed.

20. A red rose as a symbol for love is very eternal.

SPEAKING APPLICATION

Take turns with a partner. Say sentences that incorrectly use absolute modifiers. Your partner should restate your sentences correctly.

WRITING APPLICATION

Write three sentences with overstated absolute modifiers. Then, exchange papers with a partner. Your partner should revise the overstated absolute modifiers in your sentences.

MISCELLANEOUS PROBLEMS *in* USAGE

Knowing how to avoid common word usage problems will help you to write clearly and precisely.

WRITE GUY *Jeff Anderson, M.Ed.*

WHAT DO YOU NOTICE?

Think about how words are used as you zoom in on sentences from the Modoc myth "When Grizzlies Walked Upright" as retold by Richard Erdoes and Alfonso Ortiz.

MENTOR TEXT

The mountains of snow and ice became their lodge. He made a big fire in the center of the mountain and a hole in the top so that the smoke and sparks could fly out.

Now, ask yourself the following questions:

- How do writers sometimes confuse the word *their*?
- Why is the word *that* used with *so* in the second sentence?

The possessive pronoun *their* is often confused with the adverb *there* and the contraction *they're* because they sound the same even though the spellings and meanings are different. Used alone, *so* is a coordinating conjunction like *and* or *but*. When used to mean "in order to," *so* should be paired with *that* or *as*.

Grammar for Writers Writers should check how they have used words that may be easily confused to ensure their writing is clear. A little extra time spent reviewing and editing text will polish your writing.

Their books have been there for a while.

You're right there, but they're going to pick them up soon.

9.1 Negative Sentences

In English, only one *no* is needed in a sentence to deny or refuse something. You can express a negative idea with words such as *not* or *never* or with contractions such as *can't, couldn't,* and *wasn't.* (The ending *-n't* in a contraction is an abbreviation of *not.*)

Recognizing Double Negatives

Using two negative words in a sentence when one is sufficient is called a **double negative.** While double negatives may sometimes be used in informal speech, they should be avoided in formal English speech and writing.

RULE 9.1.1

> Do not use **double negatives** in formal writing.

The following chart provides examples of double negatives and two ways each can be corrected.

DOUBLE NEGATIVE	CORRECTIONS
Dave couldn't fix nothing.	Dave could fix nothing. Dave couldn't fix anything.
He didn't have no training in repairs.	He had no training in repairs. He didn't have any training in repairs.
He never asked no one for help.	He never asked anyone for help. He asked no one for help.

Sentences that contain more than one clause can correctly contain more than one negative word. Each clause, however, should contain only one negative word.

EXAMPLES   The band **didn't** make the final round, but the musicians **weren't** discouraged.

They knew they **hadn't** practiced enough; they **wouldn't** do that again.

Forming Negative Sentences Correctly

There are three common ways to form negative sentences.

Using One Negative Word The most common ways to make a statement negative are to use one **negative word,** such as *never, no,* or *none,* or to add the contraction *-n't* to a helping verb.

> Use only one **negative word** in each clause.

RULE 9.1.2

DOUBLE NEGATIVE She **wouldn't never** learn that by herself.

PREFERRED She **would never** learn that by herself.

She **wouldn't ever** learn that by herself.

Using *But* in a Negative Sense When *but* means "only," it usually acts as a negative. Do not use it with another negative word.

DOUBLE NEGATIVE There **wasn't but** one part in the play left to cast.

PREFERRED There was **but** one part in the play left to cast.

There was **only** one part in the play left to cast.

Using *Barely, Hardly,* and *Scarcely* Each of these words is negative. If you use one of these words with another negative word, you create a double negative.

> Do not use *barely, hardly,* or *scarcely* with another negative word.

RULE 9.1.3

DOUBLE NEGATIVE They **didn't barely** make minimum wage.

PREFERRED They **barely** made minimum wage.

DOUBLE NEGATIVE My family **doesn't hardly** celebrate birthdays.

PREFERRED My family **hardly** celebrates birthdays.

DOUBLE NEGATIVE I **hadn't scarcely** seen your car coming.

See Practice 9.1A   PREFERRED I **had scarcely** seen your car coming.

Using Negatives to Create Understatement

Sometimes a writer wants to express an idea indirectly, either to minimize the importance of the idea or to draw attention to it. One such technique is called **understatement.**

RULE 9.1.4

> Understatement can be achieved by using a negative word and a word with a negative prefix, such as *un-*, *in-*, *im-*, *dis-*, and *under-*.

EXAMPLES Mark did **not attend** practice **infrequently**.

He is **hardly unaware** of the time needed to master the jump shot.

He's **not inexperienced** at basketball.

These examples show that the writer is praising the people or things he or she is discussing. In the first example, the writer states that Mark actually attends practice frequently. In the second example, the writer states that he is aware of amount of time needed to master the jump shot. In the third example, the writer states that he is experienced at basketball.

If you choose to use understatement, be sure to use it carefully so that you do not sound critical when you wish to praise.

EXAMPLES It seemed familiar, but the new movie about pirates **wasn't unexciting**.

Some of the stars **weren't untalented**, although I might have cast different people.

In both examples above, the writer is actually making a negative statement. In the first example, although the writer feels that while the movie was familiar, it was still somewhat exciting. In the second example, the writer seems to think that, while the stars were talented, other people could have been better cast.

See Practice 9.1B

PRACTICE 9.1A > **Revising Sentences to Avoid Double Negatives**

Read each sentence. Then, rewrite each sentence to correct the double negative.

EXAMPLE   Eric can't have no dairy foods.

ANSWER   *Eric can't have any dairy foods.*

1. Miguel will never let nobody help him.

2. You won't never find a more loyal friend than Jasmine.

3. After tomorrow, we won't have no more classes.

4. There wasn't nobody there when we arrived.

5. You shouldn't have no more trouble with the car.

6. Neither of those boys don't know the way to the library.

7. We can never ask no questions during a test.

8. I can't find none of the game pieces for this board game.

9. I couldn't hardly believe it when I heard the news.

10. There weren't any seats nowhere in the auditorium.

PRACTICE 9.1B > **Using Negatives to Create Understatement**

Read each item. Then, use each item to create understatement.

EXAMPLE   undercooked

ANSWER   *The meat wasn't undercooked, even though it was chewy.*

11. underestimated

12. impassive

13. unmoved

14. inaccurate

15. undeveloped

16. immovable

17. dissatisfied

18. insincere

19. immature

20. underfed

SPEAKING APPLICATION

Take turns with a partner. Say sentences that contain double negatives. Your partner should listen to and correct your sentences to avoid the double negatives.

WRITING APPLICATION

Use items 13, 16, and 19 to write other sentences that contain double negatives. Then, exchange papers with a partner. Your partner should correct your sentences.

9.2 Common Usage Problems

(1) a, an The use of the article *a* or *an* is determined by the sound of the word that follows it. *A* is used before consonant sounds, while *an* is used before vowel sounds. Words beginning with *hon-, o-,* or *u-* may have either a consonant or a vowel sound.

EXAMPLES	**a** hero (*h* sound)
	a one-hour lecture (*w* sound)
	an honest opinion (no *h* sound)
	an omen (*o* sound)
	an underwater expedition (*u* sound)

(2) accept, except *Accept,* a verb, means "to receive." *Except,* a preposition, means "to leave out" or "other than."

VERB	I **accept** your offer to go to the store.
PREPOSITION	I'd be happy to shop for anything **except** shoes.

(3) adapt, adopt *Adapt* means "to change." *Adopt* means "to take as one's own."

EXAMPLES	Farmers **adapt** others' techniques to their soil.
	They often **adopt** new techniques, too.

(4) affect, effect *Affect* is almost always a verb meaning "to influence." *Effect,* usually a noun, means "a result." Sometimes, *effect* is a verb meaning "to bring about" or "to cause."

VERB	Natural disasters **affect** farmers' success.
NOUN	Farmers know the **effects** of drought.
VERB	Hot summers also **effect** changes in the harvest.

(5) aggravate *Aggravate* means "to make worse." Avoid using this word to mean "annoy."

INCORRECT	The noise of the lawnmower **aggravated** me.
PREFERRED	The drought is **aggravating** the water quality.

(6) ain't   *Ain't,* which was originally a contraction for
am not, is no longer considered acceptable in standard English.
Always use *am not,* and never use *ain't.* The exception is in
certain instances of dialogue.

(7) all ready, already   *All ready,* which consists of two separate
words used as an adjective, means "ready." *Already,* which is an
adverb, means "by or before this time" or "even now."

ADJECTIVE	Is everyone **all ready** to begin practicing?
ADVERB	We've started **already**.

(8) all right, alright   *Alright* is a nonstandard spelling. Make
sure you use the two-word form.

INCORRECT	Business in the downtown stores was **alright** during the sale.
PREFERRED	Business in the downtown stores was **all right** during the sale.

(9) all together, altogether   *All together* means "together as a
single group." *Altogether* means "completely" or "in all."

EXAMPLES	My family went to the park **all together**.
	The flowers made an **altogether** beautiful display.

(10) among, between   Both of these words are prepositions.
Among shows a connection between three or more items.
Between generally shows a connection between two items.

EXAMPLES	Schools of brightly colored fish swam **among** the coral reefs.
	They swam **between** the rocks and the higher formations, trying to avoid the sharks.

See Practice 9.2A

(11) anxious   This adjective implies uneasiness, worry, or fear.
Do not use it as a substitute for *eager.*

INCORRECT	The environmentalists were **anxious** for change.
PREFERRED	They were **anxious** about the effects of pollution.

(12) anyone, any one, everyone, every one   *Anyone* and *everyone* mean "any person" or "every person." *Any one* means "any single person (or thing)"; *every one* means "every single person (or thing)."

EXAMPLES

Anyone can be an environmentalist.

Any one person can make a difference in helping to protect our planet.

Everyone has a responsibility to keep the planet safe.

Every one of us can recycle and live responsibly.

(13) anyway, anywhere, everywhere, nowhere, somewhere   These adverbs should never end in *-s*.

INCORRECT   Before the fence was set up, my dog could wander **anywheres** in the neighborhood.

PREFERRED   Before the fence was set up, my dog could wander **anywhere** in the neighborhood.

(14) as   Do not use the conjunction *as* to mean "because" or "since."

INCORRECT   Our recycling drive was not successful **as** we couldn't get enough people to work.

PREFERRED   Our recycling drive was not successful **because** we couldn't get enough people to work.

(15) as to   *As to* is awkward. Replace it with *about*.

INCORRECT   There is some doubt **as to** whether I'll be able to complete my project on time.

PREFERRED   There is some doubt **about** whether I'll be able to complete my project on time.

(16) at   Do not use *at* after *where*. Simply eliminate *at*.

INCORRECT   **Where** is my homework **at**?

PREFERRED   **Where** is my homework?

(17) at, about Avoid using *at* with *about*. Simply eliminate *at* or *about*.

INCORRECT	My favorite television show is on **at about** 9:00.
PREFERRED	My favorite television show is on **at** 9:00.

(18) awful, awfully *Awful* is used informally to mean that something is "extremely bad." *Awfully* is used informally to mean "very." Both words are overused and should be replaced with more descriptive words. In standard English speech and writing, *awful* should only be used to mean "inspiring fear or awe in someone."

OVERUSED	I'd made an **awful** mess of my report.
PREFERRED	I'd made a **terrible** mess of my report.
OVERUSED	Marcia was **awfully** angry with Denise.
PREFERRED	Marcia was **extremely** angry with Denise.
OVERUSED	The weather report was **awful**.
PREFERRED	The weather report was **dreadful**.

(19) awhile, a while *Awhile* is an adverb that means "for a short time." *A while,* is a noun, means "a period of time." It is usually used after the preposition *for* or *after*.

ADVERB	Some plants can grow **awhile** without sun.
	We waited **awhile** until our number was called.
NOUN	They may grow for **a while** in the shade, but most plants need sunlight.
	In **a while**, our waiting will be over.

(20) beat, win When you *win*, you "achieve a victory in something." When you *beat* someone or something, you "overcome an opponent."

INCORRECT	The runner in lane 2 **won** the other runners.
PREFERRED	The runner in lane 2 **beat** the other runners.
	The runner in lane 2 wants to **win** the race.

See Practice 9.2B

PRACTICE 9.2A > **Recognizing Usage Problems 1–10**

Read each sentence. Then, choose the correct item to complete each sentence.

EXAMPLE   Can we (adopt, adapt) that city's plan to benefit our small town?

ANSWER   *adapt*

1. I (ain't, am not) going to the baseball game today.
2. Human population growth can (affect, effect) endangered species.
3. Amanda has (already, all ready) finished the test.
4. I sat (among, between) two of my teammates on the bench.
5. He will (accept, except) the award.
6. Tree pollen (aggravates, annoys) my allergy symptoms.
7. We traveled (all together, altogether) to the beach.
8. Sue said it was (alright, all right) for me to borrow her book.
9. It would be (a, an) honor to serve in your administration.
10. The town recently (adopted, adapted) a new policy for meetings.

PRACTICE 9.2B > **Recognizing Usage Problems 11–20**

Read each sentence. Then, choose the correct expression to complete each sentence.

EXAMPLE   The answer is (somewheres, somewhere) in this book.

ANSWER   *somewhere*

11. I was (awfully, extremely) tired after the race.
12. (As, Because) the park is close by, we decided to walk there.
13. I didn't have time to go to the mall (anyway, anyways).
14. Jamal (beat, won) all of his opponents in the tournament.
15. Tom and Raymond have known each other for quite (a while, awhile).
16. The party will begin (at about, at) 6:00 P.M.
17. Please share your suggestions (as to, about) how to organize the room.
18. Do you know where the softball field (is at, is located)?
19. (Every one, everyone) of the players attended the game.
20. Some of the students were so (eager, anxious) about the exam that they stayed up late studying.

SPEAKING APPLICATION

Take turns with a partner. Choose the pair of words in parentheses from sentence 2, 5, or 10, and tell your partner your choice. Your partner should say two sentences, using both words correctly.

WRITING APPLICATION

Use sentences 12, 13, 14, and 15 as models to write four similar sentences. Exchange papers with a partner. Your partner should choose the correct word that completes each of your sentences.

(21) because   Do not use *because* after the phrase *the reason*. Say "The reason is that" or reword the sentence.

INCORRECT   The **reason** I'm going to the library **is because** I have to do some research.

PREFERRED   The **reason** I'm going to the library **is** to do some research.

(22) being as, being that   Avoid using either of these expressions. Use *because* instead.

INCORRECT   **Being as** I was going past the store, I bought some lunch.

PREFERRED   **Because** I was going past the store, I bought some lunch.

(23) beside, besides   *Beside* means "at the side of" or "close to." *Besides* means "in addition to."

EXAMPLES   The equipment was lying **beside** the bleachers.

No one **besides** the team could use it.

(24) bring, take   *Bring* means "to carry from a distant place to a nearer one." *Take* means "to carry from a near place to a far one."

EXAMPLES   Mike will **bring** my homework home while I'm sick.

I'll **take** it back to school when I return.

(25) can, may   Use *can* to mean "have the ability to." Use *may* to mean "have permission to" or "to be likely to."

ABILITY   You **can** go to the library to find a book.

PERMISSION   You **may** also borrow my book.

POSSIBILITY   You **may** find a better book in the school library.

(26) clipped words   Avoid using clipped or shortened words, such as *gym* and *photo* in formal writing.

INFORMAL   I have many **photos** of my favorite singers.

FORMAL   I have many **photographs** of my favorite singers.

(27) different from, different than   *Different from* is preferred in standard English.

INCORRECT   New York's rainfall is **different than** Miami's.
PREFERRED   New York's rainfall is **different from** Miami's.

(28) doesn't, don't   Do not use *don't* with third-person singular subjects. Instead, use *doesn't*.

INCORRECT   He **don't** want to leave until the game is over.
PREFERRED   He **doesn't** want to leave until the game is over.

(29) done   *Done* is the past participle of the verb *do*. It should always take a helping verb.

INCORRECT   Jack **done** his homework in complete silence.
PREFERRED   Jack **has done** his homework in complete silence.

(30) due to   *Due to* means "caused by" and should be used only when the words *caused by* can be logically substituted.

INCORRECT   **Due to** hunting, wolves almost became extinct.
PREFERRED   The wolves' near extinction was **due to** hunting.

See Practice 9.2C

(31) each other, one another   These expressions usually are interchangeable. At times, however, *each other* is more logically used in reference to only two and *one another* in reference to more than two.

EXAMPLES   Students working in groups rely on **one another** when they assign tasks.
A pair of students often benefit from **each other's** knowledge and suggestions.

(32) farther, further   *Farther* refers to distance. *Further* means "additional" or "to a greater degree or extent."

EXAMPLES   The **farther** I swam, the more my muscles ached.
Clearly, I needed to **further** develop my strength.

(33) fewer, less   Use *fewer* with things that can be counted. Use *less* with qualities and quantities that cannot be counted.

EXAMPLES   **fewer** telephones, **less** communication

(34) get, got, gotten   These forms of the verb *get* are acceptable in standard English, but a more specific word is preferable.

INCORRECT   **get** nominated, **got** elected, **have gotten** laws passed

PREFERRED   **was** nominated, **won** the election, **passed** laws

(35) gone, went   *Gone* is the past participle of the verb *go* and is used only with a helping verb. *Went* is the past tense of *go* and is never used with a helping verb.

INCORRECT   The birds **gone** south for the winter.

They should **have went** before the cold weather.

PREFERRED   The birds **went** south for the winter.

They should **have gone** before the cold weather.

(36) good, lovely, nice   Replace these overused words with a more specific adjective.

WEAK   **good** description, **lovely** room, **nice** painting

BETTER   **vivid** description, **cozy** room, **realistic** painting

(37) in, into   *In* refers to position. *Into* suggests motion.

EXAMPLES   Broadway is **in** New York City.

We have to go **into** the subway to go uptown.

(38) irregardless   Avoid this word in formal speech and writing. Instead, use *regardless*.

(39) just   When you use *just* as an adverb to mean "no more than," place it immediately before the word it modifies.

INCORRECT   Bob **just** went to the corner store.

PREFERRED   Bob went **just** to the corner store.

(40) kind of, sort of   Do not use these phrases in formal speech.

See Practice 9.2D   Instead, use *rather* or *somewhat*.

PRACTICE 9.2C ▷ **Recognizing Usage Problems 21–30**

Read each sentence. Then, choose the correct expression to complete each sentence.

EXAMPLE The twins are quite different (from, than) each other.

ANSWER *from*

1. If we (don't, doesn't) leave soon, we'll be late for the movie.

2. (Beside, Besides) the regular menu, the restaurant offers daily specials.

3. The teacher asked us to (bring, take) extra pencils to class tomorrow.

4. The problems with the laptop computer were (because of, due to) software errors.

5. Denise (done, has done) a lot of work for that charity.

6. We selected milk (being as, because) it provides calcium and other minerals.

7. The official class (photo, photograph) will be taken on Friday, April 4.

8. The caretaker said we (can, may) visit the mansion only on weekends.

9. I left my cellphone (beside, besides) my keys.

10. The reason we're late is (because, that) we got lost.

PRACTICE 9.2D ▷ **Revising Sentences to Correct Usage Problems 31–40**

Read each sentence. Then, rewrite each sentence, correcting the errors in usage.

EXAMPLE How much further from here is the lake?

ANSWER *How much farther from here is the lake?*

11. We have less dollars in our bank account since we took a vacation.

12. Van is a good dancer.

13. I was kind of tired by the end of the trip.

14. We will have practice irregardless of the weather.

15. Please move the bikes from the porch in the garage.

16. Myra just had one test today.

17. My mom got a new shirt for me.

18. Without farther delay, I will begin my speech.

19. Luke had went upstairs to look for his backpack.

20. Molly and Tamara enjoy one another's company.

SPEAKING APPLICATION

Take turns with a partner. Say sentences with usage problems. Your partner should correct each of your sentences.

WRITING APPLICATION

Write a paragraph about a topic of your choice. Include sentences that contain usage problems. Exchange papers with a partner. Your partner should correct the usage problems in your paragraph.

(41) lay, lie The verb *lay* means "to put or set (something) down." Its principal parts—*lay, laying, laid, laid*—are followed by a direct object. The verb *lie* means "to recline." Its principal parts—*lie, lying, lay, lain*—are not followed by a direct object.

LAY	Mike asked me to **lay** the camera down.
	His artistic training **is laying** a foundation for his career.
	He **laid** the equipment bag on the ground.
	He **has laid** his tripod on the ground, too.
LIE	I like to **lie** on the ground and watch the clouds.
	The root of that tree **is lying** above the ground.
	Up above, I could see that a snake **lay** on a branch.
	The acorns from the tree **have lain** on the ground all winter.

(42) learn, teach *Learn* means "to receive knowledge." *Teach* means "to give knowledge."

EXAMPLES	That film can help you **learn** about the rain forest.
	Ecologists **teach** us how to conserve effectively.

(43) leave, let *Leave* means "to allow to remain." *Let* means "to permit."

INCORRECT	Some people **leave** their dogs run loose.
PREFERRED	Some people **let** their dogs run loose.

(44) like, as *Like* is a preposition meaning "similar to" or "such as." It should not be used in place of the conjunction *as*.

INCORRECT	That exhibit looks **like** a rain forest should look.
PREFERRED	That exhibit looks **as** a rain forest should look.
	That exhibit looks **like** a rain forest.

(45) loose, lose *Loose* is usually an adjective or part of such idioms as *cut loose, turn loose,* or *break loose. Lose* is always a verb and usually means "to miss from one's possession."

EXAMPLES	The tire is **loose**, and the bicycle is wobbling.
	A wobbling bike could cause you to **lose** your balance.

(46) maybe, may be *Maybe* is an adverb meaning "perhaps."
May be is a helping verb connected to a main verb.

ADVERB **Maybe** we can begin our recycling project soon.

VERB It **may be** this year's most successful project.

(47) of Do not use *of* after a helping verb such as *should, would,
could,* or *must.* Use *have* instead. Do not use *of* after *outside,
inside, off,* and *atop.* Simply eliminate *of.*

INCORRECT The octopus **would of** avoided us if it had seen us.

PREFERRED The octopus **would have** avoided us if it had seen us.

(48) OK, O.K., okay In informal writing, *OK, O.K.,* and *okay* are
acceptably used to mean "all right." Do not use them in standard
English speech or writing, however.

INFORMAL The principal said the dress code was **okay**.

PREFERRED The principal said the dress code was **acceptable**.

(49) only *Only* should be placed immediately before the word it
modifies. Placing it elsewhere can lead to confusion.

EXAMPLES **Only** one person went to the store.
(No one else went to the store.)

One person went **only** to the store.
(One person went nowhere but the store.)

(50) ought Do not use *ought* with *have* or *had.*

INCORRECT Simon **hadn't ought** to have told me a lie.

PREFERRED Simon **ought not** to have told me a lie.

See Practice 9.2E

(51) outside of Do not use this expression to mean "besides"
or "except."

INCORRECT No one remembers that actor's name **outside of** me.

PREFERRED No one remembers that actor's name **except** me.

(52) plurals that do not end in -s The English plurals of
certain nouns from Greek and Latin are formed as they were
in their original language. Words such as *criteria*, *media*, and
phenomena are plural. Their singular forms are *criterion*, *medium*,
and *phenomenon*.

INCORRECT	One **criteria** for success in schoolwork is paying attention in class.
PREFERRED	One **criterion** for success in schoolwork is paying attention in class.
	You should learn all of the **criteria** for success in schoolwork.

(53) precede, proceed *Precede* means "to go before." *Proceed*
means "to move or go forward."

EXAMPLES	The darkening sky **preceded** the thunderstorm.
	After the storm was over, the townspeople **proceeded** to clean up the damage.

(54) principal, principle As an adjective, *principal* means "most
important" or "chief." As a noun, it means "a person who has
controlling authority," as in a school. *Principle* is always a noun
that means "a fundamental law."

ADJECTIVE	The **principal** goal of a sailor is to sail safely.
NOUN	My dad is the **principal** on the marina's board.
NOUN	My dad's company follows the **principles** of good management by treating its employees well.

(55) real *Real* means "authentic." In formal writing, avoid using
real to mean "very" or "really."

INCORRECT	That new action movie was **real** exciting.
PREFERRED	That new action movie was **extremely** exciting.

(56) says *Says* should not be used as a substitute for *said*.

INCORRECT	Yesterday, the teacher **says** to read the next chapter.
PREFERRED	Yesterday, the teacher **said** to read the next chapter.

(57) seen *Seen* is a past participle and must be used with a helping verb.

INCORRECT	We **seen** the bright colors in the coral reef.
PREFERRED	We **had seen** the bright colors in the coral reef.

(58) set, sit *Set* means "to put (something) in a certain place." Its principal parts—*set, setting, set, set*—are usually followed by a direct object. *Sit* means "to be seated." Its principal parts—*sit, sitting, sat, sat*—are never followed by a direct object.

SET	**Set** the tools on the lawn.
	Tim **is setting** the shovel down by the garden.
	He **will set** the rake there, too.
	I **have** already **set** the seed packages by their rows.
SIT	Tim likes to **sit** in the rocking chair.
	He **is sitting** in it right now.
	He **will sit** in it when he stops work.
	His dad **has sat** in that chair many times, too.

(59) so When *so* is used as a coordinating conjunction, it means *and* or *but*. Avoid using *so* when you mean "so that."

INCORRECT	Hawks use their eyesight **so** they can find food.
PREFERRED	Hawks use their eyesight **so that** they can find food.

(60) than, then Use *than* in comparisons. Use *then* as an adverb to refer to time.

EXAMPLES	I'm driving better today **than** when I first started.
	I learned to start slowly, **then** accelerate.

(61) that, which, who Use these relative pronouns in the following ways: *that* and *which* refer to things; *who* refers only to people.

EXAMPLES	The bus **that** we take stops at every corner.
	Its route, **which** is very long, is also very popular.
	The driver **who** drives in the morning and afternoon talks to everyone he picks up.

(62) their, there, they're   *Their,* a possessive pronoun,
always modifies a noun. *There* can be used either as an expletive
at the beginning of a sentence or as an adverb showing place or
direction. *They're* is a contraction of *they are.*

PRONOUN   The musicians in the band were all improvising **their**
own solos.

EXPLETIVE   **There** will be a lot of people in the audience, and
everyone wants to hear each performer play.

ADVERB   The amplifiers will be placed over **there** , at the front and
sides of the stage.

CONTRACTION   I'm sure **they're** going to put on a great show.

(63) them   Do not use *them* as a substitute for *those.*

INCORRECT   **Them** trees are taller than any I've seen.

PREFERRED   **Those** trees are taller than any I've seen.

(64) to, too, two   *To,* a preposition, begins a phrase or an
infinitive. *Too,* an adverb, modifies adjectives and other adverbs
and means "very" or "also." *Two* is a number.

PREPOSITION   **to** the Arctic, **to** the North Pole

INFINITIVE   **to** study the polar ice, **to** see arctic seals

ADVERB   **too** cold, **too** dangerous

NUMBER   **two** polar bears, **two** pairs of gloves

(65) when, where   Do not use *when* or *where* immediately after
a linking verb. Do not use *where* in place of *that.*

INCORRECT   Spring floods are **when** rivers overflow their banks.

Wheat fields are **where** the floodwater goes.

PREFERRED   Spring floods **happen when** rivers overflow their banks.

See Practice 9.2F

Wheat fields are **the places** the floodwater goes.

PRACTICE 9.2E ▷ Recognizing Usage Problems 41–50

Read each sentence. Then, choose the correct item to complete each sentence.

EXAMPLE Grandma (learned, taught) me all she knew about cooking.

ANSWER *taught*

1. (May be, Maybe) we will go to the movies tonight.

2. It is not (acceptable, okay) to cheat on a test.

3. If you had given me your phone number, I would (have, of) called you.

4. (Leave, Let) your shoes by the door before you come inside.

5. I (lain, laid) the blanket over him.

6. I was the (only one, one only) to raise my hand.

7. Greg acted (as if, like) he cared.

8. The cat is (laying, lying) in the sun.

9. We (hadn't ought, ought not) to have spent so much money.

10. Young Billy keeps wiggling his (lose, loose) tooth.

PRACTICE 9.2F ▷ Revising Sentences to Correct Usage Problems 51–65

Read each sentence. Then, rewrite each sentence, correcting the errors in usage.

EXAMPLE Please, carefully sit that bowl in the sink.

ANSWER *Please, carefully set that bowl in the sink.*

11. Two o'clock is when we will have the election for class president.

12. There bicycles are in the garage.

13. Them students are in my math class.

14. By the lake is where we always meet.

15. I like their first album better then their second album.

16. I met the author that wrote my favorite book.

17. My cousin plans too visit two colleges next weekend.

18. The teacher approved our topic and told us to precede with our research.

19. I took a nap so I wouldn't be tired.

20. The chairperson of the company is also the principle stockholder.

SPEAKING APPLICATION

Reread each sentence in Practice 9.2E. Discuss with a partner usage errors you've made in past writing assignments.

WRITING APPLICATION

Use sentences 13, 14, and 17 as models to write similar sentences. Exchange papers with a partner. Your partner should correct your usage problems.

PRACTICE 1 ▷ Combining and Varying Sentences

Read the sentences. Then, rewrite each sentence according to the instructions in parentheses.

1. William ran around the track. (Invert the subject-verb order.)

2. Tiffany needed a flashlight. She also needed a sleeping bag to go camping. (Create a compound direct object, and start with an infinitive.)

3. The view is amazing at the top of the mountain. The weather is also amazing. (Create a compound subject, and start with a phrase.)

4. Kevin wore trunks. He also wore goggles when he went swimming. (Create a compound direct object, and start with a dependent clause.)

5. The sandpipers strutted toward the ocean. (Invert the subject-verb order.)

6. Clara wore a dress. She also wore high-heeled shoes to go dancing. (Create a compound direct object, and start with an infinitive.)

7. Jody fell asleep in class. Jody got caught falling asleep in class. (Create a compound verb, and start with a phrase.)

8. Crowds of people pushed and shoved through the mall. (Invert the subject-verb order.)

9. Carla raised her hand before time ran out. She also answered the question correctly. (Create a compound verb, and start with a phrase.)

10. I always eat a healthy breakfast in the morning. Sarah also eats a healthy breakfast. (Create a compound subject, and start with a phrase.)

PRACTICE 2 ▷ Revising Pronoun and Verb Usage

Read the sentences. Then, revise each sentence to eliminate problems in pronoun and verb usage. You may reorder, add, or eliminate words.

1. Tom and Hank usually take pride in his appearance.

2. Either Clarence or Jenna make the decisions regarding this project.

3. Mark and Julio becomes friends at the end of the movie.

4. Greg and Susie hope their test results is high.

5. A boy would have to be adventurous to enjoy their first camping experience.

6. Don't read scary stories to a little girl; it could give them nightmares.

7. Who do you see the most?

8. Both Cindy and Sara is taking advanced calculus.

9. We think it best if Pablo figures out the problem for themselves.

10. I'm worried about mine car because the mechanic overcharges us sometimes.

PRACTICE 3 ▷ Revising for Correct Use of Active and Passive Voice

Read the sentences. Then, revise each sentence to be in the active voice. You may reorder, add, or delete words.

1. The package was sent the next day by Alex.

2. Class was interrupted by the students in the hallway.

3. That problem was solved yesterday by Carlos.

4. The meeting was moved to four o'clock.

5. It was thought by many people, but it was said by Alia.

Continued on next page ▶

Cumulative Review   Chapters 4–9

 Correcting Errors in Pronoun and Verb Usage

Read the sentences. Then, revise each sentence, correcting all errors in agreement, verb usage, and pronoun usage. If a sentence is already correct, write *correct*.

1. Joseph and Daryl runs the track tomorrow.
2. Either Lola or Matt have to do it.
3. Even though Lydia wanted to win prom queen, her thought Tammy deserves it.
4. Swimming and jogging is part of a healthy exercise regimen.
5. Her and me went hiking next week in the mountains.
6. If you don't stretch before exercising, I may injure yourself.
7. I answer the phone because she was responsible for taking messages.
8. Each of us have a responsibility for the success of our task.
9. Sally was generous to buy Karen's ticket.
10. If a person gets lost, they should stay put.

 Using Comparative and Superlative Forms Correctly

Read the sentences. Then, write the appropriate comparative or superlative degree of the modifier in parentheses.

1. Trevor is (old) than David.
2. Of the two cousins, I would say Jane is the (wise).
3. Yards are (long) than feet.
4. There are (few) cassette tapes in stores than there used to be.
5. Nick got the (high) score in the class on the geometry final exam.

 Avoiding Double Negatives

Read the sentences. Then, choose the word in parentheses that makes each sentence negative without forming a double negative.

1. I don't have (no, a) clue.
2. She (has, does not have) no response to the question.
3. Ben never (didn't take, took) any more than his share.
4. He didn't see (nothing, anything).
5. Jeanne (did, didn't) have anything to eat.

PRACTICE 7 **Avoiding Usage Problems**

Read the sentences. Then, choose the correct expression to complete each sentence.

1. We will (bring/take) a fruit salad to the barbecue.
2. Karla is concerned that the temperature will (affect/effect) the experiment.
3. The family will (accept/except) the award on William's behalf.
4. The school needs to (adapt/adopt) a new dress code policy.
5. She (all ready/already) fed the dog.
6. I (did/done) my chores in the morning.
7. Andrew was afraid the team would (loose/lose) the basketball game.
8. The fish swam (among/between) the coral.
9. Can (anyone/any one) of the members speak Spanish?
10. (Everyone/Every one) will come over after the ceremony.

CHAPTER 10

CAPITALIZATION

Correct use of the conventions of capitalization can guide your readers through your text and improve the clarity of your writing.

WRITE GUY *Jeff Anderson, M.Ed.*

WHAT DO YOU NOTICE?

Think about capitalization as you zoom in on sentences from the book *The Woman Warrior* by Maxine Hong Kingston.

MENTOR TEXT

They should have been crying hysterically on their way to Vietnam. "If I see one that looks Chinese," she thought, "I'll go over and give him some advice."

Now, ask yourself the following questions:

- Why are the words *Vietnam* and *Chinese* capitalized?
- Why is the contraction *I'll* capitalized?

The word *Vietnam* is capitalized because it is a proper noun that names a specific place. Since the word *Chinese* is an adjective derived from the proper noun *China*, it is capitalized and classified as a proper adjective. The pronoun *I* is always capitalized no matter what its location in a sentence. The same rule applies when *I* is part of a contraction, such as in the case of *I'll*.

Grammar for Writers Writers can use capitalization to signal the beginning of a sentence or quotation or to highlight a specific name. Without correct capitalization, a text would be much more difficult to read and understand.

I'm planning a vacation. What is ideal?

Well, I know that Ideal is a nice town in South Dakota.

10.1 Capitalization in Sentences

Just as road signs help to guide people through a town, capital letters help to guide readers through sentences and paragraphs. Capitalization signals the start of a new sentence or points out certain words within a sentence to give readers visual clues that aid in their understanding.

Using Capitals for First Words

Always capitalize the first word in a sentence.

Capitalize the first word in declarative, interrogative, imperative, and exclamatory sentences.

DECLARATIVE **T**hey will be here in one hour.

INTERROGATIVE **H**ow did you find it?

IMPERATIVE **W**atch where you walk.

EXCLAMATORY **H**e scored a home run!

Capitalize the first word in interjections and incomplete questions.

INTERJECTIONS **T**hat's terrific!

INCOMPLETE QUESTIONS **W**hy? **W**hat?

The word *I* is always capitalized, whether it is the first word in a sentence or not.

Always capitalize the pronoun *I*.

EXAMPLE My brother and **I** went shopping.

> Capitalize the first word after a colon only if the word begins a complete sentence. Do not capitalize the word if it begins a list of words or phrases.

10.1.4 RULE

SENTENCE
FOLLOWING
A COLON
He reached for the chair: **H**e was unable to continue standing.

LIST
FOLLOWING
A COLON
She put the following items in the trunk: **a** bedspread, a pillow, and a towel.

> Capitalize the first word in each line of traditional poetry, even if the line does not start a new sentence.

10.1.5 RULE

EXAMPLE
I think that I shall never see
A poem lovely as a tree. – Joyce Kilmer

See Practice 10.1A

Using Capitals With Quotations

There are special rules for using capitalization with **quotations.**

> Capitalize the first word of a **quotation.** However, do not capitalize the first word of a continuing sentence when a quotation is interrupted by identifying words or when the first word of a quotation is the continuation of a speaker's sentence.

10.1.6 RULE

EXAMPLES
Linda asked, "**W**ould you please pick me up at five?"

"**A**s I was typing," he said, "**t**he phone would not stop ringing."

Betsy mentioned that he is "**t**he smartest man she knows."

See Practice 10.1B

PRACTICE 10.1A > Capitalizing Words

Read each sentence. Then, write the word or words that should be capitalized in each sentence.

EXAMPLE   oh, no! i forgot to mail the letter!

ANSWER   *Oh, I*

1. should we ask for directions?

2. the storm abated: the wind died down and the sun came out.

3. we learned about Columbus's three ships: *the Nina, the Pinta,* and *the Santa Maria.*

4. did you remember to bring the notes for today's meeting?

5. mom repeated her request: please clean your room.

6. did you buy a new sweater? what color is it?

7. we still need to buy these items for the party: balloons, juice, and napkins.

8. did you pass the driver's license test?

9. mrs. Jamadar gave me some tomatoes from her garden.

10. that was a remarkable story!

PRACTICE 10.1B > Using Capitals With Quotations

Read each sentence. Then, write the word or words in each sentence that should be capitalized.

EXAMPLE   my mother asked, "do you have practice this afternoon?"

ANSWER   *My, Do*

11. the story began, "once upon a time, there was a girl named Anne."

12. Franklin D. Roosevelt said, "the only thing we have to fear is fear itself."

13. "that history test was really hard," Julia said.

14. "i think that she was right," Ron said, "when she told me to check my facts."

15. Ms. Smith replied, "yes, it is true. i have been to Spain three times."

16. Milly asked, "will you still be here when i get back?"

17. "foul ball!" yelled the umpire.

18. After learning that school was closed, Robert said, "let's go play outside in the snow!"

19. He replied, "of course you want to go to the game. your favorite team is playing."

20. "as it started to rain," Sam said, "i realized I had left my umbrella on the bus."

SPEAKING APPLICATION

Take turns with a partner. Say a variety of sentences about your favorite band. Your partner should indicate, with a nod of his or her head, each time you say a word that should be capitalized.

WRITING APPLICATION

Write a conversation between you and your teacher about an upcoming exam. Be sure to use correct capitalization in your quotations.

10.2 Proper Nouns

Capitalization make important words stand out in your writing, such as the names of people, places, countries, book titles, and other proper names. Sometimes proper names are used as nouns and sometimes as adjectives modifying nouns or pronouns.

Using Capitals for Proper Nouns

Nouns, as you may remember, are either **common** or **proper.**

Common nouns, such as *sailor, brother, city,* and *ocean,* identify classes of people, places, or things and are not capitalized.

Proper nouns name specific examples of people, places, or things and should be capitalized.

> Capitalize all **proper** nouns.

RULE 10.2.1

EXAMPLES   **M**elissa   **P**rofessor **D**oolittle   **G**overnor **P**erez

Second **S**treet   **H**ull **H**ouse   **A**lbany

Of Human Bondage   *R.M.S. Titanic*

Names
Each part of a person's name—the given name, the middle name or initial standing for that name, and the surname—should be capitalized. If a surname begins with *Mc* or *O',* the letter following it is capitalized (McAdams, O'Reilly).

> Capitalize each part of a person's name even when the full name is not used.

RULE 10.2.2

EXAMPLES   **S**ally **F**ield   **Q**.**T**. **K**ettle   **H**arry **B**. **R**ichards

Capitalize the proper names that are given to animals.

EXAMPLES   **F**licka   **S**pot   **C**uddles

Geographical and Place Names

If a place can be found on a map, it should generally be capitalized.

> **Capitalize geographical and place names.**

Examples of different kinds of geographical and place names are listed in the following chart.

GEOGRAPHICAL AND PLACE NAMES	
Streets	Madison Avenue, First Street, Green Valley Road
Towns and Cities	Dallas, Oakdale, New York City
Counties, States, and Provinces	Champlain County, Texas, Quebec
Nations and Continents	Austria, Kenya, the United States of America, Asia, Mexico, Europe
Mountains	the Adirondack Mountains, Mount Washington
Valleys and Deserts	the San Fernando Valley, the Mojave Desert, the Gobi
Islands and Peninsulas	Aruba, the Faroe Islands, Cape York Peninsula
Sections of a Country	the Northeast, Siberia, the Great Plains
Scenic Spots	Gateway National Park, Carlsbad Caverns
Rivers and Falls	the Missouri River, Victoria Falls
Lakes and Bays	Lake Cayuga, Gulf of Mexico, the Bay of Biscayne
Seas and Oceans	the Sargasso Sea, the Indian Ocean
Celestial Bodies and Constellations	Mars, the Big Dipper, moon, Venus
Monuments and Memorials	the Tomb of the Unknown Soldier, Kennedy Memorial Library, the Washington Monument
Buildings	Madison Square Garden, Fort Hood, the Astrodome, the White House
School and Meeting Rooms	Room 6, Laboratory 3B, the Red Room, Conference Room C

Capitalizing Directions

Words indicating direction are capitalized only when they refer to a section of a country.

EXAMPLES   Go **W**est, young man, and find your fortune.

Albany is **n**orth of New York City.

Capitalizing Names of Celestial Bodies

Capitalize the names of celestial bodies except *moon* and *sun*.

EXAMPLE   The **s**un is more than one hundred times larger than Earth.

Capitalizing Buildings and Places

Do not capitalize words such as *theater, hotel, university,* and *park*, unless the word is part of a proper name.

EXAMPLES   We are staying at the Waldorf Astoria **H**otel.

How far is the **h**otel from the airport?

Events and Times

Capitalize references to historic events, periods, and documents as well as dates and holidays. Use a dictionary to check capitalization.

> **Capitalize the names of specific events and periods in history.**

RULE 10.2.4

SPECIAL EVENTS AND TIMES	
Historic Events	the Battle of Waterloo, World War I
Historical Periods	the Manchu Dynasty, Reconstruction
Documents	the Bill of Rights, the Magna Carta
Days and Months	Monday, June 22, the third week in May
Holidays	Labor Day, Memorial Day, Veterans Day
Religious Holidays	Rosh Hashanah, Christmas, Easter
Special Events	the World Series, the Holiday Antiques Show

Capitalizing Seasons

Do not capitalize seasons unless the name of the season is being used as a proper noun or adjective.

EXAMPLES   My favorite place is New England in the **f**all.

We hope to go to the **S**ummer Olympics.

RULE

10.2.5

Capitalize the names of organizations, government bodies, political parties, races, nationalities, languages, and religions.

VARIOUS GROUPS	
Clubs and Organizations	Rotary, Knights of Columbus, the Red Cross, National Organization for Women
Institutions	the Museum of Fine Arts, the Mayo Clinic
Schools	Kennedy High School, University of Texas
Businesses	General Motors, Prentice Hall
Government Bodies	Department of State, Federal Trade Commission, House of Representatives
Political Parties	Republicans, the Democratic party
Nationalities	American, Mexican, Chinese, Israeli, Canadian
Languages	English, Italian, Polish, Swahili
Religions and Religious References	Christianity: God, the Holy Spirit, the Bible Judaism: the Lord, the Prophets, the Torah Islam: Allah, the Prophets, the Qur'an, Mohammed Hinduism: Brahma, the Bhagavad Gita, the Vedas Buddhism: the Buddha, Mahayana, Hinayana

References to Mythological Gods When referring to mythology, do not capitalize the word *god* (the *gods* of Olympus).

RULE

10.2.6

Capitalize the names of awards; the names of specific types of air, sea, and spacecraft; and brand names.

EXAMPLES   the **F**reedom **A**ward   the **G**ood **C**onduct **M**edal

Raisin **N**ut cereal   **G**emini **V**

See Practice 10.2A

See Practice 10.2B

PRACTICE 10.2A **Identifying Proper Nouns**

Read each sentence. Then, underline the proper noun or nouns in each sentence.

EXAMPLE   Mr. Kennedy is my next-door neighbor.

ANSWER   *Mr. Kennedy is my next-door neighbor.*

1. On their trip to South Dakota, the Green family went to Mount Rushmore.

2. When they went to Aruba, Anna and Choi stayed on the western side of the island.

3. We studied World War I and World War II with Professor Smith.

4. Samuel Morse invented Morse code.

5. Alexis visited The Museum of Modern Art during her summer vacation.

6. The *Odyssey* was written by Homer.

7. Is Jupiter the largest planet in our solar system?

8. We saw the Washington Redskins play last Sunday.

9. My father has been a member of the Elks Club for many years.

10. My cousin Nicole is fluent in French.

PRACTICE 10.2B **Capitalizing Proper Nouns**

Read each sentence. Then, write the word or words in each sentence that should be capitalized.

EXAMPLE   My friend elizabeth lives in new york.

ANSWER   *Elizabeth, New York*

11. The tudors ruled england from 1485 to 1603.

12. The walsh family visited the grand canyon.

13. My father is lithuanian, and my mother is hungarian.

14. Nick mcnulty was accepted to boston college and dartmouth.

15. On our summer vacation, we saw the st. louis arch, which is known as the gateway to the west.

16. The nobel prize was founded by alfred nobel.

17. st. patrick's day is a national holiday in ireland.

18. Sandra wished to speak to someone in the department of health and human services.

19. The *mayflower* brought the pilgrims to massachusetts from england.

20. Do the alps span both switzerland and france?

SPEAKING APPLICATION

Take turns with a partner. Tell about a historical event. Your partner should identify the proper nouns that you use.

WRITING APPLICATION

Use sentence 14 as a model to write three similar sentences. Replace the proper nouns in sentence 14 with other proper nouns.

Using Capitals for Proper Adjectives

A **proper adjective** is either an adjective formed from a proper noun or a proper noun used as an adjective.

> **RULE 10.2.7**
>
> Capitalize most **proper adjectives**.

PROPER ADJECTIVES FORMED FROM PROPER NOUNS	**A**ustralian kangaroo	**C**haucer play
	Canadian trip	**E**nglish settlers
	Spanish ambassador	**I**talian food
PROPER NOUNS USED AS ADJECTIVES	the **S**enate floor	the **R**iley speeches
	Chekhov festival	a **B**ible class
	the **G**reens' house	**N**ew **Y**ork pizza

Some proper adjectives have become so commonly used that they are no longer capitalized.

EXAMPLES	**h**erculean **e**ffort	**f**rench **f**ries
	pasteurized **m**ilk	**q**uixotic **h**ope
	venetian **b**linds	**t**eddy **b**ear

Brand names are often used as proper adjectives.

> **RULE 10.2.8**
>
> Capitalize a **brand name** when it is used as an adjective, but do not capitalize the common noun it modifies.

EXAMPLES	**T**imo **w**atches	**S**unset **c**ameras
	Super **C**ool **s**hirts	**L**onglasting **r**efrigerator

Multiple Proper Adjectives

When you have two or more proper adjectives used together, do not capitalize the associated common nouns.

> **Do not capitalize a common noun used with two proper adjectives.**

ONE PROPER ADJECTIVE	TWO PROPER ADJECTIVES
Colorado River	Snake and Colorado rivers
William Street	William, Monroe, and Lemon streets
Gowanus Canal	Gowanus and Erie canals
Lacey Act	Lacey and Higher Education acts
Atlantic Ocean	Atlantic and Indian oceans
Sussex County	Sussex and Union counties
Cook Islands	Cook and Gilbert islands

Prefixes and Hyphenated Adjectives

Prefixes and hyphenated adjectives cause special problems. Prefixes used with proper adjectives should be capitalized only if they refer to a nationality.

> **Do not capitalize prefixes attached to proper adjectives unless the prefix refers to a nationality. In a hyphenated adjective, capitalize only the proper adjective.**

EXAMPLES
all-American   Anglo-American

English-speaking   pro-Italian

American Chinese-language newspaper

pre-Renaissance   Sino-Russian

pre-Columbian architecture   Indo-Iranian

See Practice 10.2C
See Practice 10.2D

PRACTICE 10.2C ▷ Capitalizing Proper Adjectives

Read each sentence. Then, write the word or words in the sentence that should be capitalized.

EXAMPLE   Have you been to that new japanese restaurant yet?

ANSWER   *Japanese*

1. Manuel's class is studying greek mythology.

2. My neighbor has two dogs: an irish setter and an italian greyhound.

3. Meet me in the library after spanish class.

4. Is your cousin of german descent?

5. Do you enjoy french food?

6. Our theater class will perform a shakespearean play.

7. We will visit the italian city of Rome during our trip.

8. I called Mom to tell her I was at the flynns' house.

9. We have an antique victorian chair in our living room.

10. Diana enjoys studying native american pottery styles.

PRACTICE 10.2D ▷ Revising Sentences to Correct Capitalization Errors

Read each sentence. Then, rewrite each sentence using conventions of capitalization.

EXAMPLE   I'd like to visit the grand canyon during our trip to arizona.

ANSWER   *I'd like to visit the Grand Canyon during our trip to Arizona.*

11. At the entrance of the city, one can see the stadium where the baltimore ravens play.

12. A cold front came down from lake Ontario to cover new England.

13. The United States expanded its territory and settled the west.

14. Nelly ate dinner in little italy on sunday.

15. Many people confuse london bridge with tower bridge.

16. Lupe visited the national gallery of art in Washington, d.c.

17. There is a hotel, called hotel de glace, near Quebec city made entirely out of ice.

18. I'm not sure whether I will take spanish or french next semester.

19. The museum display included information about the pleistocene epoch.

20. The science club will meet in room 102 on wednesday afternoons.

SPEAKING APPLICATION

Discuss with a partner the importance of capitalization. Suggest three ways capitalization makes reading easier and helps with comprehension.

WRITING APPLICATION

Write 10 sentences. In each sentence, include a proper adjective. Be sure to use conventions of capitalization.

10.3 Other Uses of Capitals

Even though the purpose of using capital letters is to make writing clearer, some rules for capitalization can be confusing. For example, it may be difficult to remember which words in a letter you write need to start with a capital, which words in a book title should be capitalized, or when a person's title—such as Senator or Reverend—needs to start with a capital. The rules and examples that follow should clear up the confusion.

Using Capitals in Letters

Capitalization is required in parts of personal letters and business letters.

> **Capitalize the first word and all nouns in letter salutations and the first word in letter closings.**

10.3.1 RULE

SALUTATIONS
Dear **A**lice,

Dear **G**entlemen:

Dear **D**r. **D**err:

My **D**ear **A**unt,

CLOSINGS
With **h**umble **a**pologies,

Your **s**incere **f**riend,

Always **y**ours,

Best **w**ishes,

Using Capitals for Titles

Capitals are used for titles of people and titles of literary and artistic works. The charts and rules on the following pages will guide you in capitalizing titles correctly.

Capitalize a person's title only when it is used with the person's name or when it is used as a proper name by itself.

WITH A PROPER NAME **C**ongressman **G**rover went to visit the troops.

AS A PROPER NAME I'm glad you can join us, **U**ncle.

IN A GENERAL REFERENCE The **s**enator decided not to run for another term.

The following chart illustrates the correct form for a variety of titles. Study the chart, paying particular attention to compound titles and titles with prefixes or suffixes.

SOCIAL, BUSINESS, RELIGIOUS, MILITARY, AND GOVERNMENT TITLES	
Commonly Used Titles	Sir, Madam, Miss, Professor, Doctor, Reverend, Bishop, Sister, Father, Rabbi, Corporal, Major, Admiral, Mayor, Governor, Ambassador
Abbreviated Titles	*Before names*: Mr., Mrs., Ms., Dr., Hon. *After names*: Jr., Sr., Ph.D., M.D., D.D.S., Esq.
Compound Titles	Vice President, Secretary of State, Lieutenant Governor, Commander in Chief
Titles With Prefixes or Suffixes	ex-Congressman Randolph, Governor-elect Loughman

Some honorary titles are capitalized. These include First Lady of the United States, Speaker of the House of Representatives, Queen Mother of England, and the Prince of Wales.

10.3.3 RULE

> Capitalize certain honorary titles even when the titles are not followed by a proper name.

EXAMPLE   The **p**resident and **F**irst **L**ady visited with the **q**ueen of England.

Occasionally, the titles of other government officials may be capitalized as a sign of respect when referring to a specific person whose name is not given. However, you usually do not capitalize titles when they stand alone.

EXAMPLES   We thank you, **G**overnor, for this very special gift.

Sixteen **s**enators voted for this bill.

10.3.4 RULE

> Relatives are often referred to by titles. These references should be capitalized when used with or as the person's name.

WITH THE PERSON'S NAME   In the winter, **A**unt **J**oyce used to take us skating.

AS A NAME   He says that **G**randfather enjoys bowling with his grandchildren.

10.3.5 RULE

> Do not capitalize titles showing family relationships when they are preceded by a possessive noun or pronoun.

EXAMPLES   their **a**unt   his **g**randfather   Barbara's **m**other

Capitalize the first word and all other key words in the titles of books, periodicals, poems, stories, plays, paintings, and other works of art.

The following chart lists examples to guide you in capitalizing titles and subtitles of various works. Note that the articles (*a*, *an*, and *the*) are not capitalized unless they are used as the first word of a title or subtitle. Conjunctions and prepositions are also left uncapitalized unless they are the first or last word in a title or subtitle or contain four letters or more. Note also that verbs, no matter how short, are always capitalized.

TITLES OF WORKS	
Books	*The Red Badge of Courage* *Profiles in Courage* *All Through the Night* *John Ford: The Man and His Films* *Heart of Darkness*
Periodicals	*International Wildlife, Allure,* *Better Homes and Gardens*
Poems	"The Raven" "The Rime of the Ancient Mariner" "Flower in the Crannied Wall"
Stories and Articles	"Editha" "The Fall of the House of Usher" "Here Is New York"
Plays and Musicals	*The Tragedy of Macbeth* *Our Town* *West Side Story*
Paintings	*Starry Night* *Mona Lisa* *The Artist's Daughter With a Cat*
Music	*The Unfinished Symphony* "Heartbreak Hotel" "This Land Is Your Land"

10.3.7 RULE

> Capitalize titles of educational courses when they are language courses or when they are followed by a number or preceded by a proper noun or adjective. Do not capitalize school subjects discussed in a general manner.

WITH CAPITALS	**I**talian	**H**onors **A**lgebra
	Psychology 105	**B**iology 4
	Geology 202	**F**rench

WITHOUT CAPITALS	**g**eology	**e**conomics
	algebra	**h**istory
	biology	**m**ath

EXAMPLES

This year, I will be taking **p**sychology, **R**ussian, **H**onors **M**ath, and **w**orld **h**istory.

Bill's favorite classes are **a**rt **h**istory, **I**talian, and **a**lgebra.

He does like **p**hysical **e**ducation, but not as much as **m**ath.

After **G**erman class, I have to rush across the hallway to **w**oodworking.

See Practice 10.3A
See Practice 10.3B

PRACTICE 10.3A > Capitalizing Titles

Read each sentence. Then, write the word or words that should be capitalized.

EXAMPLE   Allie's favorite painting is *light at two lights* by Edward Hopper.

ANSWER   *Light at Two Lights*

1. uncle cory enjoys visiting museums.

2. "Theme for english b" was written by Langston Hughes.

3. I met delegate Simmons at the event.

4. My grandmother introduced me to her friend mrs. Addison.

5. Our class is reading *of Mice and Men.*

6. Did senator Smith attend the meeting?

7. My last two classes are honors biology and math.

8. Have you read *the great gatsby?*

9. Last week dean Horvath lead the pledge of allegiance.

10. My sister enrolled in history 101 and spanish.

PRACTICE 10.3B > Using All of the Rules of Capitalization

Read the sentence. Then, rewrite the sentences, using the conventions of capitalization.

EXAMPLE   when it comes to generosity, mrs. cavanaugh has no equal.

ANSWER   *When it comes to generosity, Mrs. Cavanaugh has no equal.*

11. sophia thought that the spanish rice was delicious.

12. My academic advisor said biology 100 is a prerequisite for medicine 203.

13. Thank you for coming, mrs. lewis.

14. "when was the last time you saw lieutenant colonel alexander?" asked general fulton.

15. On our class trip, we will visit baltimore, maryland.

16. I met dean levits at a conference last june.

17. i couldn't see the english garden behind the tudor house.

18. The stars in orion's belt can clearly be seen tonight.

19. I sent the letter to my lawyer, Stella Notte, j.d.

20. We will attend a basketball game at madison square garden in new york city.

SPEAKING APPLICATION

Discuss with a partner the importance of capitalizing titles. Answer the question: When is a title not capitalized?

WRITING APPLICATION

Write a short story. In each sentence, include a title, proper noun, or proper adjective. Be sure to correctly use conventions of capitalization.

CHAPTER 11

PUNCTUATION

Understanding the conventions of punctuation will help you organize and connect ideas in your writing.

WRITE GUY *Jeff Anderson, M.Ed.*

WHAT DO YOU NOTICE?

Note examples of punctuation as you zoom in on this sentence from *The Autobiography* by Benjamin Franklin.

MENTOR TEXT

> While my care was employed in guarding against one fault, I was often surprised by another; habit took the advantage of inattention; inclination was sometimes too strong for reason.

Now, ask yourself the following questions:

- Why is a comma inserted after the word *fault*?
- Why are semicolons used to separate items in this sentence?

The comma inserted after *fault* serves to separate a subordinate clause, *while my care was employed in guarding against one fault,* from the main, or independent, clause, *I was often surprised by another.* The semicolons are used to separate related main clauses and take the place of coordinating conjunctions.

Grammar for Writers Writers who correctly use punctuation craft understandable text, whether a sentence is short or long. Before publishing your writing, check that your punctuation helps it flow smoothly.

What did the semicolon say to the comma?

Hmm . . . "What's the hurry? Slow down a little."

11.1 End Marks

End marks tell readers when to pause and for how long. They signal the end or conclusion of a sentence, word, or phrase. There are three end marks: the **period (.)**, the **question mark (?)**, and the **exclamation mark (!)**.

Using Periods

A **period** indicates the end of a declarative or imperative sentence, an indirect question, or an abbreviation. The period is the most common end mark.

RULE 11.1.1 Use a **period** to end a declarative sentence, a mild imperative sentence, and an indirect question.

A **declarative sentence** is a statement of fact or opinion.

DECLARATIVE SENTENCE This is a warm day.

An **imperative sentence** gives a direction or command. Often, the first word of an imperative sentence is a verb.

MILD IMPERATIVE SENTENCE Complete the reading assignment.

An **indirect question** restates a question in a declarative sentence. It does not give the speaker's exact words.

INDIRECT QUESTION Jane asked me if I should come along.

Other Uses of Periods

In addition to signaling the end of a statement, periods can also signal that words have been shortened, or abbreviated.

RULE 11.1.2 Use a period after most abbreviations and after initials.

PERIODS IN ABBREVIATIONS	
Titles	Dr., Sr., Mrs., Mr., Gov., Maj., Rev., Prof.
Place Names	Ave., Bldg., Blvd., Mt., Dr., St., Ter., Rd.
Times and Dates	Sun., Dec., sec., min., hr., yr., A.M.
Initials	E. B. White, Robin F. Brancato, R. Brett

Some abbreviations do not end with periods. Metric measurements, state abbreviations used with ZIP Codes, and most standard measurements do not need periods. The abbreviation for inch, *in.,* is the exception.

EXAMPLES   mm, cm, kg, L, C, CA, TX, ft, gal

The following chart lists some abbreviations with and without periods.

ABBREVIATIONS WITH AND WITHOUT END MARKS	
approx. = approximately	misc. = miscellaneous
COD = cash on delivery	mph = miles per hour
dept. = department	No. = number
doz. = dozen(s)	p. or pg. = page; pp. = pages
EST = Eastern Standard Time	POW = prisoner of war
FM = frequency modulation	pub. = published, publisher
gov. or govt. = government	pvt. = private
ht. = height	rpm = revolutions per minute
incl. = including	R.S.V.P. = please reply
ital = italics	sp. = spelling
kt. = karat or carat	SRO = standing room only
meas. = measure	vol. = volume
mfg. = manufacturing	wt. = weight

Sentences Ending With Abbreviations When a sentence ends with an abbreviation that uses a period, do not put a second period at the end. If an end mark other than a period is required, add the end mark.

| EXAMPLES | Be sure to speak with Barrie Fine Jr. |
| | Is that Mark Tanner Sr.? |

See Practice 11.1A

Do not use periods with acronyms, words formed with the first or first few letters of a series of words.

| ACRONYMS | USA (United States of America) |
| | ECM (European Common Market) |

Use a period after numbers and letters in outlines.

EXAMPLE

I. Maintaining your pet's health

    A. Diet

        1. For a puppy

        2. For a mature dog

    B. Exercise

Using Question Marks

A **question mark** follows a word, phrase, or sentence that asks a question. A question is often in inverted word order.

Use a question mark to end an interrogative sentence, an incomplete question, or a statement intended as a question.

INTERROGATIVE SENTENCE	Is the day over yet?
	When are we going out tonight?
INCOMPLETE QUESTION	Many kinds of animals travel in packs. Why?
	I will buy you dinner. Where?

Use care, however, in ending statements with question marks. It is better to rephrase the statement as a direct question.

STATEMENT WITH A QUESTION MARK	The sun hasn't risen yet **?**
	We are having vegetables with lunch **?**
REVISED INTO A DIRECT QUESTION	Hasn't the sun risen yet **?**
	Are we having vegetables with lunch **?**

Use a period instead of a question mark with an **indirect question**—a question that is restated as a declarative sentence.

EXAMPLE	Kate wanted to know when Tim was coming **.**
	She wondered if they would be on time **.**

Using Exclamation Marks

An **exclamation mark** signals an exclamatory sentence, an imperative sentence, or an interjection. It indicates strong emotion and should be used sparingly.

> Use an **exclamation mark** to end an exclamatory sentence, a forceful imperative sentence, or an interjection expressing strong emotion.

11.1.6 RULE

EXCLAMATORY SENTENCE	Look at the blue water **!**
FORCEFUL IMPERATIVE SENTENCE	Don't stop the water **!**

An interjection can be used with a comma or an exclamation mark. An exclamation mark increases the emphasis.

EXAMPLES	Wow **!** It was a great meal **.**
	Oh **!** It was a great show **.**
WITH A COMMA	Wow **,** it was a great meal **.**

See Practice 11.1B

PRACTICE 11.1A **Using Periods Correctly in Sentences**

Read each sentence. Then, rewrite each sentence, adding periods where needed. If a sentence is correct, write *correct*.

EXAMPLE   F Scott Fitzgerald wrote The Great Gatsby

ANSWER   *F. Scott Fitzgerald wrote The Great Gatsby.*

1. Leo asked Kate if she heard the noise

2. The Washington Monument was finished on Dec 6, 1884.

3. Her fiance gave Mimi a 2-kt diamond engagement ring.

4. Kent W. Burkes Sr led the parade

5. Dr. Benton's office is on Sixth St and Orange Ave

6. Leilani was born in Honolulu, Hawaii

7. You'll need 3 m of ribbon for your project.

8. Irvin told me about his trip to Mt McKinley.

9. Dinner is always at 6:00 PM on Tuesdays.

10. Ms Cabrera wants us to bring healthy snacks

PRACTICE 11.1B **Using Question Marks and Exclamation Marks Correctly in Sentences**

Read each sentence. Then, write the correct end mark for each item.

EXAMPLE   Wow, what a performance

ANSWER   /

11. What is your favorite baseball team

12. How long will it take

13. Stop yelling

14. Mia, leave the room

15. What a pleasant surprise

16. How long is the play

17. When will the rain stop

18. Walk carefully

19. Where is Liechtenstein

20. Stop thief

SPEAKING APPLICATION

Take turns with a partner. Say sentences that contain abbreviations for titles, times and dates, and initials. Your partner should tell where periods would be used if the sentences were written.

WRITING APPLICATION

Write two sentences that use question marks and two sentences that use exclamation marks. Identify each sentence as *interrogative*, *exclamatory*, *forceful imperative*, or *sentence with an interjection*.

11.2 Commas

A **comma** tells the reader to pause briefly before continuing a sentence. Commas may be used to separate elements in a sentence or to set off part of a sentence.

Commas are used more than any other internal punctuation mark. To check for correct comma use, read a sentence aloud and note where a pause helps you to group your ideas. Commas signal to readers that they should take a short breath.

Using Commas With Compound Sentences

A **compound sentence** consists of two or more main or independent clauses that are joined by a coordinating conjunction, such as *and, but, for, nor, or, so,* or *yet.*

> Use a **comma** before a conjunction to separate two or more independent or main clauses in a **compound sentence.**

11.2.1 RULE

Use a comma before a conjunction only when there are complete sentences on both sides of the conjunction. Do not use a comma if the conjunction joins a compound subject, a compound verb, prepositional phrases, or subordinate clauses.

EXAMPLE

John is practicing for his game , but I won't be

independent clause   independent clause

able to attend.

In some compound sentences, the main or independent clauses are very brief, and the meaning is clear. When this occurs, the comma before the conjunction may be omitted.

EXAMPLES

Jon typed carefully but he still had spelling errors.

Kate would like to visit Mom in May but she can't get a ticket.

In other sentences, conjunctions are used to join compound subjects or verbs, prepositional phrases, or subordinate clauses. Because these sentences have only one independent clause, they do not take a comma before the conjunction.

CONJUNCTIONS WITHOUT COMMAS	
Compound Subject	Bess and Sandra met for lunch on the beach.
Compound Verb	The group laughed and chatted as they danced at prom.
Two Prepositional Phrases	The bird flew through the room and out the door.
Two Subordinate Clauses	I enjoy shopping trips only if they are at the mall and I get what I want.

A **nominative absolute** is a noun or pronoun followed by a participle or participial phrase that functions independently of the rest of the sentence.

RULE 11.2.2

Use a comma after a **nominative absolute**.

The following example shows a comma with a nominative absolute.

EXAMPLE   Important symptoms having been missed **,**
I decided to call the doctor.

Avoiding Comma Splices

Remember to use both a comma and a coordinating conjunction in a compound sentence. Using only a comma can result in a **run-on sentence** or a **comma splice**. A **comma splice** occurs when two or more complete sentences have been joined with only a comma. Either punctuate separate sentences with an end mark or a semicolon, or find a way to join the sentences. (See Section 11.3 for more information on semicolons.)

RULE 11.2.3

Avoid comma splices.

INCORRECT   The rain beat down on the flowers **,** many petals broke under the downpour.

CORRECT   The rain beat down on the flowers **.** Many petals broke under the downpour.

Using Commas in a Series

A **series** consists of three or more words, phrases, or subordinate clauses of a similar kind. A series can occur in any part of a sentence.

> **Use commas to separate three or more words, phrases, or clauses in a series.**

11.2.4 RULE

Notice that a comma follows each of the items except the last one in these series. The conjunction *and* or *or* is added after the last comma.

SERIES OF WORDS	The wildlife included birds, squirrels, deer, and snakes.
SERIES OF PREPOSITIONAL PHRASES	The directions led them through the streets, around the buildings, and through the center of town.
SUBORDINATE CLAUSES IN A SERIES	The radio reported that the election was over, that the turnout was good, and that the results were surprising.

If each item (except for the last one) in a series is followed by a conjunction, do not use commas.

EXAMPLE	I saw black bears and polar bears and brown bears.

A second exception to this rule concerns items such as *salt and pepper*, which are paired so often that they are considered a single item.

EXAMPLES	For my party, we had macaroni and cheese, franks and beans, and bacon and eggs.
	Ariel carried a big box with salt and pepper, plates and cups, and forks and knives.

Using Commas Between Adjectives

Sometimes, two or more adjectives are placed before the noun they describe.

RULE 11.2.5

Use commas to separate **coordinate adjectives,** also called **independent modifiers,** or adjectives of equal rank.

EXAMPLES a strong, tall man

a hopeful, productive, creative meeting

An adjective is equal in rank to another if the word *and* can be inserted between them without changing the meaning of the sentence. Another way to test whether or not adjectives are equal is to reverse their order. If the sentence still sounds correct, they are of equal rank. In the first example, *a tall, strong man* still makes sense.

If you cannot place the word *and* between adjectives or reverse their order without changing the meaning of the sentence, they are called **cumulative adjectives.**

RULE 11.2.6

Do not use a comma between cumulative adjectives.

EXAMPLES a new comforter cover
(*a comforter new cover* does not make sense)

many large animals
(*large many animals* does not make sense)

RULE 11.2.7

Do not use a comma to separate the last adjective in a series from the noun it modifies.

INCORRECT A large, powerful, truck picked up the soil.

CORRECT A large, powerful truck picked up the soil.

See Practice 11.2A
See Practice 11.2B

PRACTICE 11.2A **Using Commas Correctly in Sentences**

Read each sentence. Then, rewrite each sentence, adding a comma or commas where needed. Write the reason(s) for the comma usage.

EXAMPLE   Laurence has a cavity so he is going to a dentist.

ANSWER   *Laurence has a cavity, so he is going to a dentist.* — compound sentence

1. Can you come now or do you need more time?

2. We looked for the ball in the grass in the shed and under the car.

3. Startled by the ringing phone I dropped the dish.

4. I love to knit sweaters but thick fluffy socks are my specialty.

5. I didn't pick up the dry cleaning bread or mail.

6. It was a small bright colorful footstool.

7. Her hair was tied with a red curly ribbon.

8. I hoped to see Juan but he wasn't at home.

9. Her kittens purring with contentment the mother cat curled up and fell asleep.

10. Kit washed the car and then she waxed it.

PRACTICE 11.2B **Revising to Correct Errors in Comma Use**

Read each sentence. Then, rewrite each sentence, adding or deleting commas as necessary.

EXAMPLE   Sitting on a bench I read my book.

ANSWER   *Sitting on a bench, I read my book.*

11. We painted pottery, and took skating lessons in the park on our day off from school.

12. Her pom poms waving the cheerleader performed her routine.

13. Bob likes country music yet he sets his radio to the rock station.

14. He's interested in cooking, and football.

15. The mouse squeaked, and ran to grab the piece of cheese.

16. I love to play tennis and now I also enjoy ping-pong badminton and racquetball.

17. I thought Loren was a science major but she just signed up for philosophy and economics.

18. May received a bouquet of beautiful, red roses.

19. The woman looked first dashed across the street, and then ran down the block.

20. Marissa took Nahtali, Joachim, Peter, and, Derek to the science museum.

SPEAKING APPLICATION

Take turns with a partner. Tell about what you have done this morning. List the activities in a series, and use adjectives of equal rank to describe them. Your partner should tell where commas would be inserted if your description were written.

WRITING APPLICATION

Write four sentences that use commas incorrectly. Exchange papers with a partner. Your partner should correct your sentences, adding or deleting commas as necessary.

Using Commas After Introductory Material

Most material that introduces a sentence should be set off with a comma.

RULE 11.2.8

> **Use a comma after an introductory word, phrase, or clause.**

KINDS OF INTRODUCTORY MATERIAL	
Introductory Words	Yes, we do expect to speak with them soon. No, there has been no phone call. Well, I was definitely surprised by her statement.
Nouns of Direct Address	Anthony, will you speak?
Introductory Adverbs	Hurriedly, they gathered up the camping gear. Patiently, the manager explained it to them again.
Participial Phrases	Acting quickly, she averted a potential traffic accident. Waiting for the start of the marathon, we introduced ourselves and started to chat.
Prepositional Phrases	In the shade of the leafy branches, the family picked several baskets of apples. After the lengthy seminar, we were all exhausted.
Infinitive Phrases	To choose the right foods, I consulted a nutrition book. To finish my paper on time, I will have to work all weekend.
Adverbial Clauses	When she asked for a permit for the store, she was sure it would be approved. If you compete in swim meets, you may be interested in this one.

Commas and Prepositional Phrases Only one comma should be used after two prepositional phrases or a compound participial or infinitive phrase.

EXAMPLES   In the pocket in his jacket**,** he found
his keys.

Wandering in the auditorium and scared**,** the fans
asked a security guard for directions.

It is not necessary to set off short prepositional phrases. However, a comma can help avoid confusion.

CONFUSING   In the rain water soaked my clothing.

CLEAR   In the rain**,** water soaked my clothing.

Using Commas With Parenthetical Expressions

A **parenthetical expression** is a word or phrase that interrupts the flow of the sentence.

> **Use commas to set off parenthetical expressions from the rest of the sentence.**

11.2.9 RULE

Parenthetical expressions may come in the middle or at the end of a sentence. A parenthetical expression in the middle of a sentence needs two commas—one on each side; it needs only one comma if it appears at the end of a sentence.

KINDS OF PARENTHETICAL EXPRESSIONS	
Nouns of Direct Address	Will you have brunch with us**,** April? I wonder**,** Ms. Bliss**,** where we'll go for brunch.
Conjunctive Adverbs	Someone had already bought them flatware**,** however. We could not**,** therefore**,** buy all of them.
Common Expressions	I listened to Athena's side as thoughtfully as anyone else did**,** I assume.
Contrasting Expressions	Arabella is ten**,** not eleven. Daphne's warmth**,** not her beauty**,** won Joshua's heart.

Using Commas With Nonessential Expressions

To determine when a phrase or clause should be set off with commas, decide whether the phrase or clause is *essential* or *nonessential* to the meaning of the sentence. The terms *restrictive* and *nonrestrictive* may also be used.

An **essential,** or **restrictive, phrase** or **clause** is necessary to the meaning of the sentence. **Nonessential,** or **nonrestrictive, expressions** can be left out without changing the meaning of the sentence. Although the nonessential material may be interesting, the sentence can be read without it and still make sense. Depending on their importance in a sentence, appositives, participial phrases, and adjectival clauses can be either essential or nonessential. Only nonessential expressions should be set off with commas.

NONESSENTIAL APPOSITIVE	The speech was given by Bill, the oldest member of the committee.
NONESSENTIAL PARTICIPIAL PHRASE	The long journey, one that many traveled, crosses the entire continent.
NONESSENTIAL ADJECTIVAL CLAUSE	The mountain, which is covered with flowers in the summer, is popular with skiers.

Do not use commas to set off essential expressions.

ESSENTIAL APPOSITIVE	The part was played by the famous actress Meryl Streep.
ESSENTIAL PARTICIPIAL PHRASE	The woman baking the chicken is my mother.
ESSENTIAL ADJECTIVAL CLAUSE	The book that my teacher suggested would alter my conclusions.

See Practice 11.2C
See Practice 11.2D

PRACTICE 11.2C > Placing Commas Correctly in Sentences

Read each sentence. Then, rewrite each sentence, adding commas where they are needed.

EXAMPLE   Actually she hasn't finished her lunch yet I think.

ANSWER   *Actually, she hasn't finished her lunch yet, I think.*

1. After her mother gave her a reassuring nod the child swam across the pool.

2. Looking slightly bemused the professor applauded the student's satirical speech.

3. Although she liked the plan she wasn't sure that the committee would approve it.

4. Luckily no one was absent yesterday.

5. When Paige arrived at the campsite she checked the cabin for broken windows.

6. The preface "An Introduction to Physics" will help you understand the text.

7. Mary will win honors for her project I am quite sure.

8. To pay for a new car stereo Will got a job after school.

9. An estimated 200 people almost all women received an award from the council last year.

10. The most beautiful vistas including the one where I took the picture can be seen from Lauver's Lookout.

PRACTICE 11.2D > Revising Sentences for Proper Comma Use

Read each sentence. Then, rewrite each sentence, adding or deleting commas as necessary.

EXAMPLE   Absent-mindedly Jonna, poured orange juice not milk on her cereal.

ANSWER   *Absent-mindedly, Jonna poured orange juice, not milk, on her cereal.*

11. No there aren't any blueberry muffins left.

12. Sleepily Trent pulled on his pajamas and climbed into bed.

13. Seamounts, underwater mountains that do not break the surface of the water are my favorite marine feature to study.

14. This, *Saturday Evening Post* cover was created by the famous artist Norman Rockwell.

15. To win, the game you have to know your opponent's weaknesses.

16. China, is the most densely populated country, in the world.

17. Will, you change the radio station Jorge?

18. This river the longest in the state, currently has over 60 beaver dams.

19. After their lengthy discussion the men, all shook hands.

20. In the dusky glow of the evening Ryan looked relaxed, not at all impatient.

SPEAKING APPLICATION

With a partner, reread all of the sentences in Practice 11.2C. Discuss the purpose of each comma in all ten sentences.

WRITING APPLICATION

Write a story that includes at least five different ways to use commas, including introductory material, parenthetical expressions, and nonessential expressions.

Using Commas With Dates, Geographical Names, and Titles

Dates usually have several parts, including months, days, and years. Commas separate these elements for easier reading.

RULE 11.2.10

When a date is made up of two or more parts, use a comma after each item, except in the case of a month followed by a day.

EXAMPLES   The journey began on June 6, 2010, and the preparations began on March 12, 2009.

The job began on January 1 and ended two weeks later.
(no comma needed after the day of the month)

Commas are also used when the month and the day are used as an appositive to rename a day of the week.

EXAMPLES   Monday, April 13, was the first day of the class.

Ben will arrive on Saturday, April 19, and will stay until Sunday.

When a date contains only a month and a year, commas are unnecessary.

EXAMPLES   I will leave in July 2011.

Ashley will visit Germany in May 2009.

If the parts of a date have already been joined by prepositions, no comma is needed.

EXAMPLE   The historic newspaper printed its first edition in June of 1890.

> When a geographical name is made up of two or more parts, use a comma after each item.
>
> RULE 11.2.11

EXAMPLES   My sister who lives in Orlando, Florida, has a job working with the dolphins.

See Practice 11.2E

We're going to Montreal, Quebec, Canada, for our road trip.

> When a name is followed by one or more titles, use a comma after the name and after each title.
>
> RULE 11.2.12

EXAMPLE   I see that Carlos Monegro, P.A., works there.

A similar rule applies with some business abbreviations.

EXAMPLE   Eastern Smith, Inc., started publishing in 2001.

Using Commas in Numbers

Commas make large numbers easier to read by grouping them.

> With large numbers of more than three digits, use a comma after every third digit starting from the right.
>
> RULE 11.2.13

EXAMPLES   10,000 gallons, 1,600 miles, 1,246,314 pennies

> Do not use a comma in ZIP Codes, telephone numbers, page numbers, years, serial numbers, or house numbers.
>
> RULE 11.2.14

ZIP CODE	17458	YEAR NUMBER	1980
TELEPHONE NUMBER	(908) 962-2644	SERIAL NUMBER	105-256-815
PAGE NUMBER	Page 2651	HOUSE NUMBER	6494 Lake Street

See Practice 11.2F

PRACTICE 11.2E Using Commas With Dates and Geographical Names

Read each sentence. Then, rewrite each sentence to show where to correctly place commas in dates and geographical names.

EXAMPLE Galveston Texas is located on the Gulf of Mexico.

ANSWER *Galveston, Texas, is located on the Gulf of Mexico.*

1. Next Monday is January 20 2009.

2. The summer of 2008 was the last time Melanie went to Hartford Connecticut.

3. We will land in London England on Thursday March 5.

4. The package was sent to London Ontario Canada.

5. There was a flood in Annapolis Maryland on December 3 1993.

6. The ceremony will take place on Friday October 8.

7. The address on the envelope is for Canberra New South Wales Australia.

8. Penny went to Mexico City Mexico in June 2007.

9. The show opened on April 4 2000 and will close on May 10 2009

10. I will vacation in Paris France from Monday December 1 to Friday December 5.

PRACTICE 11.2F Editing Sentences for Proper Comma Usage

Read each sentence. Then, rewrite each sentence, adding or deleting commas where they are needed.

EXAMPLE I have lived in Valencia Spain and Okinawa Japan.

ANSWER *I have lived in Valencia, Spain, and Okinawa, Japan.*

11. This Wednesday November, 3 Janet is going to see her family in Topeka Kansas.

12. Mei was hired by Friendly Publishers Inc.

13. On May 16 2007 Professor Helen H. Fitzpatrick Ph.D. received tenure from Colgate University.

14. Russell's car has 85672 miles on it but it's still running well.

15. December 8 1998 is the date, Natasha's family emigrated from St. Petersburg Russia.

16. Exactly 2000 babies were born in that country in the year 2000.

17. Gianna, the girl next door, was Bargain City's 1000000th customer last Friday July 5.

18. This Tuesday August 5 Kelly comes home from Montreal Quebec Canada.

19. There are 13485 residents in Smithtown New York.

20. Dr. Moses Leverly M.D. will perform the operation next Thursday January 3.

SPEAKING APPLICATION

Discuss with a partner the reason for punctuation in writing. Then, discuss how commas help us when we read aloud.

WRITING APPLICATION

Write four sentences that show comma use with dates, geographical names, titles, and numbers.

Using Commas With Addresses and in Letters

Commas are also used in addresses, salutations of friendly letters, and closings of friendly or business letters.

> **Use a comma after each item in an address made up of two or more parts.**

Commas are placed after the name, street, and city. No comma separates the state from the ZIP Code. Instead, insert an extra space between them.

EXAMPLE   The package was delivered to Carlos Lopez,

25 Valley Road, Dallas, Texas 75201.

Fewer commas are needed when an address is written in a letter or on an envelope.

EXAMPLE   Mr. John Black

55 Highway Lane

Brooklyn, NY 11201

> **Use a comma after the salutation in a personal letter and after the closing in all letters.**

See Practice 11.2G

| SALUTATIONS | Dear Uncle Teddy, | Dear Amanda, |
| CLOSINGS | Sincerely, | With love, |

Using Commas in Elliptical Sentences

In **elliptical sentences,** words that are understood are left out. Commas make these sentences easier to read.

> **Use a comma to indicate the words left out of an elliptical sentence.**

EXAMPLE   Tia celebrates her anniversary formally; Bette**,**
          casually.

The words *celebrates her anniversary* have been omitted from
the second clause of the sentence. The comma has been inserted
in their place so the meaning is still clear. The sentence could
be restated in this way: *Tia celebrates her anniversary formally;*
Bette celebrates her anniversary casually.

Using Commas With Direct Quotations

Commas are also used to indicate where **direct quotations** begin
and end. (See Section 11.4 for more information on punctuating
quotations.)

**Use commas to set off a direct quotation from the rest of a
sentence.**

EXAMPLES   "You showed up late**,**" commented Beth's mother.

          She said**,** "The committee meeting ran longer than
          I had hoped**.**"

          "I hope**,**" Kyle's father said**,** "that his best friend
          doesn't forget to call**.**"

Using Commas for Clarity

Commas help you group words that belong together.

Use a comma to prevent a sentence from being misunderstood.

UNCLEAR   Near the freeway developers were building a
          condo complex.

CLEAR   Near the freeway**,** developers were building a
          condo complex.

Misuses of Commas

Because commas appear so frequently in writing, some people are tempted to use them where they are not needed. Before you insert a comma, think about how your ideas relate to one another.

MISUSED WITH AN ADJECTIVE AND A NOUN	In the morning, I have a large, hot, cup of tea.
CORRECT	In the morning, I have a large, hot cup of tea.
MISUSED WITH A COMPOUND SUBJECT	Following the party, my sister Jane, and our cousin Rita, invited Bill to the barbeque.
CORRECT	Following the party, my sister Jane and our cousin Rita invited Bill to the barbeque.
MISUSED WITH A COMPOUND VERB	He watched as she spoke, and listened carefully.
CORRECT	He watched as she spoke and listened carefully.
MISUSED WITH A COMPOUND OBJECT	She chose a car with four doors, and a sunroof.
CORRECT	She chose a car with four doors and a sunroof.
MISUSED WITH PHRASES	Finding the skates, and hoping they were hers, Sally tried them on.
CORRECT	Finding the skates and hoping they were hers, Sally tried them on.
MISUSED WITH CLAUSES	He discussed what elements are crucial to winning, and which players are most valuable.
CORRECT	He discussed what elements are crucial to winning and which players are most valuable.

See Practice 11.2H

PRACTICE 11.2G Adding Commas in Addresses and Letters

Read each item. Then, add commas where needed.

EXAMPLE   Dear Aunt Edith

ANSWER   *Dear Aunt Edith,*

1. The Inn at the Lake Colorado Springs Colorado.

2. Hugs and kisses
   Julianna

3. To my dear little brother

4. Donna Marie Dean 14 Kinnelon Street Jupiter Florida

5. Dear Aunt Lucy Cousin Maisy and Cousin Gracie

6. Mary's Igloo Alaska

7. Wishing you all the best
   Robert Winston Jr.

8. Fulton on the Water Suite 10C

9. Lake Manitoba Winnipeg Canada

10. Daniel Chambers
    144 Oak Avenue Apt. 4D
    Winston-Salem NC 27101

PRACTICE 11.2H Revising Sentences With Misused Commas

Read each sentence. Then, if a sentence contains a misused comma, rewrite it to show correct comma usage. If the sentence is correct, write *correct.*

EXAMPLE   As she opened the package, with great care, Nia was excited.

ANSWER   *As she opened the package with great care, Nia was excited.*

11. If I cannot find anyone I'll just, go home.

12. Mother bought a computer, and a printer.

13. My chores include vacuuming the rug, and making the beds, and doing laundry.

14. Joe Novak Jr. put on his suit, knotted his tie and grabbed, his briefcase.

15. Jerry delivered the flowers, and then drove off in his van.

16. After school, I take a long, leisurely walk.

17. Gloria, and Leigh, are preparing for graduation.

18. Ravi can't pack his bowling ball, or his helmet.

19. In the room are Justine, and her parents.

20. Watching the movie, hoping that it would end soon, Jose was glad when the phone rang.

SPEAKING APPLICATION

After correcting the items above, read them aloud with a partner. Discuss why each comma is needed.

WRITING APPLICATION

Write ten sentences with misused commas. Exchange papers with a partner. Your partner should rewrite the sentences with the commas placed correctly.

11.3 Semicolons and Colons

The **semicolon** (;) is used to join related independent clauses. Semicolons can also help you avoid confusion in sentences with other internal punctuation. The **colon** (:) is used to introduce lists of items and in other special situations.

Using Semicolons to Join Independent Clauses

Semicolons establish relationships between two independent clauses that are closely connected in thought and structure. A semicolon can also be used to separate independent clauses or items in a series that already contain a number of commas.

> **Use a semicolon to join related independent clauses that are not already joined by the conjunctions *and, but, for, nor, or, so,* or *yet.***

11.3.1 RULE

EXAMPLE   We explored the old house together; we were amazed at all the antiques we found inside.

Do not use a semicolon to join two unrelated independent clauses. If the clauses are not related, they should be written as separate sentences with a period or another end mark to separate them.

Note that when a sentence contains three or more related independent clauses, they may still be separated with semicolons.

EXAMPLE   The window shattered; the screen broke; the roof disappeared.

Semicolons Join Clauses Separated by Conjunctive Adverbs or Transitional Expressions

Conjunctive adverbs are adverbs that are used as conjunctions to join independent clauses. **Transitional expressions** are expressions that connect one independent clause with another one.

> **Use a semicolon to join independent clauses separated by either a **conjunctive adverb** or a **transitional expression.****

11.3.2 RULE

CONJUNCTIVE ADVERBS	*also, besides, consequently, first, furthermore, however, indeed, instead, moreover, nevertheless, otherwise, second, then, therefore, thus*
TRANSITIONAL EXPRESSIONS	*as a result, at this time, for instance, in fact, on the other hand, that is*

Place a semicolon *before* a conjunctive adverb or a transitional expression, and place a comma *after* a conjunctive adverb or transitional expression. The comma sets off the conjunctive adverb or transitional expression, which introduces the second clause.

EXAMPLE   She never forgets her notes; in fact, she is the most prepared.

Because words used as conjunctive adverbs and transitions can also interrupt one continuous sentence, use a semicolon only when there is an independent clause on each side of the conjunctive adverb or transitional expression.

EXAMPLES   He visited a hundred restaurants and shops over two weeks; therefore, he had no time to write.

We were astounded, however, by Brett's painting of the blue sky.

Using Semicolons to Avoid Confusion

Sometimes, semicolons are used to separate items in a series.

Use semicolons to avoid confusion when independent clauses or items in a series already contain commas.

When the items in a series already contain several commas, semicolons can be used to group items that belong together. Semicolons are placed at the end of all but the last complete item in the series.

INDEPENDENT CLAUSES
The canal, reportedly teaming with fish, was a legend; and the frustrated, tired fisherman would find it only in sea stories.

ITEMS IN A SERIES
On our trip to the city, my brother visited a friend, who works in the mall; our former neighbors, who live across town; and the Smiths, who own the town coffee shop.

Semicolons appear most commonly in a series that contains either nonessential appositives, participial phrases, or adjectival clauses. Commas should separate the nonessential material from the word or words they modify; semicolons should separate the complete items in the series.

APPOSITIVES
I sent word to Mr. Lee, my language teacher; Mr. Will, my math teacher; and Mr. Dee, my soccer coach.

PARTICIPIAL PHRASES
I developed a passion for reading from my English teachers, learning about literature; from going to the library, reading British authors; and from bookstores, reading different novels.

ADJECTIVAL CLAUSES
The white yacht that I purchased has a sleeping compartment, which holds two people; a kitchen, which was just installed; and a greatroom, which is furnished.

Using Colons

The **colon (:)** is used to introduce lists of items and in certain special situations.

> **Use a colon after an independent clause to introduce a list of items. Use commas to separate three or more items.**

Independent clauses that appear before a colon often include the words *the following, as follows, these,* or *those.*

EXAMPLES
For our experiment, we had to interview the following experts: a biologist, a chemist, and a physiologist.

> **Do not use a colon after a verb or a preposition.**

INCORRECT
Cindy regularly orders: shoes, makeup, and purses online.

CORRECT
Cindy regularly orders shoes, makeup, and purses online.

> **Use a colon to introduce a quotation that is formal or lengthy or a quotation that does not contain a "he said/she said" expression.**

EXAMPLE
Oliver Wendell Holmes Jr. wrote this about freedom: "It is only through free debate and free exchange of ideas that government remains responsive to the will of the people and peaceful change is effected."

Even if it is lengthy, dialogue or a casual remark should be introduced by a comma. Use the colon if the quotation is formal or has no tagline.

A colon may also be used to introduce a sentence that explains the sentence that precedes it.

> **Use a colon to introduce a sentence that summarizes or explains the sentence before it.**

RULE 11.3.7

EXAMPLE His explanation for being late was believable:
He ran out of gas on the way.

Notice that the complete sentence introduced by the colon starts with a capital letter.

> **Use a colon to introduce a formal appositive that follows an independent clause.**

RULE 11.3.8

EXAMPLE I had finally decided where to move: Maine.

The colon is a stronger punctuation mark than a comma. Using the colon gives more emphasis to the appositive it introduces.

> **Use a colon in a number of special writing situations.**

RULE 11.3.9

SPECIAL SITUATIONS REQUIRING COLONS	
Numerals Giving the Time	3:30 A.M. 5:15 P.M.
References to Periodicals (Volume Number: Page Number)	*People* 25:12 *National Geographic* 45:15
Biblical References (Chapter Number: Verse Number)	Proverbs 3:5
Subtitles for Books and Magazines	*A User's Guide for Cars: Antique Cars and Their Parts*
Salutations in Business Letters	Dear Ms. Adams: Dear Sir:
Labels Used to Signal Important Ideas	**Danger:** Firing Range

See Practice 11.3A
See Practice 11.3B

PRACTICE 11.3A **Adding Semicolons and Colons to Sentences**

Read each item. Then, rewrite each item, adding semicolons and colons where they are needed.

EXAMPLE   The computer-generated voice said "The time is 427 P.M."

ANSWER   *The computer-generated voice said: "The time is 4:27 P.M."*

1. It is 215 P.M.

2. Ken will be our guide Mark will drive the car.

3. Dear Mr. Stark

4. Sydney is in New South Wales Perth is in Western Australia.

5. Let me reiterate my statement Keep this door locked at all times.

6. We wanted to start our vacation as soon as possible therefore, we left very early.

7. Diana wants to start working soon in fact, she has already had three interviews.

8. Manuel wants to apply to several schools Dartmouth, Harvard, Yale, and Brown.

9. Captain Ford demands one thing obedience.

10. For the hike, I will need a warm hat, strong, sturdy boots, and a bottle of water.

PRACTICE 11.3B **Using Semicolons and Colons**

Read each sentence. Then, rewrite each sentence, replacing the incorrect comma with a semicolon or a colon.

EXAMPLE   Which branch of the military is he in, Army, Air Force, Navy, or Marines?

ANSWER   *Which branch of the military is he in: Army, Air Force, Navy, or Marines?*

11. Peter has researched his report for two months, he will present it soon.

12. Thelma hurt her foot, therefore, she will not play basketball this season.

13. I like soccer, football, and baseball, however, they will never replace lacrosse.

14. Heather wants only healthy foods, carrots, celery, and apples.

15. The show starts at 4,15 P.M.

16. Mel ordered the following items, milk, eggs, bread.

17. Tiara wants to be like her big brother, he travels the world.

18. The wind died down, thus, we rowed to shore.

19. Warning, The floor is wet.

20. George's favorite animal is a tiger, his brother likes sharks.

SPEAKING APPLICATION

Take turns with a partner. Say sentences that would require colons or semicolons if they were written. Your partner should tell which punctuation would be needed for each of your sentences.

WRITING APPLICATION

Write two paragraphs about something that happened in English class last year. Use colons and semicolons to combine sentences in your paragraphs.

11.4 Quotation Marks, Underlining, and Italics

Quotation marks (" ") set off direct quotations, dialogue, and certain types of titles. Other titles are **underlined** or set in *italics*, a slanted type style.

Using Quotation Marks With Quotations

Quotation marks identify spoken or written words that you are including in your writing. A **direct quotation** represents a person's exact speech or thoughts. An **indirect quotation** reports the general meaning of what a person said or thought.

> A **direct quotation** is enclosed in quotation marks.

DIRECT QUOTATION

"When I learn to paint," said the student, "I'll go to the studio every day."

> An **indirect quotation** does not require quotation marks.

INDIRECT QUOTATION

The student said that when she learns to paint, she'll go to the studio every day.

Both types of quotations are acceptable when you write. Direct quotations, however, generally result in a livelier writing style.

Using Direct Quotations With Introductory, Concluding, and Interrupting Expressions

A writer will generally identify a speaker by using words such as *he asked* or *she said* with a quotation. These expressions, called **conversational taglines** or **tags,** can introduce, conclude, or interrupt a quotation.

Direct Quotations With Introductory Expressions

Commas help you set off introductory information so that your reader understands who is speaking.

RULE 11.4.3

> **Use a comma after short introductory expressions that precede direct quotations.**

EXAMPLE   My friend warned , "If you drive my car, you'll be responsible for it. "

If the introductory conversational tagline is very long or formal in tone, set it off with a colon instead of a comma.

EXAMPLE   At the end of the school year, Jane shared her desire : "I plan to become a teacher and help children read and think. "

Direct Quotations With Concluding Expressions

Conversational taglines may also act as concluding expressions.

RULE 11.4.4

> **Use a comma, question mark, or exclamation mark after a direct quotation followed by a concluding expression.**

EXAMPLE   "If you buy a new car, you'll be responsible for filling it with gas , " my father warned .

Concluding expressions are not complete sentences; therefore, they do not begin with capital letters. Closing quotation marks are always placed outside the punctuation at the end of direct quotations. Concluding expressions generally end with a period.

Divided Quotations With Interrupting Expressions

You may use a conversational tagline to interrupt the words of a direct quotation, which is also called a **divided quotation.**

> Use a comma after the part of a quoted sentence followed by an interrupting conversational tagline. Use another comma after the tagline. Do not capitalize the first word of the rest of the sentence. Use quotation marks to enclose the quotation. End punctuation should be inside the last quotation mark.

11.4.5 RULE

EXAMPLE   "If you buy a new car, " my father warned, "you'll be responsible for filling it with gas. "

> Use a comma, question mark, or exclamation mark after a quoted sentence that comes before an interrupting conversational tagline. Use a period after the tagline.

11.4.6 RULE

EXAMPLE   "You bought a new car, " stated my father.
"You are responsible for filling it with gas. "

Quotation Marks With Other Punctuation Marks

Quotation marks are used with commas, semicolons, colons, and all of the end marks. However, the location of the quotation marks in relation to the punctuation marks varies.

> Place a comma or a period *inside* the final quotation mark.
> Place a semicolon or colon *outside* the final quotation mark.

11.4.7 RULE

EXAMPLES   "Sprinkles was a great kitten, " sighed my sister.

We just learned about his "groundbreaking medical discovery"; we are very pleased.

> Place a question mark or an exclamation mark inside the final quotation mark if the end mark is part of the quotation. Do not use an additional end mark.

11.4.8 RULE

EXAMPLE   Ben wondered, "How could I lose the contest? "

RULE 11.4.9

Place a question mark or exclamation mark outside the final quotation mark if the end mark is part of the entire sentence, not part of the quotation.

EXAMPLE   We were outraged when we heard, "Go back"!

Using Single Quotation Marks for Quotations Within Quotations

As you have learned, double quotation marks (" ") should enclose the main quotation in a sentence. The rules for using commas and end marks with double quotation marks also apply to **single quotation marks.**

RULE 11.4.10

Use **single quotation marks (' ')** to set off a quotation within a quotation.

EXAMPLES   "I recall Tiff quoting Macy, 'If it gets any busier, how will we find parking?'" John said.

"The surgeon said, 'It was successful!'" Ben explained.

Punctuating Explanatory Material Within Quotations

Explanatory material within quotations should be placed in brackets. (See Section 11.7 for more information on brackets.)

RULE 11.4.11

Use brackets to enclose an explanation located within a quotation. The brackets show that the explanation is not part of the original quotation.

EXAMPLE   The volunteer said, "This bridge is a link between two towns [Cane and Falls]."

See Practice 11.4A
See Practice 11.4B

PRACTICE 11.4A Using Quotation Marks

Read each sentence. Then, rewrite each sentence, inserting quotation marks where needed.

EXAMPLE   The professor said, Prepare to work hard this semester.

ANSWER   *The professor said, "Prepare to work hard this semester."*

1. Start running, said the coach, when you see my signal.

2. Are the final drafts due next week? Zeke inquired.

3. Donna cheered, Go team, go!

4. The actress must have said, 'Thank you' a dozen times, said the newscaster.

5. Did Aaron say, Lock all the doors?

6. I thought Raj said that he didn't want any juice, but he actually said, Yes, please.

7. Please leave your name and number, was the recorded message.

8. I can't see! wailed the child.

9. Maybe, Brenda suggested optimistically, I could finish the job.

10. Michael said that I said, Surprise! but I didn't.

PRACTICE 11.4B Revising for the Correct Use of Quotation Marks

Read each sentence. Then, rewrite each sentence, correcting the misuse of quotation marks.

EXAMPLE   "Howard said, No one has given me any instructions."

ANSWER   *Howard said, "No one has given me any instructions."*

11. "Yuen said," I think it's going to rain tomorrow.

12. "It is doubtful, said Mandy, that I will be home on time."

13. Yes! Tom exclaimed "as he rounded the bases."

14. "I heard Bethany yell, Home free! at the top of her lungs, said Greg."

15. Truth be told, said Ving, "I loved your performance tonight."

16. "Were you confused when I said, No?"

17. "Is your favorite painting a van Gogh? she asked."

18. "Don't forget to wear sunblock," said Mother. It's very sunny outside.

19. "Who would be crazy enough to pass up an opportunity like that? asked Nikki."

20. "Tom proclaimed, I passed!" when he received his grades.

SPEAKING APPLICATION

Take turns with a partner. Say sentences with direct quotations and indirect quotations. Your partner should tell which sentences would need quotation marks if they were written.

WRITING APPLICATION

Write a dialogue between two people at a bookstore. Include at least six lines of dialogue.

Using Quotation Marks for Dialogue

A conversation between two or more people is called a **dialogue.**

RULE 11.4.12 **When writing a dialogue, begin a new paragraph with each change of speaker.**

The snow slowly fell over the top of the distant mountain, as the sun set in the west.

Dan sat by the fireplace and talked with his brother about his future.

"I'm going to the city," said Dan. "I think I'll like the atmosphere better; you know I don't like to be bored."

"Have you found a place yet?" asked Matt. "Can I have your couch?"

"It's all yours," said Dan. "It is fine with me if I never see it again."

RULE 11.4.13 **For quotations longer than a paragraph, put quotation marks at the beginning of each paragraph and at the end of the final paragraph.**

John McPhee wrote an essay about a canoe trip on the St. John River in northern Maine. He introduces his readers to the river in the following way:

"We have been out here four days now and rain has been falling three. The rain appears to be ending. Breaks of blue are opening in the sky. Sunlight is coming through, and a wind is rising.

"I was not prepared for the St. John River, did not anticipate its size. I saw it as a narrow trail flowing north, twisting through balsam and spruce—a small and intimate forest river, something like the Allagash . . . ."

Using Quotation Marks in Titles

Generally, quotation marks are used around the titles of shorter works.

> Use quotation marks to enclose the titles of short written works.

WRITTEN WORKS THAT USE QUOTATION MARKS	
Title of a Short Story	"The Black Cat" by Edgar Allen Poe "A Very Tight Place" by Stephen King
Chapter From a Book	"Of Alliances" in *War and Peace* "The Duty of Subjects" in *War and Peace*
Title of a Short Poem	"Fire and Ice" by Robert Frost
Essay Title	"The Over-Soul" by Ralph Waldo Emerson
Title of an Article	"Plugging the Gaps" by Katie Paul

> Use quotation marks around the titles of episodes in a television or radio series, songs, and parts of a long musical composition.

ARTISTIC WORK TITLES THAT USE QUOTATION MARKS	
Episode	"The Chairman" from *60 Minutes*
Song Title	"Hound Dog" by Elvis Presley
Part of a Long Musical Composition	"Spring" from *The Four Seasons* "E.T. Phone Home" from *E.T. The Extra-Terrestrial* soundtrack

> Use quotation marks around the title of a work that is mentioned as part of a collection.

The title *Plato* would normally be underlined or italicized. In the example below, however, the title is placed in quotation marks because it is cited as part of a larger work.

EXAMPLE   "Plato" from *Great Books of the Western World*

Using Underlining and Italics in Titles and Other Special Words

Underlining and **italics** help make titles and other special words and names stand out in your writing. Underlining is used only in handwritten or typewritten material. In printed material, italic (slanted) print is generally used instead of underlining.

RULE 11.4.17

> Underline or italicize the titles of long written works and the titles of publications that are published as a single work.

WRITTEN WORKS THAT ARE UNDERLINED OR ITALICIZED	
Title of a Book	*Great Expectations*
Title of a Newspaper	*The Chicago Tribune*
Title of a Play	*Les Misérables* *A Doll's House*
Title of a Long Poem	*To The Same*
Title of a Magazine	*Life*

The portion of a newspaper title that should be italicized or underlined will vary from newspaper to newspaper. *The New York Times* should always be fully capitalized and italicized or underlined. Other papers, however, can be treated in one of two ways: the *Los Angeles Times* or the Los Angeles *Times*. You may want to check the paper's Web site for correct formatting.

RULE 11.4.18

> Underline or italicize the titles of movies, television and radio series, long works of music, and works of art.

ARTISTIC WORKS THAT ARE UNDERLINED OR ITALICIZED	
Title of a Movie	*Grease, Breakfast at Tiffany's*
Title of a Television Series	*The Honeymooners* *The Addams Family*
Title of a Long Work of Music	*Paris in D Major*
Title of an Album (on any media)	*Born in the USA*
Title of a Painting	*Starry Night, Café Terrace*
Title of a Sculpture	*Apollo and Daphne* *Aphrodite of Cindus*

> **Do not underline, italicize, or place in quotation marks the name of the Bible, its books and divisions, or other holy scriptures, such as the Torah and the Qu'ran.**

11.4.19 RULE

EXAMPLE   Blair read from John in the New Testament .

Government documents should also not be underlined or enclosed in quotation marks.

> **Do not underline, italicize, or place in quotation marks the titles of government charters, alliances, treaties, acts, statutes, speeches, or reports.**

11.4.20 RULE

EXAMPLE   The Taft-Hartley Labor Act was passed in 1947.

> **Underline or italicize the names of air, sea, and space craft.**

11.4.21 RULE

EXAMPLE   Were there dogs aboard the *Titanic* ?

> **Underline or italicize words, letters, or numbers (figures) used as names for themselves.**

11.4.22 RULE

EXAMPLES   Her *i's* and her *I's* look too much like *1's* .

Avoid sprinkling your speech with *you know* .

> **Underline or italicize foreign words and phrases not yet accepted into English.**

11.4.23 RULE

See Practice 11.4C
See Practice 11.4D

EXAMPLE   "*Bonne chance* ," she said, meaning "good luck" in French.

PRACTICE 11.4C **Using Punctuation in Titles and Dialogue**

Read each sentence. Then, rewrite each sentence, adding correct punctuation where needed. If any words need to be italicized, underline those words.

EXAMPLE   I'd like to see the re-make of Hitchcock's Vertigo said Paul.

ANSWER   *"I'd like to see the re-make of Hitchcock's Vertigo," said Paul.*

1. The Venus de Milo is a famous statue.

2. The class is learning to sing the Star-Spangled Banner.

3. Stephen thought that he would go see An Inconvenient Truth at the movie theater.

4. My copy of Science Today was just delivered said Stephanie.

5. Laura is playing the part of Ophelia in our production of Hamlet.

6. Have you ever been aboard the USS Intrepid?

7. "Melanie complained, The assignment took me the whole weekend to complete."

8. Rich replied, Yeah, me, too."

9. I thought it was pretty interesting, said Miles.

10. Interesting but long, said Melanie.

PRACTICE 11.4D **Revising Punctuation in Titles and Dialogue**

Read each sentence. Then, rewrite the sentence, using correct punctuation. If any words need to be italicized, underline those words.

EXAMPLE   Sue will direct the play Waiting for Godot.

ANSWER   *Sue will direct the play Waiting for Godot.*

11. "The song Thin Fields" is based on an English famine.

12. Did Ming really say that his favorite play is The Iliad?

13. "I plan on seeing The Phantom of the Opera in June, said Tiffany."

14. Sarah asked, "Did Hemingway write the short story Out of Season?"

15. The Fantastic Voyage is tied to the dock.

16. My favorite Star Trek episode is titled The Trouble With Tribbles.

17. Meghan asked John, Are you prepared for the algebra test today?

18. "John replied, I studied all weekend."

19. Liam chimed in, "So did I, but I'm still not sure about word problems.

20. Meghan answered, I bet we all do fine."

SPEAKING APPLICATION

Take turns with a partner. Say sentences that contain both dialogue and titles. For each sentence, your partner should indicate which words would be put in quotation marks and/or italicized if the sentences were written.

WRITING APPLICATION

Write a dialogue between two friends discussing their favorite songs and movies. Be sure to use correct punctuation.

11.5 Hyphens

The **hyphen** (-) is used to combine words, spell some numbers and words, and show a connection between the syllables of words that are broken at the ends of lines.

Using Hyphens in Numbers

Hyphens are used to join compound numbers and fractions.

> **Use a hyphen when you spell out two-word numbers from twenty-one through ninety-nine.**

RULE 11.5.1

EXAMPLES   forty - four inches   fifty - seven yards

> **Use a hyphen when you use a fraction as an adjective but not when you use a fraction as a noun.**

RULE 11.5.2

ADJECTIVE   The recipe called for one - half cup of water.

NOUN   Three quarters of the report on India is complete.

> **Use a hyphen between a number and a word when they are combined as modifiers. Do not use a hyphen if the word in the modifier is possessive.**

RULE 11.5.3

EXAMPLES   The staff took a 30 - minute break after lunch.

The team put 16 weeks' worth of training in before the game.

> **If a series of consecutive, hyphenated modifiers ends with the same word, do not repeat the modified word each time. Instead, use a suspended hyphen (also called a dangling hyphen) and the modified word only at the end of the series.**

RULE 11.5.4

EXAMPLE   The sixth - and seventh - grade students came.

Using Hyphens With Prefixes and Suffixes

Hyphens help your reader easily see the parts of a long word.

RULE 11.5.5

Use a hyphen after a prefix that is followed by a proper noun or proper adjective.

The following prefixes are often used before proper nouns: *ante-*, *anti-*, *mid-*, *post-*, *pre-*, *pro-*, and *un-*.

EXAMPLES   pre - Civil War   mid - December

RULE 11.5.6

Use a hyphen in words with the prefixes *all-*, *ex-*, and *self-* and words with the suffix *-elect*.

EXAMPLES   all - knowing   governor - elect

Many words with common prefixes are no longer hyphenated. Check a dictionary if you are unsure whether to use a hyphen.

Using Hyphens With Compound Words

Hyphens help preserve the units of meaning in compound words.

RULE 11.5.7

Use a hyphen to connect two or more words that are used as one compound word, unless your dictionary gives a different spelling.

EXAMPLES   master - at - arms   follow - up

mother - in - law   two - year - old

RULE 11.5.8

Use a hyphen to connect a compound modifier that appears before a noun. The exceptions to this rule include adverbs ending in *-ly* and compound proper adjectives or compound proper nouns that are acting as an adjective.

EXAMPLES WITH HYPHENS	EXAMPLES WITHOUT HYPHENS
a well-made raincoat	widely distributed products
the bright-eyed class	socialized healthcare
an up-to-date list	the North American Continent

When compound modifiers follow a noun, they generally do not require the use of hyphens.

EXAMPLE   The trucks were **well made.**

However, if a dictionary spells a word with a hyphen, the word must always be hyphenated, even when it follows a noun.

EXAMPLE   The attendance list was up-to-date.

Using Hyphens for Clarity

Some words or group of words can be misread if a hyphen is not used.

> **Use a hyphen within a word when a combination of letters might otherwise be confusing.**

11.5.9 RULE

EXAMPLES   weak-kneed, well-being, well-to-do

> **Use a hyphen between words to keep readers from combining them incorrectly.**

11.5.10 RULE

See Practice 11.5A   INCORRECT   the air conditioning-unit

See Practice 11.5B   CORRECT   the air-conditioning unit

PRACTICE 11.5A > Using Hyphens Correctly

Read each sentence. Then, write the words that need hyphenation, adding hyphens where necessary.

EXAMPLE   My brother in law sold me his car.

ANSWER   *brother-in-law*

1. Rose just met her four year old cousin for the first time.

2. Mr. Klein is a well respected teacher at the high school.

3. Two thirds of the senior students plan on attending the last minute study session.

4. One of the coowners sold his share of the business.

5. George is still interested in board games even though he is thirty three years old.

6. I enjoyed the performance even though a reviewer deemed it second rate.

7. The cruise we took to New Zealand was all inclusive.

8. I will celebrate my twenty first birthday on December 17.

9. Manuel works two part time jobs to earn extra money.

10. The low end model of the radio is inexpensive but may not operate very long.

PRACTICE 11.5B > Revising Sentences With Hyphens

Read each sentence. Then, rewrite each sentence, correcting any error in hyphenation. If the punctuation is correct, write *correct*.

EXAMPLE   That political party has ultra conservative ideas.

ANSWER   *That political party has ultra-conservative ideas.*

11. The governor elect had close ties to the attorney-general.

12. My great great-grandfather was a blacksmith in his day.

13. I walked into the dimly-lit room hoping to find the light-switch.

14. The editor-in chief of the local newspaper is an Ivy League graduate.

15. The fact that he is selfeducated is a testament to his perseverance.

16. Max lost the race by only one-hundredth of a second.

17. Rhiannon told us that she aspires to be a singer song-writer.

18. It is a little known fact that Monique is an accomplished-piano player.

19. The computers in the school all have up-to date programs installed.

20. I didn't remember to add one half cup of milk to the batter.

SPEAKING APPLICATION

Take turns with a partner. Describe the place where you grew up. Include hyphenated words in your sentences. Your partner should listen for and identify the hyphenated words.

WRITING APPLICATION

Write a paragraph describing someone you admire. Use at least four hyphenated words not used in Practice 11.5B in your paragraph.

Using Hyphens at the Ends of Lines

Hyphens help you keep the lines in your paragraphs more even, making your work easier to read.

Dividing Words at the End of a Line
Although you should try to avoid dividing a word at the end of a line, if a word must be broken, use a hyphen to show the division.

> **If a word must be divided at the end of a line, always divide it between syllables.**

11.5.11 RULE

EXAMPLE   Kate got up early the last day of June, hop-

ing to see everything that had been planned.

> **A hyphen used to divide a word should never be placed at the beginning of the second line. It must be placed at the end of the first line.**

11.5.12 RULE

INCORRECT   The boat sailed around the island and col

-lected passengers at each stop.

CORRECT   The boat sailed around the island and col-

lected passengers at each stop.

Using Hyphens Correctly to Divide Words

One-syllable words cannot be divided.

> **Do not divide one-syllable words even if they seem long or sound like words with two syllables.**

11.5.13 RULE

INCORRECT   tre-at   mou-se   fe-nce

CORRECT   treat   mouse   fence

Do not divide a word so that a single letter or the letters -ed stand alone.

INCORRECT	a-larm	stud-y	a-loud	abandon-ed
CORRECT	alarm	study	aloud	abandoned

Avoid dividing proper nouns and proper adjectives.

INCORRECT	Fe-lix	Af-rican
CORRECT	Felix	African

Divide a hyphenated word only after the hyphen.

INCORRECT   We happily made plans to invite my moth-
er-in-law to see the children.

CORRECT   We happily made plans to invite my mother-in-
law to see the children.

Avoid dividing a word so that part of the word is on one page and the remainder is on the next page.

Often, chopping up a word in this way will confuse your readers
or cause them to lose their train of thought. If this happens,
rewrite the sentence or move the entire word to the next page.

See Practice 11.5C
See Practice 11.5D

PRACTICE 11.5C ▷ Using Hyphens to Divide Words

Read each word. If a word has been divided incorrectly, write the word, putting the hyphen in the correct place, or writing it as one word if it cannot be divided. If the word has been divided correctly, write *correct*.

EXAMPLE   dre-am

ANSWER   *dream*

1. African-American
2. ap-pear
3. a-bove
4. Ju-lia
5. em-pty-handed
6. sev-enteen
7. cor-rectly
8. guilt-y
9. Ital-ian
10. blue-berry

PRACTICE 11.5D ▷ Correcting Divided Words at the End of Lines

Read each sentence. Then, for each sentence, rewrite the incorrectly divided word, putting the hyphen in the correct place, or writing it as one word if it cannot be divided.

EXAMPLE   A peacock has brighter-colored feat-hers than a peahen.

ANSWER   *fea-thers*

11. The new student in chemistry class answer-ed almost all the questions correctly.
12. Mr. Walters wants the exhibit to be a se-cret until the unveiling.
13. Collecting all the mail once a day is a timesa-ving procedure.
14. Drama, music, band, and other extracurr-icular activities are educational programs.
15. Mike can't leave until his older brother Jer-ry comes home.
16. Giorgio bought his grandmother a knitt-ed shawl.
17. The night was so hot, but the air-condit-ioned room was comfortable.
18. I can see spring flowers—tulips and daff-odils—poking up through the soil.
19. "During our next summer vacation," said Tim-othy, "I'll be working at the town pool."
20. Jenny spent her summer at a camp far a-way from the city.

SPEAKING APPLICATION

Take turns with a partner. Say five words not used in Practice 11.5C. Your partner should tell where each word can be divided.

WRITING APPLICATION

Write a paragraph about the importance of eating healthy foods. Be sure to include divided words at the ends of lines.

11.6 Apostrophes

The **apostrophe (')** is used to form possessives, contractions, and a few special plurals.

Using Apostrophes to Form Possessive Nouns

Apostrophes are used with nouns to show ownership or possession.

RULE 11.6.1

> **Add an apostrophe and -*s* to show the possessive case of most singular nouns.**

EXAMPLES

the shoes of the girl   the girl**'**s shoes

the leash of the dog   the dog**'**s leash

Even when a singular noun already ends in -*s,* you can usually add an apostrophe and -*s* to show possession. However, names that end in the *eez* sound get an apostrophe, but not an -*s.*

EXAMPLE   The Ganges**'** source is in the Himalayas.

For classical references that end in -*s,* only an apostrophe is used.

EXAMPLES   Confucius**'** writings   Zeus**'** crown

RULE 11.6.2

> **Add an apostrophe to show the possessive case of plural nouns ending in -*s* or -*es.***

EXAMPLE   the branches of the trees   the trees**'** branches

RULE 11.6.3

> **Add an apostrophe and an -*s* to show the possessive case of plural nouns that do not end in -*s* or -*es.***

EXAMPLE   the toys of the children

the children's toys

Add an apostrophe and -s (or just an apostrophe if the word is a plural ending in -s) to the last word of a compound noun to form the possessive.

RULE 11.6.4

APOSTROPHES THAT SHOW POSSESSION	
Names of Businesses and Organizations	the Salvation Army's office the National Park's watch tower the Richardson & Associates' client list
Titles of Rulers or Leaders	Catherine the Great's victories Louis XVI's palace the head of the board's decision
Hyphenated Compound Nouns Used to Describe People	my mother-in-law's recipe the secretary-treasurer's planner the nurse-practitioner's files

---

To form possessives involving time, amounts, or the word *sake*, use an apostrophe and an -s or just an apostrophe if the possessive is plural.

RULE 11.6.5

APOSTROPHES WITH POSSESSIVES	
Time	a week's vacation three months' vacation an hour's drive
Amount	one dollar's worth twenty-five cents' worth
Sake	for Rebekah's sake for goodness' sake

**To show joint ownership, make the final noun possessive.
To show individual ownership, make each noun possessive.**

JOINT
OWNERSHIP   I enjoyed Bill and Deb᾽s documentary.

INDIVIDUAL
OWNERSHIP   Mike᾽s and Alan᾽s dry cleaning is hanging here.

Use the owner's complete name before the apostrophe to form the
possessive case.

INCORRECT
SINGULAR   Jame᾽s car

CORRECT
SINGULAR   James᾽s car

INCORRECT
PLURAL   four girl᾽s bags

CORRECT
PLURAL   four girls᾽ bags

Using Apostrophes With Pronouns

Both indefinite and personal pronouns can show possession.

**Use an apostrophe and -s with indefinite pronouns to show
possession.**

EXAMPLES   somebody᾽s dress shoes

                  each other᾽s study guides

**Do not use an apostrophe with possessive personal pronouns;
their form already shows ownership.**

EXAMPLES   his cards   our boat   his black convertible

             its mirrors   their yard   whose coat

Be careful not to confuse the contractions *who's*, *it's*, and *they're* with possessive pronouns. They are contractions for *who is*, *it is* or *it has*, and *they are*. Remember also that *whose*, *its*, and *their* show possession.

PRONOUNS	CONTRACTIONS
Whose homework is this?	*Who's* driving home tonight?
Its tires were all flat.	*It's* going to be sunny.
Their dinner is ready.	*They're* going to the movies.

Using Apostrophes to Form Contractions

Contractions are used in informal speech and writing. You can often find contractions in the dialogue of stories and plays; they often create the sound of real speech.

> Use an apostrophe in a **contraction** to show the position of the missing letter or letters.

COMMON CONTRACTIONS			
Verb + *not*	cannot could not	can't couldn't	are not will not	aren't won't
Pronoun + *will*	he will you will she will	he'll you'll she'll	I will we will they will	I'll we'll they'll
Pronoun + *would*	she would he would you would	she'd he'd you'd	I would we would they would	I'd we'd they'd
Noun or Pronoun + *be*	you are she is they are	you're she's they're	I am Jane is dog is	I'm Jane's dog's

Still another type of contraction is found in poetry.

EXAMPLES   e'en *(even)*   o'er *(over)*

Other contractions represent the abbreviated form of *of the* and *the* as they are written in several different languages. These letters are most often combined with surnames.

EXAMPLES   O'Neil

d'Armiento

o'clock

l'Abbé

Using Contractions to Represent Speaking Styles
A final use of contractions is for representing individual speaking styles in dialogue. As noted previously, you will often want to use contractions with verbs in dialogue. You may also want to approximate a regional dialect or a foreign accent, which may include nonstandard pronunciations of words or omitted letters. However, you should avoid overusing contractions in dialogue. Overuse reduces the effectiveness of the apostrophe.

EXAMPLES   "Hey, ol' buddy. How you feelin'?"

"Don' you be foolin' me."

Using Apostrophes to Create Special Plurals

Apostrophes can help avoid confusion with special plurals.

> Use an apostrophe and **-s** to create the plural form of a letter, numeral, symbol, or a word that is used as a name for itself.

EXAMPLES   *A*'s and *an*'s cause confusion.

There are four *4*'s in that number.

I don't like to hear *if*'s or *maybe*'s.

Form groups of *4*'s or *5*'s.

I need four more *?*'s

See Practice 11.6A
See Practice 11.6B

PRACTICE 11.6A Identifying the Use of Apostrophes

Read each sentence. Then, tell if each apostrophe is used to form a *possessive,* a *contraction,* or a *special plural.*

EXAMPLE   Who's in charge of the fundraiser at school next week?

ANSWER   *contraction*

1. Ben and Sara's dog, Max, is a miniature poodle.
2. Steven received 3 *A*'s and 2 *B*'s on his report card.
3. The Williamses' sailboat is docked at the Center Point marina.
4. Katrina's backpack can't hold many books.
5. Matt's comic book is the latest issue.
6. That New York ZIP Code has three *1*'s.
7. The cat's hiding under my bed.
8. Somebody's computer was left on overnight.
9. I can't believe it's Friday already.
10. When you revise your paper, try to take out any unnecessary *and*'s.

PRACTICE 11.6B Revising to Add Apostrophes

Read each sentence. Then, rewrite each sentence, adding apostrophes where they are needed.

EXAMPLE   Garret received all *As* on his reports and research papers.

ANSWER   *Garret received all A's on his reports and research papers.*

11. The way Rob writes his *ps* and *qs* is very similar.
12. That sweater is someone elses, not mine.
13. When you revise your paper, try to delete some of the *thats*.
14. I went to Erics house after school yesterday.
15. Didnt Candace tell Ms. Oconnor that shed be back by eight oclock?
16. Sometimes, Max mixes up his *6s* and his *9s*.
17. I think *Zs* are the most difficult letter to write in cursive.
18. Our new neighbors pool is bigger than ours.
19. Its a beautiful day in Houston, Texas.
20. The childs outside, playing with her older siblings.

SPEAKING APPLICATION

Take turns with a partner. Say different sentences with words that indicate possession, contractions, and special plurals. Your partner should tell how each word uses an apostrophe.

WRITING APPLICATION

Write five sentences with words that require apostrophes. The words should show possession, contractions, and special plurals.

11.7 Parentheses and Brackets

Parentheses enclose explanations or other information that may be omitted from the rest of the sentence without changing its basic meaning or construction. Using parentheses is a stronger, more noticeable way to set off a parenthetical expression than using commas. **Brackets** are used to enclose a word or phrase added by a writer to the words of another.

Parentheses

Parentheses help you group material within a sentence.

RULE 11.7.1

Use parentheses to set off information when the material is not essential or when it consists of one or more sentences.

EXAMPLE   End-of-the-month reports **(** on economics and trade **)** showed much improvement over last month.

RULE 11.7.2

Use parentheses to set off numerical explanations such as dates of a person's birth and death and around numbers and letters marking a series.

EXAMPLES   Jill Collins invented many types of pie with the help of her husband, Rick **(** 1946–2008 **)**.

Go home and pack these items: **(** 1 **)** toothbrush, **(** 2 **)** pajamas, **(** 3 **)** sneakers.

Which is your favorite team: **(** a **)** Yankees, **(** b **)** Red Sox, or **(** c **)** Phillies?

Although material enclosed in parentheses is not essential to the meaning of the sentence, a writer indicates that the material is important and calls attention to it by using parentheses.

When a phrase or declarative sentence interrupts another sentence, do not use an initial capital letter or end mark inside the parentheses.

RULE 11.7.3

EXAMPLE   Daryl finally completed his trip (the one we all planned together) and came home last night.

When a question or exclamation interrupts another sentence, use both an initial capital letter and an end mark inside the parentheses.

RULE 11.7.4

EXAMPLE   Lucy (She is one funny lady!) continues to entertain us.

When you place a sentence in parentheses between two other sentences, use both an initial capital letter and an end mark inside the parentheses.

RULE 11.7.5

EXAMPLE   America's parks are known to be breath-taking. (See the Grand Canyon as an example.) Excesses of nature are staggering to see.

In a sentence that includes parentheses, place any punctuation belonging to the main sentence after the final parenthesis.

RULE 11.7.6

EXAMPLE   The town council approved the library (after some deliberations), and they explained the new lending laws to the citizens (with some doubts about how the changes would be received).

Special Uses of Parentheses

Parentheses are also used to set off numerical explanations such as dates of a person's birth and death and numbers or letters marking a series.

EXAMPLES   Charles Dickens (1812-1870) was a popular English novelist.

Betty's phone number is (313) 515-8299.

Her group tour will take her to (1) Brazil, (2) Columbia, and (3) Argentina.

Brackets

Brackets are used to enclose a word or phrase added by a writer to the words of another writer.

> Use brackets to enclose words you insert in quotations when quoting someone else.

RULE 11.7.7

EXAMPLES   Cooper noted: "And with [E.T.'s] success, 'Phone home' is certain to become one of the most often repeated phrases of the year [1982]."

"The results of this vote [24–6] indicate overwhelming support for our building plan," she stated.

The Latin expression *sic* (meaning "thus") is sometimes enclosed in brackets to show that the author of the quoted material has misspelled or mispronounced a word or phrase.

EXAMPLE   Michaelson, citing Dorothy's signature line from *The Wizard of Oz,* wrote, "Theirs [sic] no place like home."

See Practice 11.7A
See Practice 11.7B

PRACTICE 11.7A Using Parentheses and Brackets Correctly

Read each item. Then, write a sentence in which you enclose the item in either parentheses or brackets.

EXAMPLE   around 5 o'clock

ANSWER   *We will arrive at the reception a little late (around 5 o'clock).*

1. everyone could tell

2. I can't wait!

3. at Tillman Middle School

4. known as "Hotshot" to his teammates

5. Did you know?

6. 4:00 P.M. to 6:00 P.M.

7. the former state champion

8. the one in the red dress

9. sic

10. my least favorite flavor

PRACTICE 11.7B Revising to Add Parentheses or Brackets

Read each sentence. Then, add parentheses or brackets wherever they are appropriate.

EXAMPLE   The article stated, "Mr. Jones the superintendent is up for re-election."

ANSWER   *The article stated, "Mr. Jones [the superintendent] is up for re-election."*

11. My dog Jasper is a cocker spaniel.

12. The results of the vote 145–98 indicate that Jim will be the student-council president.

13. We my sister and I are donating canned goods to a soup kitchen.

14. Once I finally fell asleep sometime around 10:00 P.M., I had very vivid dreams.

15. This museum displays artifacts from an ancient civilization Mesopotamia.

16. They our high school lacrosse team are the best team in the state.

17. Could you help me dry the dishes, please?

18. The proverb states, "Luv sic is a puppy!"

19. Lucy and Alijah They're nice girls, aren't they? are the captains of the soccer team.

20. The article said, "He the president has left to pursue other opportunities."

SPEAKING APPLICATION

Take turns with a partner. Say three phrases. Your partner should put the phrases into sentences, indicating if the phrases would be appropriate in parentheses or brackets.

WRITING APPLICATION

Write three sentences about events in world history. Your sentences should correctly use either parentheses or brackets.

11.8 Ellipses, Dashes, and Slashes

An **ellipsis** (. . .) shows where words have been omitted from a quoted passage. It can also mark a pause or interruption in dialogue. A **dash** (—) shows a strong, sudden break in thought or speech. A **slash** (/) separates numbers in dates and fractions, shows line breaks in quoted poetry, and represents *or*. A slash is also used to separate the parts of a Web address.

Using the Ellipsis

An **ellipsis** is three evenly spaced periods, or ellipsis points, in a row. Always include a space before the first ellipsis point, between ellipsis points, and after the last ellipsis point. (The plural of *ellipsis* is *ellipses*.)

RULE 11.8.1

Use an **ellipsis** to show where words have been omitted from a quoted passage.

ELLIPSES IN QUOTATIONS	
The Entire Quotation	"The Black River, which cuts a winding course through southern Missouri's rugged Ozark highlands, lends its name to an area of great natural beauty. Within this expanse are old mines and quarries to explore, fast-running waters to canoe, and wooded trails to ride."—Suzanne Charle
At the Beginning	Suzanne Charle described the Black River area in Missouri as having " . . . old mines and quarries to explore, fast-running waters to canoe, and wooded trails to ride."
In the Middle	Suzanne Charle wrote, "The Black River . . . lends its name to an area of great natural beauty. Within this expanse are old mines and quarries to explore, fast-running waters to canoe, and wooded trails to ride."
At the End	Suzanne Charle wrote, "The Black River, which cuts a winding course through southern Missouri's rugged Ozark highlands, lends its name to an area of great natural beauty . . . "

> **Use an ellipsis to mark a pause in a dialogue or speech.**

11.8.2 RULE

EXAMPLE   The coach shouted, "On your mark ... get set ... go!"

Dashes

A **dash** signals a stronger, more sudden interruption in thought or speech than commas or parentheses. A dash may also take the place of certain words before an explanation. Overuse of the dash diminishes its effectiveness. Consider the proper use of the dash in the rule below.

> **Use dashes to indicate an abrupt change of thought, a dramatic interrupting idea, or a summary statement.**

11.8.3 RULE

USING DASHES IN WRITING	
To indicate an abrupt change of thought	The magazine doesn't provide enough information on Italian cooking—by the way, where did you get the magazine?
	I cannot believe how many e-mails my mother hasn't answered—I need to talk to her about that.
To set off interrupting ideas dramatically	The school was built—you may find this hard to believe—in six months.
	The school was built—Where did they get the money and workers?—in six months.
To set off a summary statement	A solid sports background and strong writing skills—if you have these, you may be able to get a job as a sports reporter.
	To see his picture on the stage with the band—this was his dream.

Use dashes to set off a nonessential appositive or modifier when it is long, when it is already punctuated, or when you want to be dramatic.

APPOSITIVE   The cause of the damage to the bathroom tiles and the cabinets—a rare black mold—went undiscovered for months.

MODIFIER   The celebrity gossip columnist—bored with writing about spoiled movie stars—quit after the awards.

Dashes may be used to set off one other special type of sentence interrupter—the parenthetical expression.

Use dashes to set off a parenthetical expression when it is long, already punctuated, or especially dramatic.

EXAMPLE   Today, we visited a theater—what an entertaining place—in a small town.

Slashes

A **slash** is used to separate numbers in dates and fractions, lines of quoted poetry, or options. Slashes are also used to separate parts of a Web address.

Use slashes to separate the day, month, and year in dates and to separate the numerator and denominator in numerical fractions.

DATES   He listed his deployment date as 10/30/08.

My sister's first day of college was 9/2/09.

FRACTIONS   5/7   3/4   1/3

Use slashes to indicate line breaks in up to three lines of quoted poetry in continuous text. Insert a space on each side of the slash.

EXAMPLE   I used a quote from William Blake, "Tyger! Tyger! burning bright. **/** In the forests if the night," to begin my paper.

Use slashes to separate choices or options and to represent the words *and* and *or.*

EXAMPLES   Choose your bun: sesame **/** seedless **/** rye.

Each hiker should bring a water bottle and gloves **/** rope.

You can e-mail and **/** or mail the last page of the article.

Use slashes to separate parts of a Web address.

EXAMPLES   http: **//** www.fafsa.ed.gov **/**
(for financial aid for students)

http: **//** www.whitehouse.gov **/**
(the White House)

See Practice 11.8A
See Practice 11.8B

http: **//** www.si.edu **/**
(the Smithsonian Institution)

PRACTICE 11.8A Using Ellipses, Dashes, and Slashes Correctly

Read each sentence or phrase. Then, rewrite each sentence, adding dashes, ellipses, or slashes where appropriate.

EXAMPLE   I can't answer right now could you come back later?

ANSWER   *I can't answer right now—could you come back later?*

1. The home Web address for NASA is http: www.nasa.gov.

2. When I visit my grandmother who lives in Hawaii I spend a lot of time at the beach.

3. "Do you think I could uh join you?" he asked hesitantly.

4. The committee elected Eugene to be the next chairperson actually, it was a unanimous decision.

5. "Once upon a time"

6. Mr. Ramirez is the president owner of the company.

7. Italian food chicken parmesan, meatballs, and pasta is my favorite cuisine.

8. Candidates must possess a degree in French and or have worked in a French-speaking country.

9. The meteor it's shooting across the sky!

10. The glass is 34 full of milk.

PRACTICE 11.8B Revising Sentences With Ellipses, Dashes, and Slashes

Read each sentence. Then, use ellipses, dashes, or slashes to add or delete the information in parentheses to or from each sentence.

EXAMPLE   The leader is Marie. (Add *captain.*)

ANSWER   *The leader/captain is Marie.*

11. A colorful rainbow arched across the sky. (Add *and I do mean colorful.*)

12. "The team performed well and succeeded." (Delete *performed well and.*)

13. My sister is always there for me. (Add *my best friend.*)

14. Each student must have his permission slip signed by a parent. (Add *note.*)

15. I hope I get Professor Alexander next semester. (Add *the English professor.*)

16. "Despite the cold weather and the rain, the trip was a success." (Delete *and the rain.*)

17. The soccer team had the most people try out. (Add *the most popular sports team.*)

18. The show was a success. (add *it exceeded everyone's expectations.*)

19. The room will be painted blue and tan. (Add *or.*)

20. My cousin who lives in Tampa picked me up from the airport. (Delete *who lives in Tampa.*)

SPEAKING APPLICATION

Take turns with a partner. Say different sentences that, if written, would contain dashes, ellipses, or slashes. Your partner should tell which punctuation is appropriate in each sentence.

WRITING APPLICATION

Write five sentences. Alter each sentence by using dashes or slashes to add information.

PRACTICE 1 ▶ **Using Periods, Question Marks, and Exclamation Marks**

Read each sentence. Rewrite each sentence, adding question marks, periods, and exclamation marks where needed.

1. Oh, no I was supposed to be there by now
2. He didn't come home on time last night Why
3. Put your books away, and take out your pens
4. She wondered if tomorrow would be warmer
5. How coincidental it is that we should happen upon one another like this
6. That was such a dynamic interview
7. She eagerly anticipated the next performance
8. Martin Luther King Jr. was a very well-spoken individual
9. Did you have to take the earlier appointment
10. Pay attention to the instructions

PRACTICE 2 ▶ **Using Commas Correctly**

Read each sentence. Rewrite each sentence, adding commas where needed. If a sentence is correct as is, write *correct*.

1. Isaac said "I thought you attended that conference in April 2008."
2. "Katrina do you think you could loan me your dress for the dance?" Erica asked.
3. Expecting a crowd Sam arrived early.
4. The menu had appetizers salads entrees and desserts printed in an elegant font.
5. "Her birthday is May 2 1991" Kristen said.
6. Mike and Matt always got the best concert tickets because they waited in line for hours.
7. I usually bring my lunch to work but today I am going out to eat.

8. This dessert is a scrumptious, delicious end to a perfect meal.
9. "The store is over on Girard Avenue," Paul said. "The address is 616 Girard Avenue Plainville Kansas."
10. I wanted the red blouse not the green one.

PRACTICE 3 ▶ **Using Colons, Semicolons, and Quotation Marks**

Read each sentence. Rewrite each sentence, using colons, semicolons, and quotation marks where needed. If a sentence is correct as is, write *correct*.

1. Warning Dangerous curves ahead.
2. Samantha wrote her book review on *To Kill a Mockingbird* she thought the characters were well developed.
3. John said, We did a lot on our camping trip last summer swimming, fishing, hiking, and boating.
4. I usually try to get to bed by 1000 every night the alarm buzzing at 700 comes all too soon.
5. Melissa told us where the best gourmet restaurants were.
6. They each chose a topic for their science projects Fred volcanic activity Lyla erosion and Tim photosynthesis.
7. Mallory didn't want to be bothered with any more work however, she volunteered to help the team brainstorm new ideas.
8. The teacher read us O Captain! My Captain, by Walt Whitman it is a poem about Lincoln.
9. Resolved The cafeteria will no longer serve soft drinks.
10. Gus brought a list of his favorite foods hamburgers, fries, salad, and cookies.

Continued on next page ▶

Cumulative Review Chapters 10–11

 PRACTICE 4 ▷ **Using Apostrophes**

Read each sentence. Rewrite each sentence, using apostrophes where needed. If a sentence is correct as is, write *correct*.

1. I wouldnt bother Mom right now; shes busy.
2. Whos organizing this years fundraiser?
3. My brother-in-laws car is brand new.
4. Mr. Joness study had towers of books.
5. Henry brought two hundred dollars worth of supplies for the homecoming party.
6. Zeus thunderbolt is a symbol of his immense power over the other Greek gods.
7. Sabrina's project was better than theirs.
8. I dont know the answer to this problem; its too complicated.
9. Taras car needs work and is in the shop.
10. At 6 oclock, my family sits down to dinner.

PRACTICE 5 ▷ **Using Underlining (or Italics), Hyphens, Dashes, Slashes, Parentheses, Brackets, and Ellipses**

Read each sentence. Rewrite each sentence, adding underlining (or italics), hyphens, dashes, slashes, brackets, parentheses, or ellipses. If a sentence is correct as is, write *correct*.

1. My brother and I often disagree about whether Star Wars is a better film than The Empire Strikes Back.
2. Simon he sits behind me in math always seems to know the answer.
3. My grandmother a well known essayist and poet is celebrating her ninety fifth birthday next week.

4. Tommy's dad he works for an advertising agency came to school on Career Day.
5. The USS Constitution a giant ship in the U.S. Navy was nicknamed Old Ironsides.
6. Before proceeding with the lecture, the professor gave the students a five minute break.
7. In his speech, the congressman said, "They taxes will not be raised during my term."
8. The play was set during the presidential term of Theodore Roosevelt 1901–1909.
9. The Gettysburg Address states that this nation ". . . is dedicated to the proposition that all men are created equal."
10. His baby sister was born on 12 22 2005.

PRACTICE 6 ▷ **Using Capital Letters Correctly**

Read each sentence. Rewrite each sentence, using capital letters where they are needed.

1. mr. and mrs. o'callahan took a trip to dublin.
2. charles dickens, an english writer, wrote many works, including a christmas carol.
3. "i haven't been to the new american museum of art downtown yet," david said. "is it on main street or center street?"
4. the academy award for best picture went to a film that many people had not seen.
5. tina said, "today, i learned the names of many constellations, like aries and aquarius."

Modes
of Writing

Writing is a process that begins with the exploration of ideas and ends with the presentation of a final piece of writing. Often, the types of writing we do are grouped into modes according to their form and purpose.

Narration

Whenever writers tell any type of story, they are using narration. Most narratives share certain elements, such as characters, a setting, a sequence of events, and, often, a theme. The following are some types of narration:

- **Autobiographical Writing** Autobiographical writing tells a true story about an important period, experience, or relationship in the writer's life.

Effective autobiographical writing includes:
- *A series of events that involve the writer as the main character*
- *Details, thoughts, feelings, and insights from the writer's perspective*
- *A conflict or an event that affects the writer*
- *A logical organization that tells the story clearly*

Types of autobiographical writing include personal narratives, autobiographical sketches, reflective essays, eyewitness accounts, and memoirs.

- **Short Story** A short story is a brief, creative narrative.

Most short stories contain:
- *Details that establish the setting in time and place*
- *A main character who undergoes a change or learns something during the course of the story*
- *A conflict or a problem to be introduced, developed, and resolved*
- *A plot—the series of events that make up the action of the story*
- *A theme or message about life*

Types of short stories include realistic stories, fantasies, historical narratives, mysteries, thrillers, science fiction, and adventure stories.

Description

Descriptive writing is writing that creates a vivid picture of a person, place, thing, or event.

Most descriptive writing includes:

- *Sensory details—sights, sounds, smells, tastes, and physical sensations*
- *Vivid, precise language*
- *Figurative language or comparisons*
- *Adjectives and adverbs that help to paint a word picture*
- *An organization suited to the subject*

Types of descriptive writing include description of ideas, observations, travel brochures, physical descriptions, functional descriptions, remembrances, and character sketches.

Persuasion

Persuasion is writing or speaking that attempts to convince people to accept a position or take a desired action. The following are some types of persuasion:

● **Persuasive Essay**

A persuasive essay presents a position on an issue, urges readers to accept that position, and may encourage a specific action.

An effective persuasive essay:

- *Explores an issue of importance to the writer*
- *Addresses an arguable issue*
- *Is supported by facts, examples, statistics, or personal experiences*
- *Tries to influence the audience through appeals to the readers' knowledge, experiences, or emotions*
- *Uses clear organization to present a logical argument*

Forms of persuasion include editorials, position papers, persuasive speeches, grant proposals, advertisements, and debates.

● **Advertisements**

An advertisement is a planned communication that is meant to be seen, heard, or read. It attempts to persuade an audience to buy or use a product or service. Advertisements may appear in print or broadcast form.

An effective advertisement includes:

- *A concept, or central theme*
- *A device, such as a memorable slogan, that catches people's attention*
- *Language that conveys a certain view of a product or issue*

Common types of advertisements include public service announcements, billboards, merchandise ads, service ads, and public campaign literature.

Exposition

Exposition is writing that relies on facts to inform or explain. Effective expository writing reflects an organization that is well planned—one that includes a clear introduction, body, and conclusion. The following are some types of exposition:

● **Comparison-and-Contrast Essay**
A comparison-and-contrast essay analyzes similarities and differences between or among two or more things.

An effective comparison-and-contrast essay:
- *Identifies a purpose for comparing and contrasting*
- *Identifies similarities and differences between or among two or more things, people, places, or ideas*
- *Gives factual details about the subjects*
- *Uses an organizational plan suited to the topic and purpose*

● **Cause-and-Effect Essay** A cause-and-effect essay examines the relationship between events, explaining how one event or situation causes another.

A successful cause-and-effect essay includes:
- *A discussion of a cause, event, or condition that produces a specific result*
- *An explanation of an effect or result*
- *Evidence and examples to support the relationship between cause and effect*
- *A logical organization that makes the relationship between events clear*

● **Problem-and-Solution Essay** A problem-and-solution essay describes a problem and offers one or more solutions. It describes a clear set of steps to achieve a result.

An effective problem-and-solution essay includes:
- *A clear statement of the problem, with its causes and effects summarized*
- *A proposal of at least one realistic solution*
- *Facts, statistics, data, or expert testimony to support the solution*
- *A clear organization that makes the relationship between problem and solution obvious*

Research Writing

Research writing is based on information gathered from outside sources.

An effective research paper:
- *Focuses on a specific, narrow topic*
- *Presents relevant information from a variety of sources*
- *Is clearly organized and includes an introduction, body, and conclusion*
- *Includes a bibliography or works-cited list*

In addition to traditional research reports, types of research writing include statistical reports and experiment journals.

Response to Literature

When you write a response to literature, you can discover how a piece of writing affected you.

An effective response:
- *Reacts to a work of literature*
- *Analyzes the content of a literary work*
- *Focuses on a single aspect or gives a general overview*
- *Supports opinion with evidence from the text*

You might respond to a literary work in reader's response journals, literary letters, and literary analyses.

Writing for Assessment

Essays are commonly part of school tests.

An effective essay includes:
- *A clearly stated and well-supported thesis*
- *Specific information about the topic derived from your reading or from class discussion*
- *A clear organization with an introduction, body, and conclusion*

In addition to writing essays for tests, you might write essays to apply to schools or special programs, or to enter a contest.

Workplace Writing

Workplace writing communicates information in a structured format.

Effective workplace writing:
- *Communicates information concisely*
- *Includes details that provide necessary information and anticipate potential questions*

Common types of workplace writing include business letters, memorandums, résumés, forms, and applications.

Writing Effective
Paragraphs

A paragraph is a group of sentences that share a common topic or purpose. Most paragraphs have a main idea or thought.

Stating the Main Idea in a Topic Sentence

The main idea of a paragraph is directly stated in a single sentence called the topic sentence. The rest of the sentences in the paragraph support or explain the topic sentence, providing support through facts and details.

Sometimes the main idea of a paragraph is implied rather than stated. The sentences work together to present the details and facts that allow the reader to infer the main idea.

WRITING MODELS

from ***The Secret Language of Snow***
Terry Tempest Williams and Ted Major

Many types of animal behavior are designed to reduce heat loss. Birds fluff their feathers, enlarging the "dead air" space around their bodies. Quails roost in compact circles, in the same manner as musk oxen, to keep warmth in and cold out. Grouse and ptarmigan dive into the snow, using it as an insulating blanket.

> In this passage, the stated topic sentence is highlighted.

from **"The Old Demon"**
Pearl S. Buck

The baker's shop, like everything else, was in ruins. No one was there. At first she saw nothing but the mass of crumpled earthen walls. But then she remembered that the oven was just inside the door, and the door frame still stood erect, supporting one end of the roof. She stood in this frame, and, running her hands in underneath the fallen roof inside, she felt the wooden cover of the iron cauldron. Under this there might be steamed bread. She worked her arm delicately and carefully in. It took quite a long time, but even so, clouds of lime and dust almost choked her. Nevertheless she was right. She squeezed her hand under the cover and felt the first smooth skin of the big steamed bread rolls, and one by one she drew out four.

> In this passage, all the sentences work together to illustrate the implied main idea of the paragraph: The woman searches persistently until she finds food.

Writing a Topic Sentence

When you outline a topic or plan an essay, you identify the main points you want to address. Each of these points can be written as a topic sentence—a statement of the main idea of a topical paragraph. You can organize your paragraph around the topic sentence.

A good topic sentence tells readers what the paragraph is about and the point the writer wants to make about the subject matter. Here are some tips for writing a strong topic sentence.

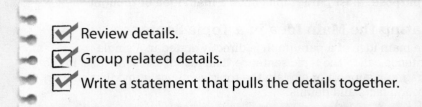

☑ Review details.

☑ Group related details.

☑ Write a statement that pulls the details together.

Writing Supporting Sentences

Whether your topic sentence is stated or implied, it guides the rest of the paragraph. The rest of the sentences in the paragraph will either develop, explain, or support that topic sentence.

You can support or develop the idea by using one or more of the following strategies:

Use Facts

Facts are statements that can be proved. They support your key idea by providing proof.

- **Topic Sentence:** Our football team is tough to beat.
- **Supporting Fact:** It wins almost all of its games.

Use Statistics

A statistic is a fact, usually stated using numbers.

- **Topic Sentence:** Our football team is tough to beat.
- **Supporting Statistic:** The football team's record is 10–1.

Use Examples, Illustrations, or Instances

An example, illustration, or instance is a specific thing, person, or event that demonstrates a point.

- **Topic Sentence:** Our football team is tough to beat.
- **Illustration:** Last week, the team beat the previously undefeated Tigers in an exciting upset game.

Use Details

Details are the specifics—the parts of the whole. They make your point or main idea clear by showing how all the pieces fit together.

- **Topic Sentence:** Our footbal team is tough to beat.
- **Detail:** There were only seconds left in last week's game, when the quarterback threw the winning pass.

Placing Your Topic Sentence

Frequently, the topic sentence appears at the beginning of a paragraph. Topic sentences can, however, be placed at the beginning, middle, or end of the paragraph. Place your topic sentence at the beginning of a paragraph to focus readers' attention. Place your topic sentence in the middle of a paragraph when you must lead into your main idea. Place your topic sentence at the end of a paragraph to emphasize your main idea.

Paragraph Patterns

Sentences in a paragraph can be arranged in several different patterns, depending on where you place your topic sentence. One common pattern is the TRI pattern (Topic, Restatement, Illustration).

- **T**opic sentence (State your main idea.)
- **R**estatement (Interpret your main idea; use different wording.)
- **I**llustration (Support your main idea with facts and examples.)

T	
R	Participating in after-school clubs is one of the ways you can meet new people. Getting involved in extracurricular activities brings you in contact with a wide range of individuals. The drama club, for example, brings together
I	students from several different grades.

Variations on the TRI pattern include sentence arrangements such as TIR, TII, IIT, or ITR.

I	
I	This month alone the service club at our high school delivered meals to thirty shut-ins. In addition, members beautified the neighborhood with new plantings. If any school-sponsored club deserves increased support, the
T	service club does.

Paragraphs
in Essays
and Other Compositions

To compose means "to put the parts together, to create." Most often, composing refers to the creation of a musical or literary work—a composition. You may not think of the reports, essays, and test answers you write as literary works, but they are compositions. To write an effective composition, you must understand the parts.

The Introduction

The introduction does what its name suggests. It introduces the topic of the composition. An effective introduction begins with a strong lead, a first sentence that captures readers' interest. The lead is followed by the thesis statement, the key point of the composition. Usually, the thesis statement is followed by a few sentences that outline how the writer will make the key point.

The Body

The body of a composition consists of several paragraphs that develop, explain, and support the key idea expressed in the thesis statement. The body of a composition should be unified and coherent. The paragraphs in a composition should work together to support the thesis statement. The topic of each paragraph should relate directly to the thesis statement and be arranged in a logical organization.

The Conclusion

The conclusion is the final paragraph of the composition. The conclusion restates the thesis and sums up the support. Often, the conclusion includes the writer's reflection or observation on the topic. An effective conclusion ends on a memorable note, for example, with a quotation or call to action.

Recognizing Types of Paragraphs

There are several types of paragraphs you can use in your writing.

Topical Paragraphs

A topical paragraph is a group of sentences that contain one key sentence or idea and several sentences that support or develop that key idea or topic sentence.

Functional Paragraphs

Functional paragraphs serve a specific purpose. They may not have a topic sentence, but they are unified and coherent because the sentences (if there is more than one) are clearly connected and follow a logical order. Functional paragraphs can be used for the following purposes:

- **To create emphasis** A very short paragraph of one or two sentences focuses the reader on what is being said because it breaks the reader's rhythm.

- **To indicate dialogue** One of the conventions of written dialogue is that a new paragraph begins each time the speaker changes.

- **To make a transition** A short paragraph can help readers move between the main ideas in two topical paragraphs.

WRITING MODEL

from **"The Hatchling Turtles"**

by Jean Craighead George

One morning each small turtle fought for freedom within its shell.

They hatched two feet down in the sand, all of them on the same day. As they broke out, their shells collapsed, leaving a small room of air for them to breathe. It wasn't much of a room, just big enough for them to wiggle in and move toward the sky. As they wiggled they pulled the sand down from the ceiling and crawled up on it. In this manner the buried room began to rise, slowly, inch by inch.

The highlighted functional paragraph emphasizes the struggle of the turtles to emerge from their shells.

Paragraph Blocks

Sometimes, you may have so much information to support or develop a main idea that it "outgrows" a single paragraph. When a topic sentence or main idea requires an extensive explanation or support, you can develop the idea in a paragraph block—several paragraphs that work together and function as a unit. Each paragraph in the block supports the key idea or topic sentence. By breaking the development of the idea into separate paragraphs, you make your ideas clearer.

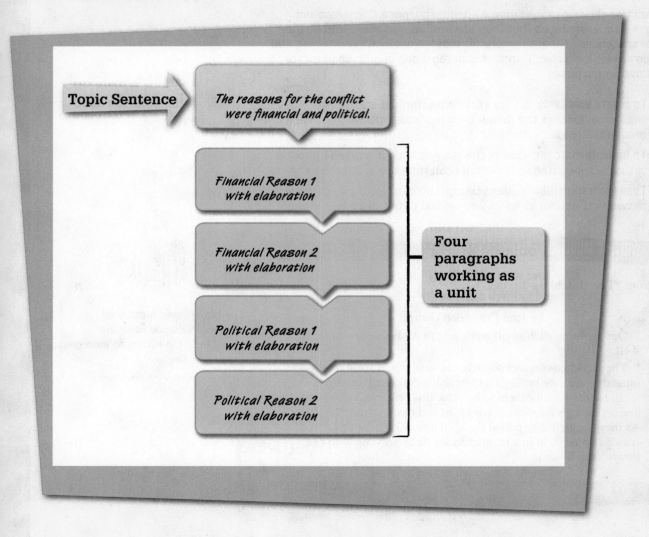

Topic Sentence → The reasons for the conflict were financial and political.

Financial Reason 1 with elaboration

Financial Reason 2 with elaboration

Political Reason 1 with elaboration

Political Reason 2 with elaboration

Four paragraphs working as a unit

Qualities
of Good Writing

The quality of your writing depends on how well you develop six important traits: ideas, organization, voice, word choice, sentence fluency, and conventions.

Ideas

Good writing begins with interesting ideas. Explore topics that you find interesting and that you think will interest others. Focus on presenting information that will be new and fresh to readers.

Organization

Organization refers to the way in which the ideas and details are arranged in a piece of writing. To enable readers to follow your ideas, choose an organization that makes sense for your topic, and stick with that organization throughout the piece of writing.

Voice

Just as you have a distinctive way of expressing yourself when you speak, you can develop a distinctive voice as a writer. Your voice consists of the topics you choose, the attitude you express toward those topics, the words you use, and the rhythm of your sentences. By developing your own voice, you let your personality come through in your writing.

Conventions

Conventions refer to the grammatical correctness of a piece of writing. Don't let errors in grammar, usage, mechanics, and spelling interfere with your message.

Word Choice

Words are the building blocks of a piece of writing. By choosing precise and vivid words, you will add strength to your writing and enable readers to follow your ideas and picture the things that you describe.

Sentence Fluency

In a piece of writing, it is important that sentences flow well from one to another. By using a variety of sentences—different lengths and different structures—and using transitions to connect them, you will create smooth rhythm in your writing.

Stages of the Writing Process

Writing is called a process because it goes through a series of changes or stages. These five stages are:

- In **prewriting**, you explore an idea by using various prewriting techniques, such as brainstorming and questioning.

- In **drafting**, you get your ideas down on paper or on the computer in roughly the format you intend.

- Once you finish your first draft, you decide on the changes, or **revisions**, you want to make.

- Finally, when you are happy with your work, you **edit** it, checking the accuracy of facts and for errors in spelling, grammar, usage, and mechanics.

- You then make a final copy and **publish** it, or share it with an audience.

You will not always progress through these stages in a straight line. You can backtrack to a previous stage, repeat a stage many times, or put the stages in a different sequence to fit your needs. To get an idea of what the writing process is like, study the following diagram. Notice that the arrows in the drafting and revising sections can lead you back to prewriting.

Prewriting
- Using prewriting techniques to gather ideas
- Choosing a purpose and an audience
- Ordering ideas

Drafting
- Putting ideas down on paper
- Exploring new ideas as you write

Publishing
- Producing a final polished copy of your writing
- Sharing your writing

Revising
- Consulting with peer readers
- Evaluating suggested changes
- Making revisions

Editing
- Checking the accuracy of facts
- Correcting errors in spelling, grammar, usage, and mechanics

Prewriting

Prewriting
- Using prewriting techniques to gather ideas
- Choosing a purpose and an audience
- Ordering ideas

No matter what kind of writing assignment you are given, you can use prewriting techniques to find and develop a topic. Some prewriting techniques will work better than others for certain kinds of assignments.

Choosing a Topic

Try some of the following ways to find topics that fit your assignment.

● **Look Through Newspapers and Magazines** In the library or at home, flip through recent magazines or newspapers. Jot down each interesting person, place, event, or topic you come across. Review your notes and choose a topic that you find especially interesting and would like to learn more about.

● **Keep an Events Log** Every day you probably encounter many situations about which you have opinions. One way to remember these irksome issues is to keep an events log. For a set period of time—a day or a week—take a small notebook with you wherever you go. Whenever you come across something you feel strongly about, write it down. After the specified time period, review your journal and select a topic.

● **Create a Personal Experience Timeline** Choose a memorable period in your life and map out the events that occurred during that period. Create a timeline in which you enter events in the order they occurred. Then, review your timeline and choose the event or events that would make the most interesting topic.

Narrowing Your Topic

Note that narrowing a topic is not an exact science. It is part of the creative process of writing, which involves experimentation and leads to discovery. Here are some specific techniques you can use.

● **Questioning** Asking questions often helps narrow your topic to fit the time and space you have available. Try asking some of the six questions that journalists use when writing news stories: *Who? What? When? Why? Where?* and *How?* Then, based on your answers, refocus on a narrow aspect of your topic.

● **Using Reference Materials** The reference materials you use to find information can also help you narrow a broad topic. Look up your subject in an encyclopedia, or find a book on it at the library. Scan the resource, looking for specific, narrow topics. Sometimes a resource will be divided into sections or chapters that each deal with a specific topic.

● **Using Graphic Devices** Another way to narrow a topic is to combine questioning with a graphic device, such as a cluster or inverted pyramid. Draw one in your notebook or journal, and write your broad topics across the top of the upside-down pyramid. Then, as the pyramid narrows to a point, break down your broad topic into narrower and narrower subcategories. The graphic shows how questions can be used to do this.

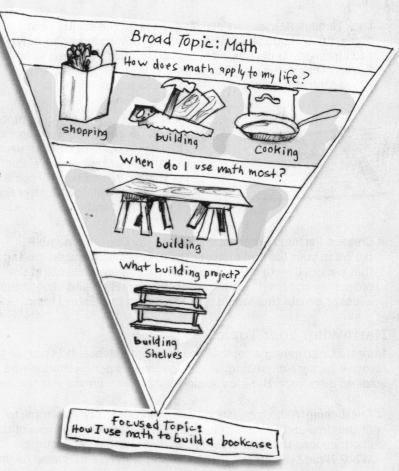

Broad Topic: Math

How does math apply to my life?

shopping   building   Cooking

When do I use math most?

building

What building project?

building Shelves

Focused Topic:
How I use math to build a bookcase

Purpose and Audience

Every piece of writing is written for an audience. Even when you write a secret in your journal, you are writing for an audience of one—yourself. To succeed in any writing task, you have to understand what your audience wants and needs to know.

Pinpointing your purpose is also essential when you write. Sometimes you write to fulfill an assignment; at other times you decide to whom you will write and why. For example, you might decide to write a letter to your sister about your bunkmates at camp. Your purpose might be to describe your bunkmates' looks and personalities. Another time you might write a letter to your principal about cellphones. Your purpose might be to convince her to ban cellphones inside your school.

● **Defining Your Purpose and Audience** Answering certain questions can help you define your purpose for writing and identify your audience.

- *What is my topic?*
- *What is my purpose for writing?*
- *Who is my audience?*
- *What does my audience already know about this topic?*
- *What does my audience need or want to know?*
- *What type of language will suit my audience and purpose?*

Gathering Details

After finding a topic to write about, you will want to explore and develop your ideas. You can do this on your own or with classmates. The following techniques may help you.

● **Interview a Classmate** Questioning a classmate can help both of you develop your topics. You can interview a friend who has a special skill. Find out how she or he developed that skill. You could also find an interview partner and question each other on an acceptable topic.

● **Fill In an Observation Chart** To come up with details to develop a piece of descriptive writing or to help you create the setting and characters for a narrative, you can fill in an observation chart. A writer created the chart that follows while wondering how to describe the school cafeteria at lunch time.

Once you have completed your own observation chart, circle the details you want to include in your piece of writing.

SUBJECT:	CAFETERIA AT LUNCHTIME				
See	Hear	Touch	Smell	Taste	
swirl of motion	kids' voices	hot melted cheese	stuff they wash the floors with	tart juice	
fluorescent lights	thuds and clunks of chairs and trays	wet plastic trays	delicious aroma of pizza	pepperoni	
colors of plastic trays	scraping of chairs	cold, wet milk cartons	apple crisp baking	mild cheese	

● **Do a Focused Freewriting** Freewriting can be used to either find or develop a topic. When it is used to develop a topic, it is called focused freewriting. Follow these four steps as you use focused freewriting to develop a topic:

1 Set a time limit. (Until you get used to freewriting, write for no more than five minutes at a time.)

2 Repeat to yourself the key words of your topic, and then write whatever comes to mind about them. Do not stop; do not read or correct what you write.

3 If you get stuck, repeat a word (even the word *stuck*), or write the last word you wrote until new ideas come. You can be sure they will.

4 When the time is up, read what you wrote. Underline parts that you like best. Decide which of these parts you will use in your piece of writing.

Drafting
- Putting ideas down on paper
- Exploring new ideas as you write

Drafting

In writing, an **organizational plan** is an outline or map that shows the key ideas and details that you want to include in the order that you want to include them. Following such a plan can help you structure your writing so that it makes a clearer and stronger impression on your audience.

Organizing Your Ideas

Often, a piece of writing lends itself to a particular order. For instance, if you are describing a scene so that readers can visualize it, spatial order may be your best option. However, if you are describing a person, you might compare and contrast the person with someone else you and your readers know, or you might reveal the person's character by describing a series of past incidents in chronological order.

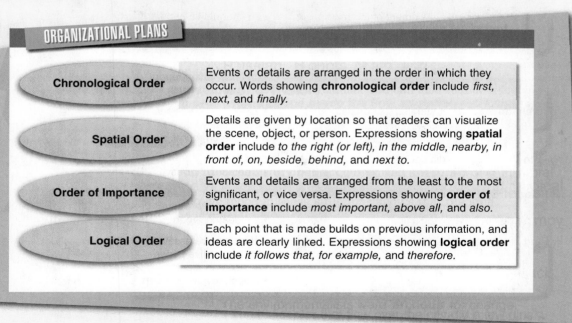

ORGANIZATIONAL PLANS

Chronological Order	Events or details are arranged in the order in which they occur. Words showing **chronological order** include *first, next,* and *finally.*
Spatial Order	Details are given by location so that readers can visualize the scene, object, or person. Expressions showing **spatial order** include *to the right (or left), in the middle, nearby, in front of, on, beside, behind,* and *next to.*
Order of Importance	Events and details are arranged from the least to the most significant, or vice versa. Expressions showing **order of importance** include *most important, above all,* and *also.*
Logical Order	Each point that is made builds on previous information, and ideas are clearly linked. Expressions showing **logical order** include *it follows that, for example,* and *therefore.*

Introductions

The introduction to your paper should include a **thesis statement**, a sentence about your central purpose or what you plan to "show" in your paper. Here is a thesis statement for a paper on the ancient Kingdom of Ghana:

> Ghana was one of the strongest, richest kingdoms of its time.

An effective written introduction draws your readers into your paper and interests them in the subject. The way you introduce your paper depends on the goal you want to achieve and the type of writing you are doing. The following are some possibilities.

GOAL	TYPE OF INTRODUCTION	COULD BE USED FOR
Be clear and direct	a statement of the main point	• an informative paper • a research report • an editorial
Appeal to readers' senses	a vivid description	• a description of a scene • an observation report • a character sketch
Get readers' attention	a startling fact or statistic	• an informative paper • a persuasive essay • a research report
Lure readers into the story quickly	dialogue	• a story • a personal narrative
Make readers wonder	a question	• an informative paper • a persuasive essay • a research report
Give your writing authority	a quotation	• a persuasive essay • an informative paper • a research report • a book review or report

Elaboration

Sometimes what you write seems to be only the bare bones of a composition. In order to flesh out your work, you must add the right details. This process is called **elaboration**.

Certain types of elaboration are more effective for certain forms of writing, but there are no hard-and-fast rules about which type of elaboration to use. You can use facts and statistics in a poem if you want to! Some types of elaboration include the following:

Facts and Statistics	Facts are statements that can be proved true. Statistics are facts that you express as numbers.
Sensory Details	Sensory details are details that appeal to the five senses—sight, hearing, touch, smell, and taste.
Anecdotes	An anecdote is a short account of an interesting or funny incident.
Examples	An example is an instance of something.
Quotations	A quotation is someone's words—often those of an expert or public figure.
Personal Feelings	Personal feelings are thoughts and emotions that are yours alone.
Memories	Memories are recollections from the past.
Observations	Observations are things you have seen or noticed firsthand.
Reasons	Reasons are explanations of why something is true.

● **Uses of Elaboration** Here is a chart showing the types of elaboration you can use and what each is used for.

TYPE OF ELABORATION		USED FOR
facts and statistics	➤	essays news stories feature articles business letters	advertisements reviews research reports
sensory details	➤	observations poems personal essays advertisements	stories plays descriptions
anecdotes	➤	journal entries personal letters news stories	personal essays feature articles
examples	➤	essays news stories business letters editorials advertisements poems	responses to literature book reports research reports feature articles reviews
quotations	➤	news stories feature articles essays	responses to literature book reports
personal feelings	➤	journal entries personal letters personal essays poems	editorials observations responses to literature persuasive essays
memories	➤	journal entries personal letters personal essays poems	descriptions observations stories
observations	➤	journal entries personal letters personal essays poems	reviews feature articles stories plays
reasons	➤	essays business letters reviews book reports news stories feature articles	editorials advertisements research reports responses to literature personal essays

Conclusions

The type of conclusion you will use depends on your subject and on your purpose. Here are some ways to end a paper effectively, with suggestions on what type of writing might best suit each type of conclusion.

● **Summarize Your Main Points** Review the most important ideas you have discussed and what you have said about them. Instead of just listing them, try to present them in a creative way. This will help you remember your key ideas.

This is a great way to conclude the following types of writing:
- *observation report*
- *personal essay*
- *research report*
- *informative essay*
- *comparison-and-contrast essay*

● **Resolve Conflicts and Problems** Bring your narrative to a close by addressing unanswered questions. Did the main character survive the battle? Did the enemies become friends?

This is especially important when you are writing the following:
- *personal narrative or autobiographical incident*
- *story or fable*
- *play*

● **Recommend an Action or Solution** You have presented your readers with an issue or problem. Now tell them what they can do about it. This will enable them to do something constructive after reading.

This is a great way to conclude these writing pieces:
- *persuasive essay*
- *letter to the editor*
- *problem-and-solution essay*

● **Offer a Final Comment or Ask a Question** Talk directly to your readers. You can do this by sharing your personal feelings, asking questions, or both. This will make your readers feel more involved.

This is a great way to conclude the following:
- *personal letter*
- *persuasive essay*
- *response to literature*
- *review*

Revising

Revising
- Consulting with peer readers
- Evaluating suggested changes
- Making revisions

When you have included all your ideas and finished your first draft, you are ready to revise it. Few writers produce perfect drafts the first time around. You can almost always improve your paper by reworking it. Here are some hints to help you revise your work.

● **Take a Break** Do not begin to revise right after you finish a draft. In a few hours or days you will be better able to see the strengths and weaknesses of your work.

● **Look It Over** When you reread your draft, look for ways to improve it. Use a pencil to mark places where an idea is unclear or the writing is jumpy or disjointed. Also, remember to let yourself know when you have written an effective image or provided a wonderful example. Write Good! next to the parts that work well.

● **Read Aloud** Your ear is a wonderful editor. Read your work aloud and listen for dull, unnecessary, or awkward parts that you did not notice when you read your work silently. Are there any passages that you stumble over as you read aloud? Try different wordings and then read them aloud with expression, emphasizing certain words. Listen and identify which wording sounds best.

● **Share Your Work** Your friends or family members can help you by telling you how your work affects them. Ask them whether your ideas are clear. What is interesting? What is boring?

When it is time to revise a draft, many writers are tempted to just correct a few spelling mistakes and combine a sentence or two. Eliminating surface errors, however, is only a small part of revising. After all, what good is a neat and perfectly spelled paper if it does not make sense or prove a point? The word *revise* means "to see again" or "to see from a new perspective." In order to revise your work, you need to rethink your basic ideas.

Revising by Rethinking

Taking a close look at the ideas in your draft is the most important part of revising. Usually, you will spot some "idea" problems. When you do, it is time to get to work. Here are some strategies to help you rethink your draft.

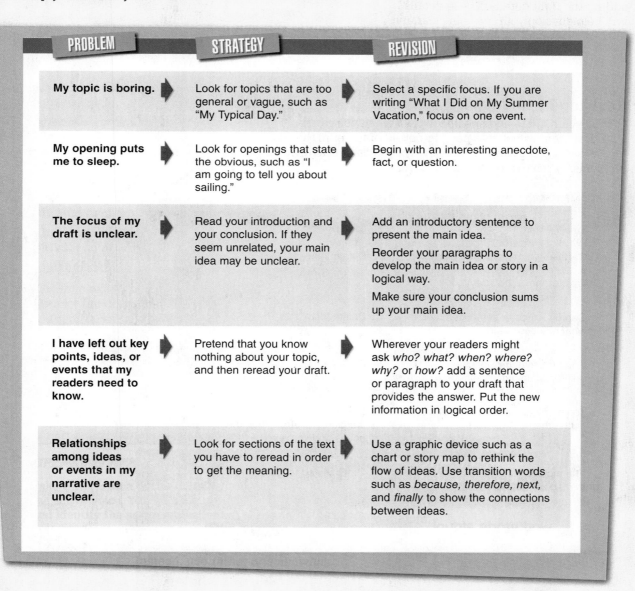

PROBLEM	STRATEGY	REVISION
My topic is boring.	Look for topics that are too general or vague, such as "My Typical Day."	Select a specific focus. If you are writing "What I Did on My Summer Vacation," focus on one event.
My opening puts me to sleep.	Look for openings that state the obvious, such as "I am going to tell you about sailing."	Begin with an interesting anecdote, fact, or question.
The focus of my draft is unclear.	Read your introduction and your conclusion. If they seem unrelated, your main idea may be unclear.	Add an introductory sentence to present the main idea. Reorder your paragraphs to develop the main idea or story in a logical way. Make sure your conclusion sums up your main idea.
I have left out key points, ideas, or events that my readers need to know.	Pretend that you know nothing about your topic, and then reread your draft.	Wherever your readers might ask *who? what? when? where? why?* or *how?* add a sentence or paragraph to your draft that provides the answer. Put the new information in logical order.
Relationships among ideas or events in my narrative are unclear.	Look for sections of the text you have to reread in order to get the meaning.	Use a graphic device such as a chart or story map to rethink the flow of ideas. Use transition words such as *because, therefore, next,* and *finally* to show the connections between ideas.

Revising by Elaborating

When you are sure your ideas are clear and in order, it is time to judge whether you have provided enough appropriate details. Remember, elaborating means developing and expanding on ideas by adding the right details. These details will help develop your ideas in clear and interesting ways.

You might choose any of the following types of details explained on page 327:

- *facts and statistics*
- *sensory details*
- *anecdotes*
- *examples*
- *quotations*
- *personal feelings*
- *memories*
- *observations*
- *reasons*

Revising by Reducing

Just as you need to add specific details when you revise your draft, you sometimes need to get rid of material that is unnecessary. Following are some ways you can solve revision problems by removing unneeded words.

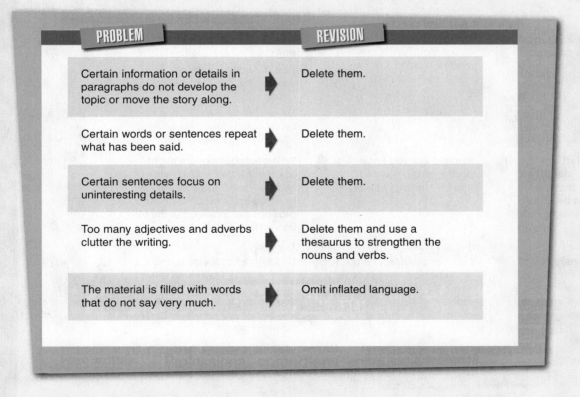

PROBLEM	REVISION
Certain information or details in paragraphs do not develop the topic or move the story along.	Delete them.
Certain words or sentences repeat what has been said.	Delete them.
Certain sentences focus on uninteresting details.	Delete them.
Too many adjectives and adverbs clutter the writing.	Delete them and use a thesaurus to strengthen the nouns and verbs.
The material is filled with words that do not say very much.	Omit inflated language.

Revising by Rewording

Choosing the right words is essential to good writing. As a final step in revising, improve your choice of words. At times, a better word will spring to mind. At other times, use a thesaurus to find words. As you rework your draft, you will reveal your own style.

The following chart can help you find the right word.

PROBLEM

Have I used the most effective word possible?

REVISION ACTIVITIES:

Choose specific nouns.
General: I wish I had some food.
Specific: I wish I had some pizza.

Choose active, colorful verbs.
General: The sick man walked to his bed.
Specific: The sick man hobbled to his bed.

Avoid the word *be*.
General: My horse is a good jumper.
Specific: My horse easily jumps four feet.

Choose the active voice.
General: Chocolate should never be fed to dogs.
Specific: Never feed dogs chocolate.

Editing

Editing
- Checking the accuracy of facts
- Correcting errors in spelling, grammar, usage, and mechanics

Here are some specific editing strategies that may help you.

Editing is the process of finding and correcting errors in grammar, usage, and mechanics. When you have finished drafting and revising your paper, here is how to edit your work.

General Tips
- Look first for mistakes that you typically make.
- Proofread your paper for one type of error at a time.
- Read your work aloud word for word.
- When in doubt, use reference sources to help you.

SPECIFIC TASKS

STRATEGY

Check Your Grammar

Have you written any run-on sentences or fragments?

Do your subjects and verbs agree?

Check that each sentence has a subject and verb. Use a comma and conjunction to connect main clauses.

Make sure that singular subjects have singular verbs and plural subjects have plural verbs.

Check Your Usage

Have you used the past forms of irregular verbs correctly?

Have you used subject and object pronouns correctly?

Watch out for irregular verb forms such as *seen, done, gone,* and *taken.*

Check that the pronouns *me, him, her, us,* and *them* are used only after verbs or prepositions.

Check Your Punctuation

Does each sentence have the correct end mark?

Have you used apostrophes in nouns, but not in pronouns, to show possession?

Have you used quotation marks around words from another source?

Look for inverted word order that may signal a question.

Use a phrase with *of* to check for possession.

Avoid plagiarism by checking your notecards to be sure.

Check Your Capitalization

Did you begin each sentence or direct quotation with a capital letter?

Have you capitalized proper nouns?

Look for an end mark and then check the next letter.

Look for the name of specific people and places.

Check Your Spelling

Did you correctly spell all words?

Use a dictionary. Look for your common errors.

Publishing
- Producing a final polished copy of your writing
- Sharing your writing

Publishing

Once you have made a final, clean copy of a piece of writing that pleases you, you may want to share it with others. What you have to say might be important or meaningful to someone else. Here are some ways you can publish your writing—that is, bring it to the public eye.

- Submit your work to a school newspaper or magazine.

- Have a public reading of your work. Perform it in one of the following ways:
  - Over the school P.A. or radio system
  - In a school assembly or talent show
  - In a group in which members take turns reading their work
  - At your local library or community center

- If your work is a play or skit, have a group of classmates or the drama club present it.

- Work with classmates to put together a class collection of written work. You can have it copied and bound at a copy shop.

- Submit your piece to a local or national writing contest.

- Send your writing to a local newspaper or area magazine.

- Publish your own work and the writings of classmates by using a computer with a desktop publishing program.

Reflecting

Your writing can help you learn about your subject or the writing process—or even yourself. Once you have completed a writing assignment, sit back and think about the experience for a few minutes.

Ask yourself questions such as the following:

- What did I learn about my subject through my writing?

- Did I experiment with writing techniques and forms? If so, were my experiments successful? If not, what held me back?

- Am I pleased with what I wrote? Why or why not?

- Did I have difficulty with any part of the writing process? If so, which part gave me trouble? What strategies did I use to overcome my difficulties?

This resource section contains tips on writing in English and information on grammar topics that are sometimes challenging for English learners.

The numbered arrows in the side margins also appear on other pages of the Grammar Handbook that provide information on writing or instruction in these same grammar topics.

EL1

Understand the Demands of Writing in a Second Language

Talk with other writers.

When you write in an unfamiliar situation, it may be helpful to find a few examples of the type of writing you are trying to produce. For example, if you are writing a letter of application to accompany a résumé, ask your friends to share similar letters of application with you and look for the various ways your friends presented themselves in writing in that situation.

Use your native language as a resource.

You can also use your native language to develop your texts. Many people, when they cannot find an appropriate word in English, write down a word, a phrase, or even a sentence in their native language and consult a dictionary later. Incorporating key terms from your native language is also a possible strategy.

A Japanese term adds perspective to this sentence.

"Some political leaders need to have *wakimae*—a realistic idea of one's own place in the world."

Use dictionaries.

Bilingual dictionaries are especially useful when you want to check your understanding of an English word or find equivalent words for culture-specific concepts and technical terms. Some bilingual dictionaries also provide sample sentences.

Learner's dictionaries, such as the *Longman Dictionary of American English,* include information about count/non-count nouns and transitive/intransitive verbs. Many of them also provide sample sentences.

Understand English idioms.

Some English idioms function like proverbs. In the United States, for example, if someone has to "eat crow," they have been forced to admit they were wrong about something. But simpler examples of idiomatic usage—word order, word choice, and combinations that don't follow any obvious set of rules—are common in even the plainest English. If you are unsure about idioms, use Google or another search engine to find out how to use them.

INCORRECT IDIOM	Here is the answer **of** your question.
ACCEPTED IDIOM	Here is the answer **to** your question.
INCORRECT IDIOM	I had jet **legs** after flying across the Pacific.
ACCEPTED IDIOM	I had jet **lag** after flying across the Pacific.

Understand Nouns in English

Perhaps the most troublesome conventions for nonnative speakers are those that guide usage of the common articles *the, a,* and *an.* To understand how articles work in English, you must first understand how the language uses **nouns.**

Proper nouns and common nouns

EL2

There are two basic kinds of nouns. A **proper noun** begins with a capital letter and names a unique person, place, or thing: *Elvis Presley, Russia, Eiffel Tower.*

The other basic kind of noun is called a **common noun.** Common nouns such as *man, country* and *tower,* do not name a unique person, place, or thing. Common nouns are not names and are not capitalized unless they are the first word in a sentence.

PROPER NOUNS

Beethoven   Michael Jordan   Honda
South Korea   Africa
Empire State Building

COMMON NOUNS

composer   athlete   vehicle   country
continent   building

Count and non-count nouns

EL3

Common nouns can be classified as either **count** or **non-count.** Count nouns can be made plural, usually by adding the letter *s* (*finger, fingers*) or by using their plural forms (*person, people; datum, data*).

Non-count nouns cannot be counted directly and cannot take the plural form (*information,* but not *informations; garbage,* but not *garbages*). Some nouns can be either count or non-count, depending on how they are used. *Hair* can refer to either a strand of hair, when it serves as a count noun, or a mass of hair, when it becomes a non-count noun.

Count nouns usually take both singular and plural forms, while non-count nouns usually do not take plural forms and are not counted directly. A count noun can have a number before it (as in *two books, three oranges*) and can be qualified with adjectives such as *many* (as in *many books*), *some* (as in *some schools*), and *few* (as in *few people volunteered*).

Non-count nouns can be counted or quantified in only two ways: either by general adjectives that treat the noun as a mass (*much* information, *some* news) or by placing another noun between the quantifying word and the non-count noun (two *kinds* of information, a *piece* of news).

CORRECT USE OF HAIR AS A COUNT NOUN

Three blonde hairs were in the sink.

CORRECT USE OF HAIR AS A NON-COUNT NOUN

My roommate spent an hour combing his hair.

INCORRECT	five horse many accident
CORRECT	five horses many accidents
INCORRECT	three breads I would like a mustard on my hot dog.
CORRECT	three loaves of bread I would like some mustard on my hot dog.

Understand Articles in English

EL4

Articles indicate that a noun is about to appear, and they clarify what the noun refers to. There are only two kinds of articles in English, definite and indefinite.

1. **the:** *The* is a **definite article,** meaning that it refers to (1) a specific object already known to the reader, (2) one about to be made known to the reader, or (3) a unique object.

2. **a, an:** The **indefinite articles** *a* and *an* refer to an object whose specific identity is not known to the reader. The only difference between *a* and *an* is that *a* is used before a consonant sound (*a man, a friend, a yellow toy*), while *an* is used before a vowel sound (*an orange, an old shoe*).

Look at these sentences, which are identical except for their articles, and imagine that each is taken from a different newspaper story.

Rescue workers lifted **the** man to safety.

Rescue workers lifted **a** man to safety.

By using the definite article *the*, the first sentence indicates that the reader already knows something about the identity of this man. The news story has already referred to him.

The indefinite article *a* in the second sentence indicates that the reader does not know anything about this man. Either this is the first time the news story has referred to him, or there are other men in need of rescue.

RULES FOR USING ARTICLES

1. *A* or *an* is not used with non-count nouns.

   INCORRECT The crowd hummed with **an** excitement.
   CORRECT The crowd hummed with excitement.

2. *A* or *an* is used with singular count nouns whose identity is unknown to the reader or writer.

   INCORRECT Detective Johnson was reading book.
   CORRECT Detective Johnson was reading **a** book.

3. *The* is used with most count and non-count nouns whose particular identity is known to readers.

   CORRECT I bought a book yesterday. **The** book is about kayaking.

4. *The* is used when the noun is accompanied by a superlative form of a modifier: for example, *best, worst, highest, lowest, most expensive, least interesting.*

   CORRECT **The** most interesting book about climbing Mount Everest is Jon Krakauer's *Into Thin Air.*

Understand Verbs and Modifiers in English

Verbs, verb phrases, and helping verbs

EL5

Verbs in English can be divided between one-word verbs like *run, speak,* and *look,* and verb phrases like *may have run, have spoken,* and *will be looking.* The words that appear before the main verbs—*may, have, will, do,* and *be*—are called **auxiliary (or helping) verbs**. Auxiliary verbs help express something about the action of main verbs: for example, when the action occurs, whether the subject acted or was acted upon, or whether or not an action occurred.

Indicating tense with *be* verbs

EL6

Like the auxiliary verbs *have* and *do, be* changes form to signal tense. In addition to *be* itself, the **be verbs** are *is, am, are, was, were,* and *been.*

To show ongoing action, *be* verbs are followed by the present participle, which is a verb ending in *-ing.*

INCORRECT	I **am think** of all the things I'd rather **be do**.
CORRECT	I **am thinking** of all the things I'd rather **be doing**.

To show that an action is being done to the subject rather than by the subject, follow *be* verbs with the past participle (a verb usually ending in *-ed, -en,* or *-t*).

INCORRECT	The movie **was direct** by John Woo.
CORRECT	The movie **was directed** by John Woo.

Auxiliary verbs that express certain conditions

EL7

The auxiliary verbs *will, would, can, could, may, might, shall, must,* and *should* express conditions like possibility, permission, speculation, expectation, and necessity. Unlike the auxiliary verbs *be, have,* and *do,* the auxiliary verbs listed above do not change form based on the grammatical subject of the sentence (*I, you, she, he, it, we, they*).

Two basic rules apply to all uses of these auxiliary verbs. First, these auxiliary verbs are always followed by the simple form of the verb. The simple form is the verb by itself, in the present tense, such as *talk* but not *talked, talking,* or *to talk.*

INCORRECT	She **should studies** harder to pass the exam.
CORRECT	She **should study** harder to pass the exam.

The second rule is that you should not use these auxiliary verbs consecutively.

INCORRECT	If you work harder at writing, you **might could** improve.
CORRECT	If you work harder at writing, you **might** improve.

1. **Speculation:** If you had flown, you **would** have arrived yesterday.

2. **Ability:** She **can** run faster than Jennifer.

3. **Necessity:** You **must** know what you want to do.

4. **Intention:** He **will** wash his own clothes.

5. **Permission:** You **may** leave now.

6. **Advice:** You **should** wash behind your ears.

7. **Possibility:** It **might** be possible to go home early.

8. **Assumption:** You **must** have stayed up late last night.

9. **Expectation:** You **should** enjoy the movie.

10. **Order:** You **must** leave the building.

EL8

Placement of Modifiers

Modifiers will be unclear if your reader can't connect them to the words to which they refer. How close a modifier is to the noun or verb it modifies provides an important clue to their relationship.

Clarity should be your first goal when using a modifier.

UNCLEAR	Many pedestrians are killed each year by motorists **not using sidewalks**.
CLEAR	Many pedestrians **not using sidewalks** are killed each year by motorists.

An **adverb**—a word or group of words that modifies a verb, adjective, or another adverb—should not come between a verb and its direct object.

AWKWARD	The hurricane destroyed **completely** the city's tallest building.
BETTER	The hurricane **completely** destroyed the city's tallest building.

Try to avoid placing an adverb between *to* and its verb. This construction is called a **split infinitive**.

AWKWARD	The water level was predicted **to not rise**.
BETTER	The water level was predicted **not to rise**.

Understand English Sentence Structure

EL9

Words derive much of their meaning from how they function in a sentence.

With the exception of **imperatives** (commands such as *Watch out!*), sentences in English usually contain a *subject* and a *predicate*. A subject names who or what the sentence is about; the predicate tells what the subject is or does.

The Lion	**is asleep.**
subject	predicate

A predicate consists of at least one main verb. If the verb is **intransitive,** like *exist*, it does not take a direct object. Some verbs are **transitive,** which means they require a **direct object** to complete their meaning.

INCORRECT The bird saw.
CORRECT The bird saw a cat.

Some verbs (*write, learn, read,* and others) can be both transitive and intransitive, depending on how they are used.

INTRANSITIVE Pilots fly.
TRANSITIVE Pilots fly airplanes.

Formal written English requires that each sentence includes a subject and a verb, even when the meaning of the sentence would be clear without it. In some cases you must supply an expletive, such as *it* and *there*.

INCORRECT Is snowing in Alaska.
CORRECT It is snowing in Alaska.